T0135480

A Component Based Platform for the Development of Hybrid Games

Von der Carl-Friedrich-Gauß-Fakultät
Technische Universität Carolo-Wilhelmina zu Braunschweig
zur Erlangung des akademischen Grades eines
Doktor-Ingenieurs (Dr.-Ing.)
genehmigte

Dissertation

von

Carsten Magerkurth

geboren am 21.01.1976 in Kronberg / Taunus

Referent: Prof. Dr. Michael Beigl, Technische Universität Braunschweig
Koreferent: Prof. Dr. Antonio Krüger, Universität des Saarlandes
Tag der Einreichung: 08. Juni 2009
Tag der mündlichen Prüfung: 30. Juni 2009

Druckjahr: 2009

Bibliografische Information der Deutschen Nationalbibliothek

Die Deutsche Nationalbibliothek verzeichnet diese Publikation in der
Deutschen Nationalbibliografie; detaillierte bibliografische Daten sind
im Internet über http://dnb.d-nb.de abrufbar.

ISBN 978-3-8325-2256-8

Logos Verlag Berlin GmbH
Comeniushof, Gubener Str. 47,
10243 Berlin
Tel.: +49 030 42 85 10 90
Fax: +49 030 42 85 10 92
INTERNET: http://www.logos-verlag.de

Acknowledgements

I would like to express my gratitude to my supervisor, Michael Beigl, who not only offered to support the thesis when the odds looked grim, but who also constantly shaped the work in the right direction and finally gave me the much needed push to cross the dip. Also, I must thank my second supervisor, Toni Krüger, for the assistance he provided at all levels of the research work. I am especially grateful for the opportunity to spend the entire week before the examination with Michael's DUS group at TU Braunschweig for the defense preparations. I have met a wonderful team there.

I would also like to thank my Hybrid Games co-workers Björn Engel, Dan Grollman, Maral Haar, Michael Wißner, Sascha Nau, Steve Hinske, Wolfgang Hinrich for their valuable contributions to this thesis. Special thanks go to Timo Engelke for his ongoing leadership and impact. Without him, Hybrid Games would not exist.

I must also acknowledge my former AMBIENTE/IPSI colleagues Carsten Röcker, Richard Etter, Richard Stenzel, Thorsten Prante, Maja Stikic, Peter Tandler for their input, but more importantly for being part of a great group that did good work and contributed to an open environment, where effective research work was facilitated. We all learned a lot from Norbert Streitz, our manager, about all things important in the research circus. His ongoing guidance and support were really crucial for this thesis.

I would like to thank my family for the support they provided me through my entire life and in particular, I must acknowledge my wife and best friend, Eveline, without whose love and assistance I would have had a hard time finishing the thesis. Also, I am grateful to my father Otto for his continued support and care. I am glad he always showed how much it mattered to him.

In conclusion, I finally want to thank my colleagues at SAP, especially Barbara Flügge, Christine Grimm, and Florian Urmetzer who kept their fingers crossed for the defense as well as Oliver Kasten and Harald Vogt who share a similar fate as I, and my team Ali Dada, Felix von Reischach, and Holger Ridinger for their understanding during the final stage of the thesis.

Abstract

The integration of information technology into the natural environments of our daily lives is proceeding rapidly. A myriad of research projects is currently exploring the challenges of providing ubiquitous computing functionality invisibly embedded in our homes and offices. This pervasiveness of the virtual domain demands novel interaction paradigms that go beyond the traditional graphical user interfaces prominent in the era of the desktop computer. These new interfaces are adaptive, flexible, distributed, scalable and seamlessly integrate physical and virtual domains to create natural and coherent interaction experiences. Bringing the computer back to the real world however introduces a new dimension of complexity with multiple displays, input devices, applications, and users to be supported simultaneously (Ballagas et al. 2003). Consequently, a growing number of augmented interface toolkits and interaction platforms have been proposed to support the dynamic change of tasks, devices, and users reducing the complexity of user interface modeling in pervasive computing environments. Typically, these approaches focus on providing and connecting non-standard interface components such as sensors or tangible controllers and integrate them with dedicated service infrastructures or existing legacy software. Physical interface components can be flexibly combined in current research prototypes such as Phidgets (Greenberg & Boyle 2002), iStuff (Ballagas et al. 2003), or Papier-Mache (Klemmer et al. 2004) and facilitate rapid prototyping of hybrid applications. However, developers still need to target specific pre-defined setups of physical interfaces and have to deal with constraints such as the availability of devices, or the consistency between physical and virtual representations of information. Furthermore, support for specific application domains such as gaming and entertainment is only beginning to be realized in the emerging generation of pervasive computing platforms.

This dissertation contributes a development and runtime platform to facilitate the realization of pervasive computing applications in the domain of hybrid games, which is one of the driving forces within the research of future networked home environments. The central thesis of this dissertation is that hybrid games benefit from a flexible and dynamically changing integration of user interfaces, because of the potential heterogeneity of end user interaction device setups. This is proven by showing that a hybrid games platform benefits from an adaptable, device independent architecture that ensures consistency among physical and digital information. The developed platform consists of several physical and graphical user interfaces specifically developed for hybrid games that effectively link properties from the real and the virtual world. These user interfaces include sentient game boards, gesture based interaction devices, smart dice cups, and other spatial or associative tangible interfaces. The respective software platform dynamically couples and coordinates interfaces and interaction devices. In contrast to most existing approaches, it supports consistency alignments across virtual and physical domains and is highly adaptive, allowing for physical reconfiguration during runtime. Game rules and mechanics are modeled independently of the concrete interaction devices and are likewise reconfigurable during runtime. Several proof-of-concept prototypes demonstrate that the development of hybrid gaming applications is greatly simplified with the platform presented in this dissertation. In order to prove the validity and goals of the platform, three formal evaluations with end-users were conducted, a formative one at the beginning of the requirements analysis and two summative ones after the deployment of final prototype applications.

Zusammenfassung

Informationstechnologien durchdringen zunehmend alle Aspekte unseres täglichen Lebens. Viele Forschungsprojekte untersuchen daher die Herausforderungen, die mit der Bereitstellung allgegenwärtiger Rechnertechnik in unseren Lebens- und Arbeitsräumen verbunden sind. Diese alles durchdringende Vernetzung des Alltags (*pervasive computing*) verlangt nach neuartigen Interaktionsparadigmen jenseits der grafischen Bedienschnittstellen traditioneller Arbeitsplatzrechner. Die neuen Bedienschnittstellen sind anpassungsfähig, verteilt, skalierbar und verflechten reale und virtuelle Welten, um kohärente Interaktionserfahrungen zu ermöglichen. Die Integration der Rechnertechnik in die reale Welt führt jedoch zu einer zusätzlichen Dimension der Komplexität, da verschiedenste Anzeigetypen, Eingabegeräte, Anwendungen und Benutzer gleichzeitig berücksichtigt werden müssen (Ballagas et al. 2003). Folgerichtig entstehen zunehmend Interaktionsplattformen und Entwicklungswerkzeuge, die die Dynamik von Aufgaben, Geräten und Benutzern in der realen Welt berücksichtigen und die Bereitstellung von Bedienschnittstellen für Pervasive Computing-Umgebungen erleichtern. Neuartige Ansätze unterstützen vor allem Interaktionskomponenten wie Sensoren, Aktuatoren oder anfassbare Bedienschnittstellen und stellen sie dedizierten Dienstinfrastrukturen oder bestehenden Anwendungen zur Verfügung. Realweltliche Komponenten können in aktuellen Forschungssystemen wie Phidgets (Greenberg & Boyle 2002), iStuff (Ballagas et al. 2003) oder Papier-Mache (Klemmer et al. 2004) flexibel kombiniert werden, um eine schnelle Prototypenentwicklung hybrider Anwendungen zu erleichtern. Entwickler müssen jedoch immer noch spezifische, vordefinierte Schnittstellenkonfigurationen berücksichtigen und sich mit Problemfällen wie der Verfügbarkeit von Geräten oder der Konsistenz virtueller und realer Informationsrepräsentationen auseinandersetzen. Darüber hinaus werden die spezifischen Elemente bestimmter Anwendungsfelder wie etwa Unterhaltungs- oder hybrider Spielanwendungen bisher erst rudimentär berücksichtigt.

Diese Dissertation stellt eine Entwicklungs- und Laufzeitplattform zur Verfügung, mit der Pervasive Computing-Anwendungen für den Bereich hybrider Spiele in vernetzten Heimumgebungen umgesetzt werden können. Die zentrale These der Dissertation besagt, dass hybride Spiele aufgrund der möglichen Verschiedenartigkeit von Gerätekonfigurationen beim Endbenutzer von einer flexiblen und dynamisch anpassbaren Integration der Interaktionskomponenten profitieren. Es wird aufgezeigt, wie eine adaptierbare, geräteunabhängige Architektur einer hybriden Spieleplattform zugute kommt, mit der die Konsistenz zwischen virtuellen und realen Informationszuständen sichergestellt wird. Die vorgestellte Plattform besteht aus mehreren anfassbaren und grafischen Bedienschnittstellen, die speziell für das Anwendungsfeld hybrider Spiele entworfen wurden und die Aspekte der realen und der virtuellen Welt zusammenbringen. Beispiele hierfür sind mit Sensorik ausgestattete Spielbretter, gestenbasierte Interaktionsgeräte, smarte Würfelbecher und andere raumbezogene oder assoziative anfassbare Bedienschnittstellen, die von einer entsprechenden Softwareplattform gekoppelt und koordiniert werden. Im Gegensatz zu existierenden Ansätzen unterstützt die Plattform den Abgleich von Konsistenzinformationen zwischen realer und virtueller Welt und stellt Rekonfigurationsmechanismen zur Laufzeit zur Verfügung. Spielmechanik und Regeln lassen sich unabhängig von konkreten Interaktionsgerätekonfigurationen modellieren und sind ebenfalls zur Laufzeit anpassbar. Mehrere Funktionsprototypen zeigen auf, dass die Entwicklung hybrider Spielanwendungen durch die Plattform vereinfacht wird. Um die Gültigkeit des Ansatzes zu demonstrieren, wurden drei formale Untersuchungen mit Endbenutzern durchgeführt, eine formative zu Beginn der Anforderungsanalyse und zwei summative Evaluationen der Funktionsprototypen.

Table of Contents

List of Tables

List of Figures

1. Introduction and Motivation

"Prototype tabs, pads and boards are just the beginning of ubiquitous computing. The real power of the concept comes not from any one of these devices; it emerges from the interaction of all of them." (Mark Weiser, 1991)

In his visionary article, Weiser predicted an emerging world of pervasive, embedded computation in which computers become part of our architectural and social environments. In this world of pervasive and ubiquitous computing, traditional desktop computers with their keyboards, mice, and monitors are augmented by dozens of additional computing devices that adapt to the properties of their physical and social context. They come in many shapes and forms, and integrate themselves into the devices and artifacts of our daily lives. These smart devices such as room elements (Prante et al. 2004), writing utensils (Millien et al. 2003), or even coffee cups (Gellersen et al. 1999) perform specific purposes that are afforded by their physical appearance. They support the users by offering context-dependent computing functionality in an unobtrusive way. For instance, a smart desk might be used like any traditional desk, e.g. one might sit at it and put sheets of paper on its surface. However, an integrated touch sensitive display of a smart desk might additionally be used for displaying information the user requires. Likewise, a smart blindman's stick (Coroama et al. 2004) can be used just like a traditional white cane, but it might provide additional information for its user by reasoning about its environment and communicating this information to the user.

Very often, these smart artifacts are much less powerful than their desktop counterparts due to being constrained by physical size or power consumption or dedicated to specific lightweight tasks. By connecting all of them with a continuous, pervasive networking technology, their single limitations are balanced by their distributed interaction and computation capabilities. The various sensors, actuators, displays, artifacts envisioned in a pervasive computing environment unleash their power when they are integrated into a coherent smart environment that is sentient about the human users' activities and tasks and offers appropriate means to assist them fulfilling these tasks. For instance, the smart blindman's stick only realizes its full potential, when all the other physical artifacts in its vicinity communicate their properties and states to it, so that it might inform its user about locked doors or reserved tables.

The way how users are supported in their tasks and how they interact with the smart environment is one of the most crucial issues for the realization of pervasive computing technologies. The design of the interaction and the human experience becomes a central research field in an environment that is populated with all kinds of different computing devices providing numerous services and autonomously communicating with each other. As Ballagas et al. (2003) point out, the interaction space becomes much more complex, since multiple heterogeneous interaction devices and multiple users involved in multiple tasks and applications have to be supported concurrently. Clearly, the traditional graphical user interface paradigms in which single user interaction is realized via windows, icons, mouse, and pointing (WIMP) is not appropriate for smart environments in which humans directly interact with each other and with many more computing devices than the desktop PC alone. Thus, in order to be accepted by the human parts of the system, interaction metaphors should adhere to the way humans interact with the real world. Humans talk to each other, point at information on whiteboards, use gestures, manipulate physical items and artifacts, walk around, and perform many other actions that relate to their physical and social environment.

1.1. Challenges for Human Computer Interaction

Abowd & Mynatt (2005) identify three profound changes to the interfaces that define the human experience with smart computing environments.

First, and most importantly, the interaction with a smart environment cannot be regarded as a solely explicit communication act as it was in the desktop era. The user input to the virtual domain of the computer system can now be implicit, which means that the natural interactions with the physical world provide sufficient input without any additional actions being necessary to inform the virtual domain. This includes the notion of tangible or graspable interfaces that "provide users concurrent access to multiple, specialized input devices which can serve as dedicated physical interface widgets, affording physical manipulation and spatial arrangements" (Fitzmaurice 1996). These tangible interfaces afford their intended usage by their physical shapes and thus allow for a natural and intuitive interaction. For instance, the sentient game board (Magerkurth et al. 2004) is operated just like a physical chess board, but implicitly communicates its state to other devices in a smart environment. In addition to these physical interfaces, many researchers are also investigating the use of various sensing technologies such as radio frequency identification (RFID), light, or inertial sensors to sense and reason about human activity in a completely implicit, even invisible way. A discussion of appropriate sensing technologies can be found in Hinckley et al. (2000).

The second major change in the interaction with pervasive computing environments lies in the distribution and scalability of output mechanisms. While input becomes more implicit to allow for humans to cope with the introduced complexities of pervasive computing, the adaptation of output to different scales and human perceptual modalities also serves the goal of realizing more natural ways of communicating information back to the users, so that they do not become distracted from their actual tasks. Weiser already identified different types and scales of displays that range from small, "inch scale" portable displays commonly found in personal digital assistants (PDAs) or mobile phones to huge wall-sized displays with extremely high resolutions as in the Princeton Display Wall (Chen et al. 2000) or the Darmstadt DynaWall (Streitz 2005). The appropriate mechanism for providing information on devices with vastly differing resolutions is one of the issues to be investigated in pervasive computing environments. Another, more important issue relates to the notion of public and private information to be conveyed via the different displays. In a multi-user setting with multiple displays it is crucial to associate displays and users appropriately, so that both public information can be easily perceived by everybody as well as private information is communicated only to the correct target person.

Due to the physical mobility of the users, small private displays as in mobile phones are preferred devices for private output, but also large public displays can be utilized for private information as e.g. the Hello.Wall (Streitz et al. 2005 b) that provides a special pattern language and supports the notion of dynamically "borrowing" other, private displays. Such interplay of private and public interaction devices is an important aspect of the distributed output capabilities of smart environments. As Greenberg et al. (2002) or Magerkurth & Stenzel (2003) have demonstrated, the coupling of private and public displays with different affordances provides unique interaction metaphors that directly relate back to Weiser's notion of the ubiquitous computing power coming only from the interaction of all the different devices. The aforementioned Hello.Wall is also an example for a so called "ambient display" that requires minimal attention and cognitive effort, because it can convey information in a peripheral way. Due to the potential number of displays in smart environments, there is a growing trend to utilize ambient displays that demand less attention from the users and leave more capacities for social interaction. Very often, these ambient displays involve other modes or modalities than visual output. For instance, the Audio Aura (Mynatt et al. 1998) uses auditory cues in a mobile device, and the AROMA awareness system even provides olfactory information (Bodnar et al. 2004).

The third important property of interaction with pervasive computing technology is the seamless integration of physical and virtual worlds. This relates to a complementary process in which physical objects are represented in the digital world and likewise the digital world of the computer is brought back to the real world. The results are hybrid information spaces in which physical and computational artifacts are merged into hybrid objects. Conceptually, Römer et al. (2004) introduce the notion of a "virtual counterpart" that exists in the virtual world as a digital representation of the physical artifact, whereas Mavrommati & Kameas (2003) refer to hyper-objects as physical objects that are digitally enhanced. Typically, some of the hybrid object's properties are represented both in the physical and in the virtual domain, while others are solely virtual or solely physical. For instance, a smart physical toolbox (Lampe et al. 2004) contains a certain set of RFID-tagged tools. Its contents are hybrid properties that are represented both in the real and in the virtual world, whereas the tools' physical states of abrasion are not digitally represented. In terms of user interaction, the seamless integration of virtual and physical worlds is often realized with techniques from the domain of Augmented Reality (AR), a term coined by Wellner (1993). With his DigitalDesk prototype he augmented the physical reality of an ordinary desk by projecting additional information from the virtual domain of a computer application over it. Complementarily, a camera tracked the writing of persons working on the table, so that a two-way communication channel between real and virtual world was established.

1.2. Emerging Application Domains

All of the presented approaches in interaction design for pervasive computing environments share the common goal of changing the way interaction is realized towards more natural and intuitive techniques that change the way the computer is perceived. Instead of the traditional Human Computer Interaction (HCI) new forms of human to information or human to human interaction emerge in a smart environment, when the computer as a primary device steps back from our perception (Streitz et al. 2005 a). To gain insights on the implications of smart environments, in which the boundaries of virtual and physical worlds dissolve and novel forms of interaction are applied, researchers around the world have begun to build up prototypical realizations of such environments.

These test sites consist of rooms or even complete cooperative buildings that are equipped with distributed pervasive computing technology aimed at assisting their inhabitants. Both home and office environments are investigated, each with unique goals and research interests. While smart offices set out to support the work and collaboration of its users with strictly task-oriented context-aware services, home environments set a stronger focus on supporting divergent leisure activities. This contrasts the design goals of efficiency and productivity with user acceptance, comfort, and well-being. Smart offices have a longer research tradition with early systems such as the Active Badges (Want et al. 1992) dating back to the late eighties and early nineties of the last century, when the notion of ubiquitous computing was just about to be coined. Large research projects such as the Intelligent Room at MIT (Torrance 1995) already came up at that time and nowadays the body of research regarding the issues of smart offices is generally better understood than those of smart home environments.

1. Introduction and Motivation

The scope of smart homes is diverse, ranging from home automation to fun and entertainment as well as assistance for people with special needs such as elderly or handicapped individuals. Today, several living labs and smart homes like the Aware Home at the Georgia Institute of Technology (Abowd et al. 2000), the Philips HomeLab (de Ruyter & Aarts 2004), or the InHaus from Fraunhofer IMS in Duisburg, Germany (Scherer et al. 2004), serve as test beds for the research of real people being supported by unobtrusive information technology in their natural environments. The experiments conducted in smart homes often involve the participants to actually move into these augmented spaces and live there for several days or even weeks. During these periods, very different technical and social aspects are investigated. This includes the deployment of appropriate sensing technologies that facilitate the environment to become aware of its occupants. For instance, the Easy Living project at Microsoft Research (Brumitt et al. 2000) was concerned with the fusion of multiple sensing modalities such as computer vision or pressure sensors integrated in sofas or chairs to optimize inhabitant tracking. In contrast to technology related research regarding e.g. sensor and communication networks, ethnographic investigations help understanding the everyday practices and needs of the inhabitants of smart home environments. These studies can inform the design and development of smart artifacts and interfaces in the home, as e.g. discussed in Hindus et al. (2001).

Three major application domains for smart home environments include the compensation for physical decline, aiding recall of past actions, and supporting awareness for extended family members (Abowd & Mynatt 2005). A fourth trend that is also driven by an enormous commercial exploitation potential is the field of smart home entertainment. The AMIGO (Ambient Intelligence for the Networked Home Environment) integrated project of the European Union (www.amigo-project.org) also addresses fun and entertainment as one of the important driving forces for the permeation of pervasive computing technology in the home.

The traditional field of computer entertainment and games has already become a booming market. Gross revenues in the entire computer entertainment market in 2003 excelled the 1,5 billion Euro mark in Germany alone (PriceWaterHouseCoopers – German Entertainment and Media Lookout, cited in Gerber 2005) with an expected increase of 15% until the year 2008. As a complementary trend to the integration of pervasive computing technologies to other home and office applications, computer games have also recently begun to leave the traditional screen oriented interaction paradigms. So called Hybrid or Pervasive Games (Benford et al. 2005) bridge the gap between virtual and physical worlds by making the physical context of the players, their locations and real-world parameters, an integral part of the gaming experience.

This dissertation picks up this emerging trend and focuses on smart home applications supporting entertainment activities and gaming. These applications are referred to as "hybrid games" because of their hybrid nature that integrates physical and virtual elements in the smart home. The central idea of hybrid games is to bring together the best elements of traditional physical games such as board games and on the other side computer entertainment. Both of these game types emphasize specific aspects of the entertainment experience. Traditional board games focus on the direct interaction between human players. They sit together around the same table, discuss, laugh, listen, and look at each other interpreting facial expressions and gestures which help understand the others' actions and create a rich social situation. Complex game rules, smart and proactive behavior, or multi-sensual stimulation, on the other side, is what computer games excel (Mandryk & Maranan 2002). The drawback of computer games, however, is the lack of social interaction in a face to face setting. Even with

4

multiplayer games that are connected e.g. via the Internet, the players' notion of each other is mostly conveyed by screen and keyboard which pales against the richness of a face-to-face group interaction. Hybrid games thus provide the chance and challenge to augment the human centered group situation of traditional physical games with the advantages of computing technology.

Streitz et al. (2005 a) identify a set of experience qualities specifically related to hybrid gaming. These include 1.) the social quality, achieved by face-to-face interaction styles, 2.) the haptic quality, related to the tangible artifacts that serve as user interfaces, 3.) the multimodal stimulation, realized by adapting the player's ambience to the flow of the game, adding to the immersion of the interaction experience, 4.) Virtual attributes of physical artifacts that can differ from game to game and augment physical artifacts in many different ways. To realize these experience qualities in a smart home environment, an infrastructure of tangible and graphical interfaces is essential to achieve the desired level of immersion.

1.3. Challenges for Application Development

Both smart home and office environments will soon become end users' realities, as the increasing availability of inexpensive computing devices and storage technologies has led to the integration of embedded computing technology into many facets of our lives. To utilize and integrate them in a coherent way, Shrobe (2005) identifies an agenda of challenges to be met in the realization of pervasive computing environments.

The first challenge lies in the provision of a comprehensive infrastructure for ubiquitous computing that includes a solid and robust middleware for distributed computing, protocols for wired and wireless communication, etc.

The second challenge lies in the development of frameworks that allow systems to respond adaptively to user interactions. He argues that no single metaphor, such as the desktop as a metaphor for the personal computer, is sufficient to cover the required range of natural interactions with pervasive computing environments. Depending on the properties of a given situation and task, different modes of interaction are natural to people. This observation is picked up in this dissertation both by providing a broad range of dedicated physical and graphical interfaces and a coordination software platform that mediates between the properties of different user interfaces.

The challenge of providing a comprehensive infrastructure is addressed in several research projects such as the Interactive Workspaces project at Stanford University (Johanson et al. 2002) and their iROS middleware or the BEACH / COAST software framework from the Ambiente division of Fraunhofer IPSI (Tandler 2004). These projects investigate the software foundations to integrate and coordinate the various input and output devices in a smart environment. As it will be pointed out in this dissertation, each of these related research projects encounter certain limitations, constraints, and disadvantages when applied to the field of pervasive entertainment applications that need to dynamically integrate both graphical and tangible interfaces.

Only few of the coordination infrastructures explicitly support the idiosyncrasies of tangible interfaces such as the physical iStuff components (Ballagas et al. 2003) interoperating with the iROS middleware. Other physical interface toolkits could potentially be integrated with a coordination infrastructure to reduce the complexities of physical interfaces and allow for rapid prototyping of hybrid applications. Such toolkits as e.g. Phidgets (Greenberg & Boyle 2002) or Papier-Mache (Klemmer et al. 2004) are already available, however with little support for multi-user applications. The dynamic nature of hybrid games with users and device setups changing frequently during an interaction session also demand support for flexible reconfiguration of input and output devices and mechanisms to ensure consistency and integrity among virtual and physical representations which are lacking in existing solutions. Especially when multiple interaction devices are present it becomes necessary to keep state representations consistent among the various nodes already below specific application layers.

Consequently, an integrative approach that addresses the appropriate orchestration of graphical and tangible interfaces in a smart home environment, that coordinates devices and interfaces ensuring consistency and integrity, and that adapts to varying device setups is required and presented in this dissertation.

1.4. Overview of the Dissertation

The dissertation is structured around the central thesis that it is essential to provide hybrid gaming applications with the capability of dynamically integrating and flexibly administrating different user interface devices, because of the potential heterogeneity of end user interaction device setups. The dissertation will first outline the novel application domain of hybrid games and motivate the need for a dedicated development and runtime platform that facilitates the realization of hybrid games. The hardware and software components that make up the platform are then discussed, followed by proof-of-concept prototypes and their respective evaluations that prove the dissertation's thesis by showing that a hybrid games platform benefits from an adaptable, device independent architecture that ensures consistency among physical and digital information.

The structure of the dissertation is shown in Figure 1.

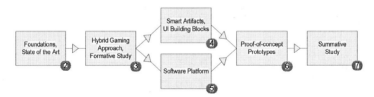

Figure 1: Structure of the dissertation

Chapter 2 of the dissertation presents the current state of the art in smart environment infrastructures and discusses the foundations of user interaction in pervasive computing environments. This discussion includes the respective middleware requirements for integrating and coordinating various types of heterogeneous user interface components and evaluates existing approaches. The theory and idiosyncrasies of tangible user interfaces are then discussed and emerging tangible and graphical user interface toolkits are evaluated. After the discussion of the state of the art of coordination and user interface middleware the need for a novel development and runtime platform in the application domain of hybrid games is motivated.

1. Introduction and Motivation

The actual theory and concept and of hybrid games is presented in Chapter 3. This discussion includes the specific perceptive qualities of hybrid games and the emerging conceptual approaches. As a central part of this chapter, a formative evaluation is presented that proves the validity of supporting the development of hybrid gaming with a respective computing infrastructure. This evaluation was conducted as a requirements analysis before the design of the platform in order to verify that end users would appreciate the concept of hybrid games as a novel form of future entertainment applications in smart environments.

Chapter 4 discusses hardware interfaces and smart artifacts developed as building blocks for the software infrastructure presented in the succeeding chapter. A number of tangible interaction devices were specifically designed and implemented to provide the affordances of well known user interfaces from the domain of traditional gaming such as game boards, dice, or magic wands. These devices can be flexibly integrated and re-combined with the game application prototypes presented in a later chapter. Additionally, the combination of tangible and graphical user interface components in smart environments as part of the so called Roomware technologies is presented with their opportunities for supporting hybrid game sessions.

The next chapter 5 discusses the complementary software platform to integrate the user interface components presented before and to provide a distributed communication and coordination infrastructure on top of which hybrid gaming applications can be implemented. It synchronizes various software components via a publish-subscribe approach and provides an operating system-, device-, and protocol-independent communication scheme, in order to cope with the anticipated heterogeneity in future smart home environments. To deal with the dynamic integration of multiple graphical and tangible interaction devices, consistency management between components is also provided as well as a definition language for game rules that allows for a high level specification of games and the alteration of game rules during runtime.

Chapter 6 presents several proof-of-concept prototypes that were developed using the software and hardware platform discussed in the previous chapters. There are four prototypes of different complexity, each focusing on different aspects and capabilities of the platform.

Two of the prototypes discussed in chapter 6 were utilized in summative evaluations discussed in chapter 7. These evaluations close the circle between the formative evaluation in chapter 3 and the development of the platform itself, proving the central thesis of this dissertation: It is not only beneficial to develop hybrid games, but the development of these games also profits greatly from a flexible and dynamically changing integration of user interfaces that is possible with the platform contributed in this dissertation.

2. State of the Art

This chapter gives an overview of the state of the art in pervasive computing user interface infrastructures and toolkits. Since the development of pervasive computing environments is more complex than that of traditional desktop applications, and development tools and techniques have not yet matured to a comparable state, the research of appropriate user interface middleware is currently an important task to lower the threshold for developing pervasive computing applications. The most prominent research approaches and projects are discussed in this chapter and also evaluated for their suitability for entertainment oriented applications in home environments.

The chapter starts with a brief discussion of the scope and requirements on user interface middleware for pervasive computing entertainment applications. These requirements provide a foundation for the forthcoming review of the respective state of the art. The discussed scope specifically addresses entertainment oriented applications that share some of the characteristics of applications in other domains, but also introduce unique issues such as an appropriate orchestration of input and output devices for dramatic purposes. The next section of this chapter reviews the major research projects that deal with the development and deployment of smart environments. These projects frame the different approaches in realizing pervasive computing applications and are typically broader than the contributions of this dissertation, addressing the entire width of issues relevant for the creation of living laboratories such as security, privacy, context awareness, positioning, and sensing technologies, or even legal constraints. Since this dissertation contributes a user interface toolkit and an appropriate communication infrastructure to support the deployment in a real smart environment, the reviewed pervasive computing projects are correspondingly discussed with a focus on their integrated communication and coordination infrastructures. An interplay of both concrete user interfaces and their coordination and communication is essential for the development of pervasive computing applications. Therefore, the concluding sections of the chapter address tangible and graphical interface toolkits that are geared towards ubiquitous computing spaces.

2.1. Scope and Requirements of Pervasive Gaming Middleware

The following sections outline both the scope and the respective requirements in the different fields that are relevant for pervasive gaming applications. According to Sommerville (2006) the process of requirements engineering generally involves four distinct stages, namely:

- Requirements elicitation
- Requirements specification
- Requirements validation and verification
- as well as requirements negotiation

The nature of a scientific process compared to a traditional software product development process clearly differs in so far, as the traditionally involved stakeholders such as domain experts and requirements analysts are to some degrees expected to exist in personal union, so that the negotiation stage is not really applicable in a scientific process. The remaining stages are specifically addressed within this dissertation in different sections. Requirements elicitation and specification are detailed in this chapter and in the next chapter following the distinction of van Vliet (2008) regarding the main source of information. Namely, in this chapter, the focus is on the domain and its relevant state of the art, whereas the formative evaluation discussed in the next chapter has a focus on the user and consequently utilizes user specific requirements elicitation techniques such as a focus group session and interviews. Requirements validation and verification is addressed informally in chapter 6 within the discussion of proof of concept prototypes and within chapter 7 that addresses an overall evaluation of this dissertation's contributions.

In order to elicit the domain relevant requirements discussed in this chapter, an analysis of the respective findings of domain experts is conducted, wherever possible. Since there are also requirements that stem from novel combinations across related fields, some requirements are motivated by argumentation, but literature review is the preferred and aimed at method.

In general, pervasive entertainment applications share many of the general characteristics of other applications in pervasive computing environments. Abowd & Mynatt (2005) identify the need for flexibly distributing output to multiple, differently scaled displays, the support for appropriate input strategies involving tangible and other non-standard interaction metaphors, and the seamless integration of virtual and physical worlds. Tandler (2004) formulates requirements from different system perspectives. Regarding human computer interaction and ubiquitous computing, he identifies the need for different forms of interaction, different user interface concepts, multiple and heterogeneous devices, multiple-computer devices, context and environmental awareness, dynamic configuration changes, adapted presentation, multiple device user interfaces as well as physical interaction.

Communication middleware and user interface toolkits need to facilitate the development of pervasive computing applications adhering to these requirements, so that distributed, adaptive, robust and flexible applications can be developed rapidly and easily without exposing the complexities of the integration of physical and social context to the developers (Ballagas et al. 2003). Entertainment and gaming applications, however, do have their idiosyncrasies and demand for additional specific requirements that are not necessarily relevant for other types of pervasive computing applications such as smart office or assistive systems for elderly or handicapped users. These specific requirements include the support for graphical and physical user interfaces, flexible device configuration, runtime adaptability in terms of devices and game rule descriptions, and an appropriate modeling of the social space.

Support for Graphical and Physical User Interfaces

Entertainment applications traditionally make strong use of graphical output to support the immersion into the game. Many of the innovations both in 3D rendering algorithms and rendering hardware are in fact driven by the highly competitive games market. While pervasive game applications need to provide rich graphical output to appeal to the users, their real potential can only be unleashed, when non-standard physical interfaces are integrated that support the social dynamics of the involved players and link between physical and virtual worlds without requiring exclusive attention. The requirement for supporting complementary graphical and physical user interfaces is abstracted from Tandler's (2004) requirements for different forms of interaction, different user interface concepts, and multiple and heterogeneous devices as well as adapted presentation. Likewise, Abowd & Mynatt (2005) identify the need for supporting heterogeneous user interfaces as a central requirement.

R2.1: Heterogeneous user interfaces – A pervasive gaming middleware shall support complementary graphical and physical user interfaces

2. State of the Art

While the combination and complementary integration of physical and graphical user interfaces forms an underlying basic requirement, both graphical and physical user interface come up with their own dedicated set of specific requirements, in our context there is an emphasis on:

> *R2.2: Rich multimedia – Graphical user interface middleware shall support high performance rendering of rich multimedia content relevant in gaming applications*

This requirement relates to the conclusion of Stewart (2007) that consumer demand is the single most powerful force in driving progress in real-time rendering for games and thus attractive graphics are a critical factor for gaming in general. This follows Ogden (1999) who notes that neither text nor icon would be adequate to present many gaming situations, but "the best, most involving way to present a situation where the player sees something out of the corner of his eye, is to present the scene to the player, and actually let him see the item out of the corner of his eye".

In order to realize attractive and believable game worlds, it is crucial to provide convincing graphical representations which are a challenge in the pervasive computing domain due to the heterogeneous and often resource-constrained nature of interaction devices (Wagner & Kellerer 2004). Likewise, the different categories, sizes, and scales of output devices demand for taking their idiosyncrasies into account. As Crabtree et al. (2004) point out, the effective orchestration of displays is a crucial point in pervasive gaming applications. For dramatic reasons, it is important to make effective use of the various output devices in a smart space. For instance, story-telling elements such as the infamous cut-scenes from contemporary computer games demand for large public displays to have the intended immersive effect. When heterogeneous interaction devices with different interaction characteristics are integrated in a pervasive gaming environment, it is essential to utilize each single device in accordance with its interaction affordances. The demand for supporting the idiosyncrasies of device and display classes has been formulated many times, beginning with Weiser (1991), but also e.g. in (Garlan 2000, Brummit et al. 2000, Sousa & Garlan 2002).

> *R2.3: Display idiosyncrasies – Graphical user interface middleware shall address the idiosyncrasies of the multitude of different-sized horizontal and vertical displays*

For physical user interfaces, a corresponding requirement can be formulated. However, the complexity of the physical space does not allow for categorizations in terms of display sizes or affordances such as the inch, foot, yard scales that pioneered the field of Pervasive Computing. Given the multitude of physical controllers available for modern video game consoles like the Nintendo Wii or the different Playstation revisions, it becomes clear that physical controllers (henceforth referred to as tangible user interfaces) come in various shapes, sizes and complexities with an almost unlimited amount of respective interaction metaphors, so that the requirement from a middleware perspective is to provide the means of integrating a diverse set of different interaction devices. This requirement is widely recognized among tangible user interface researchers and formulated e.g. in (Marquardt & Greenberg 2007, Hartmann et al. 2006, Ballagas et al. 2003), although dedicated tangible user interface middleware exists that focuses on a narrow set of interfaces (Klemmer et al. 2004) conceding that broader categories are commonly identified nonetheless.

> *R2.4: Physical versatility – Tangible user interface middleware shall support components of different complexity and interaction models*

10

The capability of integrating more than basic physical controls inevitably introduces challenges to application development with respect to dealing with the representation of physical devices and their properties. Ideally, virtual counterparts of physical devices should be available that allow for substituting hardware with software proxies and thus allow for augmenting typical graphical user interface prototyping tools with tangible interface support.

In this context, it is a crucial task to ensure that information represented in the physical domain, e.g. in the state of a tangible user interface, matches virtual representations, e.g. a graphical widget rendered on the screen. This is especially important, when multiple physical and/ or virtual components relating to the same information are integrated at the same time. While most TUI toolkits do not support simultaneously altering the same set of information from multiple access points, Hartmann et al. (2006) specifically discuss interlinking the graphical representations of physical interfaces for human "designers". Apart from that specific case, consistency in distributed systems is generally regarded as a central requirement in order to keep the overall system behavior predictable (van Vliet 2008).

> *R2.5: Domain Consistency – Tangible and graphical user interfaces that represent the same set of information must ensure consistent representations*

Flexible Device Configuration

In contrast to many smart workspaces that mostly integrate a certain set of fixed displays of various sizes and forms (cf. Russel et al. 2005), the setup of interaction devices in a hybrid game session can vary greatly, depending on what is available at a user's site. Solutions tailored to one specific site that is mostly static in its configuration might make sense in a business context, but since home entertainment naturally aims at mass market deployment the developer of a hybrid game cannot anticipate the device setup of the end user. One user might possess a certain interaction device, while another user owns a different one. When both participate in the same game session, they should be able to bring their own devices and make use of them. Accordingly, the hybrid game application should be able to operate on a minimal device setup, e.g. a single desktop PC, and adapt to a myriad of additional input and output devices. This demands for decoupled communication between application components and requires gaming applications to be defined and executed without costly reconfiguration in different physical setups. As the situation for hybrid games in this respect is largely similar to other applications in pervasive computing environments that dynamically integrate all kinds of different devices, the requirement for decoupling communication identified in e.g. Tandler (2004), Johanson et al. (2002) or Murphy et al. (2006) also relates to hybrid games and is actually also a very traditional requirement as it was introduced as early as the 1980s with the Tuplespace communication model (Gelernter 1985).

> *R2.6: Decoupled communication – Gaming applications shall be decoupled from any specific physical configurations as setups may vary considerably*

Runtime Adaptability

In an office context, many interaction situations are clearly defined and terminated. For instance, work meetings commonly have a starting point and an end point as well as an agenda that structures its proceeding. Accordingly, participants are expected to attend the meeting from beginning to end. In a home entertainment setting, interaction situations are less structured with participants joining and leaving at any time. Due to the dynamic nature of the interaction situations, interaction devices need to be flexibly integrated and be added and removed at any point in time. Since it cannot be taken for granted that private devices are always available in sufficient quantities (see flexible device configuration), the application must also be capable of dynamically reassigning private devices to different users.

In addition to the device configuration, the game applications themselves also need to be adaptable during runtime regarding their modeled rules and game mechanics. This relates to the notion of "house rules" that allow participants of the game to change certain game mechanics as a result of their own playing history. The runtime adaptability of traditional tabletop games is one of the reasons for their continuing success despite the technical superiority of computer entertainment (cf. Mandryk & Maranan 2002). Outside the gaming context, the requirement of runtime adaptability has long been identified e.g. by Coen et al. (1999) or by Shafer et al. (2001) with Garlan (2000) specifically pointing out that the problem of "the devices are likely to come and go in an unpredictable fashion" in pervasive computing environments is a key challenge to address.

> ***R2.7: Runtime adaptability – A pervasive gaming middleware shall be adaptable to changes in device configurations and application logic during runtime***

One aspect of this runtime adaptability also relates to extensibility, i.e. the capability to add more components to the game (players, devices, etc.) while a game is in progress. Although this dissertation mostly focuses on gaming in smaller areas such as single rooms, it should still be possible to extend game sessions over these more or less arbitrary boundaries and support both scenarios involving room-to-room communication as well as even more demanding setups such as Massively Multiplayer Online Role-Playing Games (MMORPG) augmented by physical aspects [this relates to end user feedback from the formative evaluation discussed in the next chapter]. These scenarios impose scalability issues that e.g. centralized architectures could not cope with. With a growing number of communicating entities issues of robustness also become relevant. Disintegration or failures of entities should not result in a complete crash of the entire system, for instance if a centralized server disappears. This relates to the differentiation between vertical, as e.g. traditional client server architectures, and horizontal, as e.g. peer-to-peer architectures, distribution within an information system (Tanenbaum 2007). Likewise, Dustdar et al. (2003) discuss this requirement in relation to different architectural styles.

> ***R2.8: Extensibility and robustness – It shall be possible to extend running game sessions with distributed communicating entities in a failsafe way***

Appropriate Modeling of Shared Information

Pervasive computing environments are built to support multiple users. While this adds new complexities, it is essential in order to support humans in their natural environments. Consequently, when dealing with multiple users, an inherent distinction between private and public information must be made. Notes taken in a negotiation meeting, for instance, must not be directed to a public display. For entertainment applications, it is often favorable to also introduce multiple degrees of privacy for game events, so that different degrees of shared, public and individual knowledge in the social domain can be utilized by a game application to foster cooperation and competition between human participants. This follows the related requirements for co-located groupware, e.g. (Greenberg et al. 1998, Morris et al. 2004).

> ***R2.9: Modeling of shared information – It shall be possible to model, process, and render information with respect to the social relationships between users***

2. State of the Art

The following table (Table 1) recapitulates the identified requirements and indicates their relevance to the related research areas. In the following sections the state of the art in smart environments projects, tangible, and graphical user interface toolkits are discussed with respect to the relevant requirements.

Table 1: Pervasive gaming middleware requirements

Req.	Label	Relevance
R2.1	Heterogeneous user interfaces	Smart Environments Projects, Tangible User Interfaces
R2.2	Rich multimedia	Smart Environments Projects, Graphical User Interfaces
R2.3	Display idiosyncrasies	Graphical User Interfaces
R2.4	Physical versatility	Tangible User Interfaces
R2.5	Domain Consistency	Tangible User Interfaces
R2.6	Decoupled communication	Smart Environments Projects
R2.7	Runtime adaptability	Smart Environments Projects, Tangible User Interfaces
R2.8	Extensibility and robustness	Smart Environments Projects
R2.9	Modeling of shared information	Smart Environments Projects

2.2. Smart Environments Projects

As pointed out, developing pervasive computing environments is a difficult and costly task that necessitates addressing issues from many different areas of computer science being integrated in an overall vision or approach. Depending on the goals of the respective research project, different focal areas will be addressed in more depth and detail than others. For instance, the focus of a project might be on a context processing software infrastructure that receives input from sensor networks trying to gain awareness of the physical and social realities in the smart environment. Other projects might address the support of certain task domains such as co-located cooperation and consequently provide the respective tools and applications that are tailored to dedicated interaction devices.

Despite the heterogeneity of the current body of smart environment research projects, most projects make contributions in the field of human computer interaction in one way or the other, since this is one of the key areas that differentiate pervasive computing from other research paradigms. Consequently, in many research projects the development of specialized user interfaces is addressed. Taking the distributed nature of pervasive computing into account, a respective coordination and communication middleware that connects the diverse interaction devices in the physical space becomes a complementary research challenge. Typically, both areas of concrete interface devices and their coordination infrastructure rely on and influence each other. The smart environments projects discussed in this section are thus presented with both regard to their general approaches and contributions as well as the integrated user interface middleware. Some of the discussed projects have developed their own graphical or tangible user interface toolkits. Since these research categories are well defined and allow a direct and appropriate comparison of features, they are left out of the discussion and presented separately in the next section of this chapter, even though there might be a natural interdependence with the other components of the middleware, such as a

13

tangible user interface toolkit making use of the smart environment's communication infrastructure.

Since there are many research activities emerging in the field of pervasive computing environments, only the significant and influential projects are discussed in depth in this section. These include the Stanford Interactive Workspaces project that develops a smart meeting room called iRoom, the i-Land project at Fraunhofer IPSI, Darmstadt, that has a similar focus, the EasyLiving project at Microsoft Research that contributes to the area of smart home environments, and the Aware Home project at Georgia Tech that also provides services residents of a smart home environment. Other projects with less scientific impact or a less related focus are briefly discussed at the end of the section.

iRoom (Stanford Interactive Workspaces)

The Interactive Workspaces project is one of the most prominent pervasive computing projects that is still active after several years of research. It was initiated at Stanford University in 1999 to explore the implications for human computer interaction in smart environments (Johanson et al. 2002). Initially, the project started by deploying a single large vertical display in a laboratory and since then has evolved into the development of a full-fledged infrastructure for a smart room, the iRoom, that contains multiple horizontal and vertical displays (R2.3), a pressure-sensitive floor, cameras, microphones, and various tangible interface components (R2.1) (Ballagas et al. 2003). The goals and contributions of the project revolve around the support of co-located meeting situations that rely on social protocols rather than on software constraints, that are widely applicable to arbitrary smart room setups, and are simple to grasp both for the end users and the developers writing components for the iRoom. Specifically, the iRoom provides applications to move data from the various devices and applications in the room, move control, so that applications can be accessed from any place in the room, and also dynamically coordinate applications, so that the output of one application might be used as an input for arbitrary other applications. The project also sets a focus on the integration of legacy applications, which are especially important in the addressed work environment context, where proprietary, domain specific applications are essential to integrate during business meetings. Obviously, R2.7 is strongly addressed by the project.

iROS – Interactive Room Operating System

To support the requirements of pervasive computing environments realizing the integration of various, different sized and shaped interaction devices in the iRoom, a coordination and communication infrastructure called "Interactive Room Operating System" (iROS) was developed that consists of several subsystems. The "Data Heap" addresses the aforementioned movement of data, the "iCrafter" addresses the movement of control, and the "Event Heap" addresses the dynamic coordination of applications. The Event Heap also forms the underlying communication infrastructure of the iROS and is required to be used by all other iROS components and subsystems. An additional subsystem called iStuff (Ballagas et al. 2003) integrates tangible interfaces with the iROS and is discussed in the later section on tangible user interface toolkits.

The Data Heap provides the conversion and transcoding of data for heterogeneous and legacy applications. It stores format information for various application data and transforms data files on the fly, e.g. providing a JPEG image instead of the original PowerPoint document for constrained devices unable to handle the latter format. The iCrafter essentially is a user interface generator that uses templates for generating simple GUIs that can be invoked from

Java or HTML pages. Finally, the Event Heap is the single most important subsystem that stores and forwards messages as events, each consisting of collections of name-type-value-fields. Events are stored in a central repository, based on a tuplespace model, to which all applications can post their own events. The selection of events by the individual applications is realized by pattern matching of fields and values, similar as in Schmidt & Gellersen (2001). By adding timestamps and expiration information to events it is ensured that unconsumed events can be garbage collected by the Event Heap. The Event Heap also implicitly provides a decoupling mechanism (R2.6) for applications, because of the indirection that is imposed by the communication through the tuplespace. Applications do not communicate directly with each other, but post events to Event Heap. This makes it possible to keep the iROS in a functioning state, if single applications crash during execution. Because of the use of a shared repository, the Event Heap does not scale well (R2.8) for large numbers of communicating entities (Johanson & Fox 2002). This however, is not a big issue in the domain of smart rooms, because the number of meaningfully interacting participants and running applications is usually quite limited. The Event Heap is also not appropriate for arbitrary types of communication. For instance, data intensive communication such as the streaming of video is not feasible with the system, it is also not designed for storing large amounts of data that is shared among applications. To cope with the heterogeneity of devices, the Event Heap is currently implemented in different forms for Windows, Linux, Palm OS, and Windows CE.

The Event Heap communication infrastructure of the iRoom realizes some of the demands of smart home environment applications. With the iCrafter and Data Heap components it is possible to adapt user interfaces dynamically during runtime, taking the characteristics of individual interaction devices into account (R2.3, R2.7). Also, it is possible to change the configuration of devices dynamically, because of the indirect communication through the tuplespace. Support for graphical and tangible user interfaces is provided with the iStuff toolkit being separately discussed later (R2.1). The major disadvantage of the Event Heap lies in its shared space implementation that does not realize a full decoupling of communicating entities (Eugster et al. 2003) and its sole reliance on events as a means of information exchange between distributed components (R2.6). This aggravates the management of shared state information between components such as a tangible interface and its graphical interface counterpart that need to maintain a coherent state. The centralized architecture of the Event Heap furthermore imposes a risk on the flexible configuration of devices as a loss of the central server results in a failure of the entire iROS (R2.8). It must be noted, though, that the loss of other components using the Event Heap only results in local failures leaving the overall system in a functional state.

i-Land (Fraunhofer IPSI)

The i-Land project at Fraunhofer IPSI in Darmstadt, Germany, (Streitz et al. 1997) started with a similar focus as the iRoom and even predates the Stanford project. The initial goal was to create a landscape of creativity and innovation addressing also architectural issues in the design of so called "cooperative buildings" that support co-located knowledge workers and project teams. Within the i-Land project, both extensive hardware and software infrastructures were developed. On the hardware side, the most notable achievement of the project is the development and trademark of the term "Roomware®" that relates to computer-augmented room elements such as doors, walls, or furniture with integrated information and communication technology. These Roomware components follow Weiser's notion of disappearing computers in so far as the computer as a device disappears and becomes invisibly integrated into the smart Roomware components, but its functionality remains ubiquitously available. Roomware thus attempts not to focus on interaction with computer technology, but to hide the technology as much as possible within physical artifacts to facilitate a natural and human centered interaction. Roomware components were built iteratively in two generations (cf. Streitz et al. 2002). The respective Roomware Laboratory in Darmstadt works as a living lab for testing an orchestration of several Roomware components and also informed the establishment of the iRoom. The DynaWall®, a wall-sized interactive surface, CommChair®, a chair with an integrated touch sensitive display, ConnecTable®, a table component that combines its smart surface with other ConnecTables, when physically attached, and InteracTable®, and interactive table with an integrated horizontal display, are currently integrated with the i-Land landscape. All Roomware components are connected via Ethernet and run a coordination and user interface infrastructure called BEACH. In addition to the graphical displays integrated in the various Roomware components, i-Land also provides support for associative tangible user interfaces (R2.1), most notably the "Passage" mechanism (Tandler 2004). The Passage mechanism allows to associate information to arbitrary physical artifacts that are measured by their weight (or by an RFID tag in a later revision of the system). These physical bookmarks to virtual information are used to quickly transfer data objects from one Roomware component to another by simply placing the artifact on dedicated spaces at the component (so called "bridges") and then performing an appropriate gesture at the touch sensitive display.

BEACH – Basic Environment for Active Collaboration with Hypermedia

The BEACH software infrastructure addresses various issues regarding co-located computer supported cooperative work (CSCW) applications. It provides a generic user interface subsystem that tailors the adaptation of information to the specific characteristics of interaction devices (R2.3), such as automatically outfitting arbitrary window objects with means of rotation on horizontal issues (tackling the problem of different viewing angles). User awareness is also addressed with an audio based subsystem that provides context clues on the spatial configuration of co-located users' workspaces (Müller-Tomfelde et al. 2003). Taking the touch sensitive displays of Roomware components into account, it also provides an incremental gesture recognition module for hand-drawn gestures. Several specialized user interface modules e.g. for creativity support (Mind Maps, MagNets) are available to augment applications with domain specific interaction capabilities. BEACH is based on the COAST framework (Schuckmann et al. 1999) that implements shared objects as a tightly coupled communication approach (!R2.6). This tight coupling of components is suitable for the relatively static setup of Roomware components, but becomes problematic in highly dynamic and distributed environments due to its reliance on a central server component (the "Mediator"). BEACH provides an application framework for developing custom applications that exploit the user interface and communication features of the BEACH software architecture. While it has been proved to be taken up easily by a growing number of student developers, the support for interoperability with legacy applications is still minimal today, hampering a deployment of BEACH in many real-life work situations. The i-Land project recently also integrated the Stanford Event Heap to interoperate with the applications in the Roomware Laboratory.

What BEACH excels at is the modeling of social spaces, reflected in a sophisticated conceptual model with multiple layers and compartments, and appropriate support in the software architecture and programming framework (R2.9). Depending on the functional attributes of individual Roomware components, a seamless transition between public and private interaction spaces can be realized in a single interaction device. For instance, a CommChair component can be provided with a shared user interface for making information on a public DynaWall private, and likewise publicize its private content on the DynaWall with a simple gesture stroke. The support for graphical and physical user interfaces is also very strong in BEACH with gesture recognition, associative tangible UIs and RFID sensors all exposed by the programming framework (R2.1). The graphical adaptation capabilities nicely take the affordances of horizontal, vertical, small, large, and PDA based displays into account, providing rotation, zooming, and transparency where appropriate (R2.3). It must be noted, however, that due to the focus on office applications and the Smalltalk based custom implementation of the graphical user interface subsystem there is no appropriate support for entertainment or multimedia applications yet implemented (!R2.2). For instance, video clips, 3D graphics, or even rotation of window objects at arbitrary angles are not feasible with the current implementation of BEACH. Finally, the mostly static nature of Roomware environments is also reflected in the lack of runtime adaptability (R2.7). While software components can be removed from a running i-Land infrastructure and later re-integrated with an automatic state synchronization, there is no reconfiguration (such as e.g. the spatial relationships to other components) possible while a component is active, because components are configured only at startup.

The work in this dissertation stems from the context of the i-Land project and contributes an alternative communication and coordination infrastructure and tangible interfaces not related to the BEACH software architecture and application framework. Since this dissertation is concerned with home entertainment applications, the former i-Land work that focused on the support of co-located collaboration in smart office spaces was not a well suited foundation any more.

Easy Living (Microsoft Research)

The now abandoned Easy Living project from the Vision Group at Microsoft Research dealt with the development of an architecture for intelligent environments that supports the dynamic aggregation of diverse interaction devices into a single coherent user experience (Brumitt et al. 2000). The research of the project mainly focused on using computer vision for the tracking of people and devices in a smart home environment. This allows for automatically providing services and user interfaces tailored to the positions of persons in a room and the computing resources nearby (R2.9). In addition to computer vision, location information was also gained from other sensing technologies and then fused to obtain better accuracy. For instance, Microsoft's own RADAR system (Bahl & Padmanabhan 2000) that allows 802.11b-enabled mobile devices to compute their location based on the signal strength of known infrastructure access points, was supported by the Easy Living project. Other potential sources for gaining location information included fingerprint sensors at well known positions or login information at computer terminals (R2.1).

The project addressed several research areas that are relevant for the provision of location aware services. Next to the perception of devices and users via various sensor technologies, the development of an appropriate world model (R2.9) for representing the relationships between the physical entities and the related services, service descriptions to support decomposition of device control, internal logic, and user interface, there was also a focus on a distributed middleware for coordinating devices and services in the environment.

The project's world model called "Easy Living Geometric Model" (EZLGM) represents physical relationships between entities in the world. It was designed to work with multiple perception technologies and abstracts the application away from the details of the respective sensing modalities. In its last published version, it could handle sub-meter localization of entities in a closed small-scale environment with larger scales still remaining an open research issue. While the inhabitant tracking functionality and the related world model are important for the proactive provision of services, the communication and coordination middleware is more relevant in the context of this dissertation.

InConcert

Easy Living used a communication middleware called InConcert that was developed at Microsoft Research in conjunction with other groups. It provides asynchronous message passing, machine independent addressing (R2.6) and XML-based message protocols. The asynchronous message passing approach was taken in order to avoid blocking. Furthermore, the asynchronous approach timely decouples senders and receivers of messages. Clients are thus not to expect reply messages as a return from the original request, but at any later point in time, thus being robust against sporadic disintegration of components. This time decoupling feature is also found in BEACH and iROS, although differently implemented.

Communication between different machines is handled by integrating a naming and lookup service into the delivery mechanism. When started, a component requests a name (an "Instance ID") and while running provides the lookup service with a periodic keep-alive message. Once the message is delivered to the correct process, its content is decoded from the respective XML description. This mechanism addresses delivery problems in common architectures such as CORBA, when the target is moved to another machine after registration. While this is not a space decoupling as found in the Event Heap of iROS, where interacting parties do not even need to know each other, it is still a contribution towards mobility that is advantageous over the BEACH communication model that does not provide a post-registration mobility. The major problem with InConcert is that state changes are not transmitted via an asynchronous event system, but by polling the respective entity. As the number of connections between services increases, polling, however, ceases to be a viable mechanism (!R2.8). Consequently, it is currently not possible with InConcert to register event requests that notify an entity, when a particular state is reached. For instance, one cannot trigger e.g. the light in the room to be turned off, when the TV program is finished without constantly polling the state of the light.

In conclusion, one of the main contributions of the Easy Living project is the provision of unobtrusive and implicit user interfaces in smart home environments that really address Weiser's notion of calm technology (R2.1). InConcert succeeds in integrating various physical interfaces and sensors with traditional graphical user interfaces in a distributed environment, although the lack of an asynchronous event system is a serious drawback compared to the aforementioned middleware solutions (!R2.8). The world model (R2.9) supports the project's focus on providing location awareness in a smart home. Since implicit, sensor based interaction is favored in contrast to explicit interaction as e.g. in the i-Land project, there are only few contributions in terms of device adapted graphical interfaces. These are addressed in detail both in the i-Land and the iRoom environments. Due to the sophisticated geometric model, shared social spaces with varying degrees of privacy can be realized elegantly.

Intelligent Room (MIT Artificial Intelligence Lab)

The Intelligent Room (previously referred to as Hal, later as AIRE Space) is part of the large Oxygen Project at MIT (http://oxygen.lcs.mit.edu), in which human centered pervasive computing technology is investigated that is envisioned to become ubiquitously available "like oxygen in the air we breathe". The Intelligent Room is a smart environment somewhat similarly set up as the Stanford iRoom. It is equipped with various interactive displays and

2. State of the Art

also traditional desktop computers. Microphone and camera arrays are mounted on the ceiling of the Intelligent Room to locate users and infer their activities. Accordingly, users can speak with, gesture to, and otherwise interact with the room (R2.1). For the interactive surfaces of the room, several dedicated sketching and design tools were developed such as ASSIST which is a sketching environment that understands and interprets mechanical engineers' sketches. Another tool, Annotea (Kahan & Koivunen 2001) is used for shared web annotations in the context of the Semantic Web. Other software applications also exist for capturing and recording co-located work meetings. Additionally, the Cricket location support system (Priyantha et al. 2000) that operates with ultrasound and RF signal transmission is deployed in the Intelligent Room.

Several software infrastructures were developed to integrate the various sensing and interaction devices distributed in the Intelligent Room. Among them are network routing oriented systems such as "CORE" (communication-oriented routing environment) or "Click" and systems for realizing pervasive computing user interfaces. These are subsumed in a related project called "Pebbles" (PDAs for Entry of Both Bytes and Locations from External Sources) that mostly deal with distributing user interfaces among multiple devices (Myers 2001). Pebbles has not developed a single toolkit or infrastructure, but contributed multiple research prototypes of applications utilizing so-called MMUIs (Multi Machine User Interfaces). The developed applications, e.g. PebblesDraw, Remote Commander, or Slideshow Commander, as well as the underlying interaction techniques such as "Semantic Snarfing" elegantly demonstrate how the individual affordances of different device classes can be used complementarily to distribute user interfaces ergonomically and naturally in a smart environment. Typical Pebbles applications are limited to one or two PDAs tightly coupled to a PC server application, thus being inappropriate for highly dynamic environments with arbitrary numbers of heterogeneous devices (!R2.6). Therefore, to provide a robust foundation for coupling various interaction devices in the Intelligent Room, an agent-based software infrastructure was developed called "Metaglue".

Metaglue

MetaGlue receives its name from the notion of computational "glue" that ties together large groups of software agents associated with the various devices and applications in the Intelligent Room (Coen et al. 1999). MetaGlue's design goals are the provision of wide-scale communication and discovery services (R2.8), the ability for users to interact with software and data from any location, and the management of sharing limited computing resources such as displays or microphones among applications. MetaGlue is implemented as an extension to the Java language, introducing a new Agent class to access MetaGlue's features. Metaglue includes a post-compiler that is run over the compiled class files to generate Metaglue agents that operate on a tweaked Java virtual machine called "Metaglue Virtual Machine". The Agent class provides a custom remote method invocation (RMI) mechanism that supports dynamic reconnection (R2.7). This allows agents to disconnect and later reconnect without losing state information, so that e.g. devices can be flexibly integrated during runtime. The states of individual Agents are stored in a centralized database to provide for persistence while being offline. Next to the database, another central component called "Catalog" is provided that serves as a simple service directory. Agents register with the Catalog when they are constructed and convey their capabilities, so that other Agents can query for capabilities instead of concrete agents introducing a layer of indirection to inter-agent communication. Finally, a hierarchical set of specialized agents called "Dealers" are available that are responsible for distributing resources to the rest of the system. This resource management

19

scheme is quite sophisticated with multiple agent prototypes that each provide different rules for resource allocation, distribution, etc.

Metaglue follows the agent metaphor more directly than the other middleware solutions discussed so far, but due to the centralized nature of several key components, it fails to provide a truly distributed infrastructure of autonomous entities (!R2.8). The communication approach is more lightweight than the other discussed solutions, and like InConcert it does not realize asynchronous messaging. Due to the lower abstraction level than all other middleware systems it might take more effort to create applications with Metaglue, especially since Metaglue does not directly support modeling or developing user interfaces, social, or physical spaces (!R2.9). The strongest contribution of Metaglue is the integrated resource management and distribution functionality that is missing or only rudimentarily realized in most of the other systems. For applications such as games, where all participating users and devices are integrated in a single global task (playing the game) this contribution is, however, not too crucial. Nonetheless, for certain scenarios such as pervasive gaming applications that "compete" with other application within a smart environment, it might even be essential to provide sophisticated resource management functionalities. Within the focus of this dissertation, however, the resource problem of other, unrelated applications is disregarded. Within a single application, however, resource configuration and device setup is indeed a crucial topic which is addressed by the contributed software platform and unrelated to Metaglue's cross-application resource management.

Other Smart Environments Projects

While the research projects discussed above are especially influential and relevant in the context of this dissertation due to their communication middleware developments, there are also other contributions to the field of pervasive computing environments with less impact or other focal points. These are not reviewed in detail, but briefly surveyed for the reader to further investigate.

The Aware Home project at Georgia Tech (Abowd et al. 2000) has a similar focus as the Easy Living project, namely to "create a home environment that is aware of its occupants whereabouts and activities". The project has developed two toolkits for context capturing and processing. INCA (Infrastructure for Capture and Access) supports the construction of applications that capture details of a live experience and provide future access to that experience by various means of searching and browsing. The Context Toolkit is a Java based toolkit for developing context aware applications with functionality to abstract and fuse heterogeneous context information. Several applications were built using the toolkits and deployed in the Aware Home living lab. Tangible and graphical interfaces and their respective coordination middleware are of lesser importance in the Aware Home project.

Another smart home project initiated at the University of Texas at Arlington is the MavHome (Managing an Adaptive Versatile Home) that mainly focuses on providing an intelligent and proactive environment for managing and integrating various home appliances (Das et al. 2002). In MavHome, the home is viewed as an intelligent agent that tries to maximize the comfort of its inhabitants while at the same time reducing resource consumption. A reasoning infrastructure is being developed to optimize the different goals of the agent. Various independent software and sensing components are distributed in the "MavPad" on-campus apartment that are connected via simple CORBA. Clearly, the contributions of the project are more related to artificial intelligence methods than on user interface infrastructures.

2. State of the Art

Although not directly concerned with the entirety of issues regarding smart environments, the Things That Think (TTT) consortium at MIT Media Lab (http://ttt.media.mit.edu/) has developed a multitude of prototypes and demonstrations targeted at pervasive computing functionality put into everyday objects. Most of these are individual applications such as smart surfaces, messenger services, or tangible interface prototypes; however a distributed Java platform called "Hive" was also developed to build TTT applications with (Minar et al. 1999). Hive is an agents platform that provides ad-hoc agent interaction, ontologies of agent capabilities, mobile agents, and a graphical interface to view the distributed system of agents. Interaction is based on Remote Procedure Calls (Java RMI) which implies synchronization coupling and makes it thus unsuitable for distributed event systems. Consequently, Hive was mostly used with static ambient displays and tangible interfaces.

Conclusions

In this section, the current state of the art in pervasive computing environments and the respective communication and coordination infrastructures were discussed. Some of the presented systems have rather a broad scope and include sophisticated functionality for adapting graphical output to the heterogeneous interaction devices in a smart environment (BEACH, iROS), while others solely focus on providing a flexible communication platform. To flexibly integrate various device components, the middleware must at least cope with temporary losses of connection and mobility of services, which is handled sufficiently by all solutions (R2.7). The communication paradigms range from tightly coupled approaches such as message passing (InConcert), remote method invocation (Metaglue), or shared data objects (BEACH) to more advanced loosely coupled approaches such as the tuplespace model of the iROS Event Heap which is thus more flexible for distributed applications (R2.6). A full decoupling of communicating entities adhering to a publish/ subscribe approach adding synchronization decoupling to the time and space decoupling of the shared tuplespace (Eugster at al. 2003) is not realized by any of the current solutions.

Most systems also adhere to centralized server components such as Metaglue's Catalog, or the Mediator of BEACH, despite their conceptual peer-to-peer distribution that, in the case of Metaglue, even explicitly follows an autonomous agent approach. One could argue that smart environments are typically limited to individual rooms or buildings and do not require a completely decentralized infrastructure that scales to millions of nodes. Provided that the central components are sufficiently robust and failsafe, the discussed solutions should therefore suffice, although Johanson & Fox (2002) explicitly point out the scalability problem of the Event Heap implementation. In the field of pervasive entertainment applications that include both stationary and mobile players and interconnect different home environments, the number of communicating entities might increase and scalability might consequently become an issue (R2.8).

The middleware platforms BEACH and iROS both address issues of individual device characteristics that need to be taken into account to provide for an adequate user interface orchestration. In both platforms, however, only basic display properties, i.e. resolution and vertical/ horizontal orientation, are modeled, although a dedicated tangible user interface toolkit for iROS exists which is discussed in the next section (R2.1, R2.3). To address the multitude of interaction devices in smart environments that do not include traditional graphical displays such as audio or tangible interfaces, it would be advisable to provide a more general model that goes beyond the exclusive use of graphical displays.

2. State of the Art

To conclude, R2.1 and R2.7 are addressed and met by most reviewed pervasive computing environments. To a certain degree, R2.6 is also realized in most systems using different communication paradigms, although no current solution realizes full time, space, and synchronization decoupling. Given the specific nature of the application domain addressed in this dissertation that is different from the office worker's focus of most reviewed systems, it is not surprising that the most predominant gaps identified relate to R2.1 and R2.2. Since R2.1 can be seen as a precondition to R2.4 and R2.5 that are relevant for the next section of this chapter, the adequate integration of tangible and graphical interfaces is especially crucial.

The identified shortcomings of the discussed middleware are addressed in the contributed communication infrastructure that is described in a later chapter of this thesis. Communication infrastructures alone, however, are only preconditions to the deployment and distribution of arbitrary numbers of tangible and graphical user interfaces in a smart environment. The design and implementation of pervasive user interfaces and interaction devices come with their own challenges and issues, and it is therefore important to be able to prototype, tweak, and evaluate user interface components easily. Since pervasive computing implies the constraints and complexities of the physical world, an appropriate toolkit support is even more crucial than with traditional graphical user interfaces on desktop PCs. The next sections therefore review the current state of the art in pervasive computing user interface toolkits, both for tangible and graphical user interfaces.

2.3. Tangible User Interfaces

Tangible user interfaces (TUIs) play an important role in the realization of pervasive computing environments. These interfaces associate physical, tangible objects with virtual information and allow for interaction metaphors that are based on the users' previous knowledge of the real world. Many physical artifacts "afford" their intended usage and thus facilitate intuitive interaction. The term "affordance" was coined by the perceptual psychologist J. J. Gibson (1979) to refer to the actionable properties between an object and an actor which are implicitly conveyed by the object. Due to the complexity of the architectural spaces in home and office environments, it is essential not to overstrain the users with completely novel forms of interaction, but to support interfaces that are natural and intuitive to the uninitiated user.

The other major advantage of tangible interfaces lies in the seamless integration of representation and control, as Ullmer & Ishii (2001) point out. Traditional graphical interfaces fundamentally distinguish between input devices for controlling or manipulating information and graphical output devices for representing and displaying information. The controls, such as keyboard or mice, are not directly related to the representation, i.e. the output on the screen. In a prototypical tangible interface such as an abacus, the control is also the representation, because there is no differentiation between input and output. By eliminating the indirection of input and output, the mental capacity needed to interact with the interface is reduced. This is especially relevant for group situations with an increased information load. Accordingly, Cohen & McGee (2004) report from the successful installation of tangible and multimodal interfaces in group applications, in which previous task distraction of graphical interfaces was found to be counterproductive. Patten & Ishii (2000) additionally report from increased performance in spatial organization tasks with a tangible user interface compared to traditional GUIs, also relating to the differences in mental processing demands.

22

2. State of the Art

While tangible interfaces provide potential benefits for the interaction in smart environments, Shaer et al. (2004) point out that the development of these interfaces is currently more challenging than building traditional graphical user interfaces. Some of the conceptual and technical difficulties identified include

Interlinked virtual and physical worlds

Traditional graphical user interfaces deal with virtual entities alone. Tangible interfaces, however, comprise both virtual and physical elements that exchange information with each other and have their own states. The challenge for the developer is both to ensure that virtual and physical state information is consistent and to determine which information to represent digitally and physically. This directly relates to the aforementioned requirement R2.5 and also relates to the classic distinction of functionality beyond and within the desktop, see e.g. Kaptelinin & Czerwinski (2007).

Multiple behaviors

The behavior of a widget in a graphical user interface is determined and encapsulated by the widget itself. Constraints can easily be formulated on what is possible in combination with other widgets and what is not. In the physical world, the developer cannot impose any constraints on how physical objects and artifacts interact with each other. Therefore, the mutual impact of physical objects must be considered, when the behavior of a certain physical object is defined.

Multiple actions

In contrast to graphical user interfaces that are commonly restricted to the six fundamental interaction tasks (select, position, orient, path, quantify, and text) as defined in Foley et al. (1984), the space of possible actions in the physical world is much larger and includes numerous activities such as stroking, tossing, pushing, tapping etc. It is thus more difficult to select and define the meaningful actions and to align them with the aforementioned affordances of the physical objects. This potentially large space of possible actions also relates to requirement R2.4.

No standard input/ output devices

There are not yet any standard mechanisms or technology bases for accomplishing a given user interface task. For instance, the identification of a physical artifact on a table surface could be implemented using computer vision, RFID, weight, etc, resulting in very different input devices that each come with unique implications for control and integration. Therefore, it can be costly and difficult to introduce novel technological solutions for tangible interfaces.

To address these and other challenges, appropriate software toolkits are necessary to unburden the developer from some of the complexities introduced with tangible interfaces. The current state of the art in tangible interface toolkits is discussed in the following sections. All of the toolkits implicitly adhere to the MCRpd interaction model developed by Ullmer & Ishii (2001) that introduces the notion of physical and virtual representation to the traditional "model-view-controller" (MVC) archetype of graphical user interfaces.

MCRpd (MIT Media Lab)

The term MCRpd stands for "model-control-representation (physical and digital)" and extends the MVC with the distribution of the representations among virtual and physical worlds (cf. Shaer 2004). While MCRpd itself is not a TUI toolkit, it elaborates on the characteristics of tangible interfaces in a way that is appropriate for the implementation of the

2. State of the Art

actual toolkits discussed below. MCRpd picks up the notion of representation sensu the external manifestation of information that can be perceived with human sensors. Representation is divided into two classes. First, there are physical representations of information embodied in physical, tangible form. Second, there are digital representations that are conveyed by a display or other standard means of computer output. Applied to the classic MVC interaction model of Smalltalk-80 that addresses GUIs, the MVC "view" is divided into the physical and virtual representation subcomponents in a tangible interface. While the "model" remains separated from the other components in both GUIs and TUIs, the GUI focuses on the separation of graphical or digital representation and control. The TUI, however, highlights the integration of physical representation and control, both being separated from the digital representation. This is due to TUI artifacts physically embodying both the control and a central representational aspect of the interface.

Two important implications of the MCRpd are related to the physical representations. First, TUI artifacts are generally persistent, i.e. the physical representation of a tangible interface does not cease to exist after the termination of the digital application. This is in contrast to any graphical interface which can be arbitrarily destroyed or duplicated. Second, both people and digital systems frequently perceive the physical state of TUI artifacts, hence it is important to ensure that the human perception does not stand in contrast to the digital perception, although the set of state parameters processed by human and digital system does not necessarily need to be identical.

Ullmer & Ishii (2001) explicitly address the importance of the digital representation as a perceptually coupled and actively mediated counterpart to the physical representation. Ideal tangible interfaces feature a balance of digital and physical representations, with the digital representations taking a major role in the display of information processed by the underlying computer application (the "model"). Traditional graphics and audio thus enhance tangible interfaces with appropriate feedback mechanisms to changes in the physical representation.

Three dominant categories interpreting the physical representations of tangible interfaces are identified by the authors. These consist of a.) spatial approaches that directly interpret the spatial configurations of tangible objects, e.g. a chess board with playing pieces on it, b.) relational approaches that interpret arbitrary other logical relationships between objects, e.g. sequences or adjacencies, and c.) the constructive assembly of modular interface elements as in traditional LEGO bricks or their computer augmented counterparts, e.g. the mediaBlocks system (Ullmer et al. 1998). These categories are sufficient to describe the majority of tangible interfaces, but are not exhaustive. Another category that has recently gained attention is that of exertion interfaces (Müller et al. 2003) in which physical effort or physical skills are measured.

A more recent interaction model than the MCRpd was proposed by Shaer et al. (2004) as the "Token and Constraints" (TAC) paradigm. It is based on the notions of physical objects (so called pyfos), tokens, variables, and constraints that stand in defining relationships to each other. The authors demonstrate that several existing tangible interfaces can be described with the TAC paradigm and propose the creation of a toolkit based on their approach, but as of today, such a toolkit has not been realized. TAC is useful as an analytical tool and a novel descriptive language, but so far its contribution for the process of developing tangible interfaces is unclear. MCRpd thus remains the standard paradigm implicitly or explicitly informing the development of TUI toolkits.

2. State of the Art

iStuff (Stanford Interactive Workspaces)

The iStuff toolkit (Ballagas et al. 2003) was developed in the Interactive Workspaces project at Stanford and addresses the need for supporting tangible and physical interfaces in smart environments. As described before, the support for interaction devices in the iRoom mainly focus on interactive surfaces and standard graphical user interfaces. Insofar, the development of the iStuff toolkit was a consequent step towards realizing smart environments with interaction capabilities beyond the graphical display (R2.1).

The iStuff toolkit picks up the communication and coordination infrastructure of the iRoom, it is thus built on top of iROS, the meta-operating system that allows for coupling different applications and devices. Communication is realized with the Event Heap that coordinates the distribution of events to the respective recipients.

In the iStuff toolkit, the physical interaction devices are called components. These components are basic input and output devices that generate or receive events via the Event Heap. Components include buttons, sliders, light bulbs, etc. They are mapped to the various applications in an iRoom by a dedicated coordinating software called PatchPanel. Each component consists of a physical device, a transceiver, and a software component called Proxy. The Proxy tackles with the device's idiosyncrasies and exposes an interface to the Event Heap. Once the Event Heap handles the communication with other components in the iRoom, the advantages of the iROS infrastructure become accessible for the iStuff toolkit, namely platform and protocol independence, support for multiple simultaneous users, and the ease of integration with other applications.

In order to fit into the Event Heap communication mechanisms, iStuff components emit iStuff events. These iStuff events are specific to each iStuff component, so that an iButton consequently emits its pressed state and an iSlider emits its position over a fixed axis. To allow applications to deal with multiple iStuff components without having to process each the various iStuff events, the abstraction software component called PatchPanel translates iStuff events to more abstract events. The PatchPanel is implemented as an Event Heap client that listens for any events matching an editable event-mapping configuration and adds new abstract events to the Event Heap. Ballagas et al. (2003) exemplify this mechanism with an application called iPong which is an adaptation of the classic arcade game to the iRos infrastructure. While initial versions of the iPong game had to explicitly process iSlider events in order to allow the paddles to be controllable by iSlider components, a later release worked with the abstracted "MovePaddle" events that were generated by the PatchPanel. This abstraction introduced by the PatchPanel facilitates the integration of arbitrary input devices with the iPong application without having to alter the iPong code. To add new iStuff components one simply needs to provide a respective event-mapping configuration to the PatchPanel (R2.6).

The iStuff components realized so far are mostly very basic devices such as knobs, sliders, or mice. They are generic enough to be utilized in many kinds of different tangible interfaces. Due to the communication via the Event Heap it is possible to coordinate components via state events, implementing basic state machines using events. However, since the Event Heap does not distribute data structures to its clients, such control structures need to be explicitly modelled in an application and thus cannot be considered part of the Event Heap (!R2.4).

25

2. State of the Art

The conceptual separation of iStuff components into proxy and physical device is a prerequisite for the rapid development of hybrid interfaces. The proxy is merely the connector between the signals of the device and the software interfaces of the Event Heap.

Given that the Event Heap existed before the iStuff components were developed, it is not surprising that the communication between iStuff components and other iROS applications is solely realized via dedicated iROS events. The advantage of this approach is clearly the reuse of the existing infrastructure and the implied interoperability. "Legacy" iROS applications can directly be controlled via iStuff components that have their specialized events transformed by the PatchPanel. The flexible (dis-)integration of iStuff components during runtime is also provided through iROS (R2.7). The major disadvantage, however, is also related to the event based communication via the Event Heap. As long as iStuff components are very simple and do not have any complex state information, their entire state can be communicated as an event.

For more complex tangible user interfaces such as e.g. a physical game board that is common in pervasive gaming applications, this is not feasible any more, especially if not only positions and object identifications are processed, but also additional state information such as object orientations or individual object states. The lack of a dedicated persistent storage of the iStuff components' physical states therefore results in two limitations: 1.) All the iStuff components are very primitive devices (!R2.4) such as knobs or buttons that can communicate their entire states over the Event Heap as events. 2.) There are no virtual counterpart components that share their states with the physical components providing sophisticated debugging or replacement functions (!R2.5), e.g. when an iStuff components disconnects or breaks. Since the functionality of the Event Heap can be exploited, arbitrary iROS snooping mechanisms could naturally be tailored to include iStuff components, so that the debugging limitation might be overcome. Regarding the simplicity of physical devices, one might argue that the Event Heap also facilitates the composition of individual components, so that more complex user interfaces can be built from the primitive individual iStuff components. While individual components can indeed be associated or aggregated and allow for interesting event chains such as linked light switches, more complex user interfaces nevertheless require the coordination of a multitude of iROS events, which is not facilitated by the toolkit.

In conclusion, the iStuff components integrate seamlessly with the previously existing iROS infrastructure and enrich the iRoom with a distributed set of simple tangible user interfaces. Especially existing iROS applications profit by the toolkit's integrated mechanisms for translating iStuff events to general iROS events, so that legacy applications can be equipped with tangible interaction techniques. This flexible legacy support is the major contribution of the iStuff components. On the downside, there are currently no appropriate virtual counterpart components (!R2.5) and the existing physical components are only very simplistic (!R2.4). Due to the implementation of the Event Heap, this is also unlikely to change in the future.

Phidgets (Calgary)

The Phidgets toolkit (Greenberg & Boyle 2002) picks up the notion of a widget as an element of a graphical user interface and applies it to the domain of tangible user interfaces. The resulting physical widgets (i.e. Phidgets) abstract and wrap physical input and output in the same way as a graphical widget. While implementation and construction details are hidden, a unified API allows accessing them in standardized way.

2. State of the Art

Each Phidget consists of a physical device that is connected to a Windows PC via a USB cable as well as a Phidget-specific COM object that implements the functionality necessary to access the specific physical device. A wire protocol for the USB line manages information exchange between the device and the host computer and handles device identification (unique ID and device type). Each device can also convey state information specific to its type. Likewise, the host computer can transmit device specific requests. Regarding the definition of a Phidget as a composite of a physical device, a wire protocol, and a COM object, the Phidget concept is largely identical to the iStuff components, where each component consists of a physical device, a transceiver, and a Proxy. Apart from iStuff components not being bound to a wired connection that might be unsuitable for mobile pervasive computing applications, their virtual counterparts also differ in scope and complexity. Each Phidget-specific COM object is not only responsible for providing a virtual interface to the physical device. It is also required to implement a simulation mode and a graphical representation through an ActiveX control. The simulation mode allows the developer or end user to use the Phidget, even if the physical device is absent .The COM object is responsible for setting its own simulation characteristics, so that the application using the Phidget continues to operate correctly with the virtual simulation of the physical device (R2.5). The ActiveX controls wrap the COM objects and provide a GUI for controlling the Phidgets and displaying their physical (or simulated) states. Since the graphical interfaces are contained in ActiveX controls, they can be used with respective interface builders such as Visual Basic and simply be dragged into arbitrary dialog resources.

To monitor and communicate with attached devices, the Phidget architecture consists of an additional component, the PhidgetManager. The PhidgetManager is a COM object that exposes an event-based programming interfaces for application developers to get notified when devices are attached or detached. Whenever a device is attached, the PhidgetManager creates an appropriate Phidget-specific COM object and returns an interface to it to allow the application to access the respective device-specific functionality.

A communication or coordination infrastructure is not directly addressed in the Phidgets project. However, Greenberg and Fitchett (2001) present an architecture extension that adds a notification server implementing a shared dictionary. Applications can publish key/value pairs into the dictionary. Likewise, applications can subscribe to particular keys via pattern matching. By publishing the Phidgets' state information into the notification server, distributed applications based on physical devices can be implemented that communicate in a decoupled fashion (R2.6). The authors give an example of capturing a person's presence with a proximity sensor, publishing it to the dictionary and then have another application subscribe to this information in turn triggering a Phidget device that rotates a physical object.

While the initial set of Phidgets consisted of only few devices such as a servo or a controllable power bar, they are still being further developed today. The Phidgets research project has been commercialized and the devices and software can be purchased on the web. Current Phidgets include servos, LC displays, RFID readers, motors, and lamps. Due to the COM implementation, bindings for several programming languages exist, such as Visual Basic, C++, or Java.

In contrast to the iStuff components, Phidgets are closer to realizing the full potential of the unification of representation and control, because object states are also persistently represented in the ActiveX controls. This allows for the sophisticated virtual counterparts that are available for the Phidgets. The simulation mode of the ActiveX controls provides appropriate control mechanisms either when a physical input component is unavailable (substitution) or when a physical output device needs to be configured, e.g. turning a lamp on and off via a widget. Missing, however, is a consistent way of dealing with the issue of both physical input devices and widgets to be used simultaneously for interaction. This means that a widget in simulation mode might substitute a physical input device that is (temporarily) disconnected, but upon reconnection it is forced to yield control back to the physical device or the physical device will not be accepted for interaction. A mechanism for ensuring consistency between virtual and physical representation is unfortunately missing (!R2.5).

The current range of supported Phidgets includes only rather basic physical components, which is due to the fact that Phidgets specifically aim at low cost, general purpose, and rapid prototyping (!R2.4). Therefore, the focus on USB communication is an appropriate design choice, since it is both cheaper and more robust than the wireless iStuff devices that also require a functioning Event Heap installed. The implementation of the virtual counterparts as ActiveX controls is also appropriate for the rapid prototyping approach, because they are interoperable with practically any development environment.

To summarize, Phidgets provide only simple physical devices (!R2.4) with more sophisticated virtual counterparts than iStuff (R2.5), but also lacking a simultaneous widget/ phidget operating mode. The interoperability with traditional GUI builders is favored over the interoperability of Phidgets among each other, so that Phidgets seem more suitable for prototyping small-scale TUIs than distributed environments of multiple user interfaces. Nonetheless, Phidgets do succeed in bridging the gap between usage within and beyond the desktop (Kaptelinin & Czerwinski 2007), although real domain consistency (R2.5) is not realized.

Papier-Mache (Berkeley)

Papier-Mache is a tangible interface toolkit that aims at facilitating the development of applications involving tangible interfaces (Klemmer et al. 2004). The focus of the project is more narrow than iSuff or Phidgets in that it only supports paper-based TUIs and RFID (!R2.4). The paper-based interfaces are either barcode-based or involve computer vision. Input from any of these sources is abstracted within the Papier-Mache software and then exposed to the applications in a technology-independent way, so that developers can retarget their applications to different input sources without any (or with only limited) changes to the program code. Papier-Mache features extensive support for debugging (R2.5). For instance, an object monitoring window can be displayed at any time that gives information about the current input objects and image input and processing.

The development of the toolkit was motivated both by a literature review and by structured interviews with TUI designers, so that design decisions of the toolkit are backed up by empirical data. These include the importance of feedback to users and developers, thus motivating the aforementioned object monitoring window. Furthermore, abstracting from the concrete input technology should result in two metaphors for authoring input behavior: Associations and Classifications. Classifications relate to the general category of physical objects. For instance, in the classic marble answering machine TUI (Ishii & Ullmer 1997) the classification relates to marbles being messages. Complementarily, the association addresses specific cases such as message X being associated with a specific call from person Y. Papier-Mache consequently classifies input and associates it with application behavior.

2. State of the Art

The toolkit is Java based (Java Media Framework) and is available under open source licenses. The physical objects represented in Papier-Mache are referred to as "Phobs". They are acquired and generated at an input layer that utilizes the different sensor technologies. The discovery of input devices and the connection to the respective hardware is taken care for automatically by Papier-Mache. Users only need to identify which of the found input sources are to be used for generating events about the Phobs' addition, updating, and removal from a sensor's view. The events are identical for any sensing technology, but different input technologies might provide different types of information, depending on the capabilities of the sensors. For instance, RFID only conveys the unique tag ID, while vision provides more information such as bounding boxes or shapes.

To model the classifications and associations, representation mappings are implemented by so called "AssociationFactories" that listen to events from the input sources. The factory receives a callback and creates respective representation instances such as audio or video signals or text for each newly detected phob. Both nouns and actions (cf. Fishkin et al. 1998) are supported as association elements.

Apart from the object monitoring output, Papier-Mache also includes the ability to create virtual placeholders for physical objects that allow for debugging applications when no sensor hardware is available. This is referred to as "Wizard of Oz Control". A similar, but more flexible debugging mechanism is also realized for the Phidgets toolkit (R2.5).

Compared to the other toolkits discussed so far, Papier-Mache has a rather limited scope, being capable to deal with only three sensor technologies of which two are practically identical in the richness of data they provide (RFID and barcodes). For these two technologies, the benefits over dealing with the input data directly come down to the (trivial) abstraction of input data, the association with virtual representation instances, and the debugging support with the Wizard of Oz Control. The vision interface provides more detailed information about the physical objects and allows for topological or spatial applications. However, neither vision nor the simple associative technologies provide for modeling different states of objects and thus the interaction supported is limited to objects being added or removed. Both iStuff and Phidgets facilitate far more variation in object states, consequently relating to the notion of physical widgets, whereas Papier-Mache replaces the widget metaphor with basic events resulting in less powerful toolkit functionality. Obviously, the toolkit is aimed at rapid prototyping with minimal coding effort at the expense of limited flexibility. The toolkit's ability to automatically find and utilize arbitrary input devices without a real query interface is also convenient, but might hamper serious deployment.

Finally, there is no communication or coordination infrastructure for the Papier-Mache toolkit which is clearly aimed at using with single desktop PCs, although due to the lack of other interactions than adding and removing objects this should be more trivial than with the other toolkits discussed so far.

Calder Toolkit (Carnegie Mellon)

A more recently developed tangible interface toolkit called "Calder" is primarily geared towards supporting product designers and consequently addresses issues such as the preservation of fluidity and flexibility in the design process as a justification and design rationale (Lee et al. 2004). The result is a hardware and software toolkit that sets out to augment typical GUI prototyping tools such as Macromedia Director or Flash with support for physical devices (R2.5). In a similar fashion to the aforementioned Phidgets and iStuff

2. State of the Art

toolkits, the Calder development environment provides a set of generic, re-usable input and output devices that are connected via a communication infrastructure and provide virtual proxy objects for interface prototyping. As an intersection between Phidgets and iStuff, both USB based wired components and wireless components using a custom radio transmission protocol are supported. The available wired components consist of a button array, a joystick, a single button, and an analog knob. The wireless components are of similar complexity and numbers with an analog knob, a button array, a tilt sensor, and a 3-LED array being available (!R2.4). To support product designers quickly prototyping with foam mockups, there are pins on the backs of the components that allow for an easy attachment of foam models. In the case of the wireless components, these pins also serve as transmit and receiver antennae.

The software infrastructure is comparably simple. Each single component registers as a standard USB Human Interface Device (HID) class with a unique serial number for identification. The interface details are packaged into a DLL that can be accessed from various programming environments. Next to Macromedia's XTRA interface, bindings and samples for C++ and Java are also provided. For the Macromedia Director application there are also surrogate GUI controls available that represent the external Calder components. This concept is identical to the Phidgets' ActiveX controls, albeit with less interoperability, since the virtual Phidgets surrogates can be integrated with any arbitrary host system.

The Calder toolkit clearly focuses on ease of use for non-computer programmers and consequently does not offer a sophisticated development infrastructure. Except for the simultaneous integration of both wireless and wired devices, the Calder Toolkit therefore does not make significant contributions over the existing Phidgets and iStuff toolkits, but lacks some of the functionality available for these toolkits.

Conclusions

For the development of distributed tangible user interfaces it is crucial to make use of appropriate middleware that reduces the complexities of pervasive computing technology. Respective communication middleware is one aspect; the other aspect addresses the abstraction and integration of diverse physical devices that each have their own idiosyncrasies. All of the discussed tangible user interface toolkits follow the approach of proxy objects that mediate between the physical state of the interaction device and the virtual representation exposed to the communication middleware. The complexity and power of these proxy objects range from basic connectors (iStuff) to more sophisticated virtual counterparts that can substitute the physical devices and provide complementary graphical user interfaces to inform about and alter the physical states of the hardware components (Phidgets). These complementary GUIs are naturally very important during application development, when the physical components might not be permanently available. Unfortunately, none of the discussed solutions provides simultaneous input with virtual and physical components, which could, for instance, augment the scope of an individual tangible interface to a distributed interface that involves local, tangible and remote, graphical interfaces realizing an extension of the smart environment to remote places. Therefore, requirement R2.5 is currently not realized in existing toolkits.

Except for the vision recognition of the Papier-Mache, all discussed toolkits provide only very primitive physical components. The rationale behind this is that these basic, general purpose components function well for a multitude of applications, e.g. turning something on and off (button) or assigning a discrete value to a variable (slider). For many concrete and meaningful applications, however, more complex tangible interfaces tailored to the specific problem domain would be more appropriate, in analogy to complex, tailored graphical widgets such as calendar controls being preferable over mere edit fields for date and time editing. The usefulness of the TUI toolkit therefore depends on the ease of adding more complex components to the set of pre-defined ones. While Papier-Mache cannot easily be augmented with custom components and i-Stuff does not provide means to store complex state information, Calder and Phidgets might be capable of integrating also more complex physical devices. Unfortunately, both toolkits fail at providing a distributed communication infrastructure to integrate the new components beyond single user applications. Interestingly, none of the discussed solutions provides generic output device control via power sockets to integrate arbitrary output devices with basic on/ off states. Also, none of the solutions except the vision recognition of Papier-Mache offers a spatial TUI component, although it has been shown that this is one of the key areas in which TUIs outperform comparable GUIs (Patten & Ishii 2000). Therefore, requirement R2.4 is also currently not realized in existing toolkits.

To provide tangible user interface support for home entertainment applications, it will naturally be necessary to develop and integrate game specific interaction devices that are not yet available among the primitive devices found in the current set of tangible interface toolkits. Due to the other limitations in the existing toolkits, most importantly the lack of appropriate communication infrastructures as well as state sharing and simultaneous input among virtual and physical components, a combination of tangible interfaces with rich virtual counterparts and a communication infrastructure is necessary that is equally appropriate for applications and arbitrary tangible interfaces of varying degrees of complexity.

2.4. Graphical User Interfaces

User Interaction in pervasive computing environments goes beyond the traditional interface metaphors of the desktop PC domain such as the Windows, Icons, Menus, and Pointers (WIMP) paradigm. Pervasive computing aims at developing user interfaces that are embedded in the physical realities of its users and provide more natural and intuitive forms of human interaction with the ultimate goal of replacing human computer interaction with human to human or human to information interaction, respectively. As Abowd & Mynatt (2005) note, the scope of user interfaces now ranges from explicit to implicit interaction and involves tangible and graphical interfaces as well as sensor technologies to make applications aware of user activities. While tangible interfaces are primarily geared towards explicit input, output commonly requires a display in order to convey information back to the users. Displays might be of auditive nature and map audio signals to the spatial features of the physical spaces (e.g. Naef et al. 2002, or Müller-Tomfelde et al. 2003), but graphical output is still the prominent modality for rendering complex information.

In pervasive computing environments, graphical output might be distributed among multiple displays and involve heterogeneous devices that scale across greatly different dimensions and resolutions. Weiser (1991) already identified three scales, the inch, the foot, and the yard with inch-sized devices resembling palmtop computers or mobile phones and yard-sized devices ranging to entire walls. The size and deployment of the graphical displays has also implications for its usage and the interactions supported for it. Small and mobile devices are often permanently associated with their users and correspondingly display private information, while large displays might be accessible from multiple users concurrently and thus display mostly public information, although techniques for presenting private information on public displays are also actively investigated (Shoemaker & Inkpen 2001, Streitz 2005). Distance and orientation are also important factors in pervasive computing displays. Depending on individual viewing angles and distance to the viewer, information might need to be rotated, scaled, contrasted, highlighted, etc in order to be appropriately perceived without significant cognitive overhead. Consequently, interaction prototypes such as the "AttrActive" windows (Denoue at al. 2003) were proposed that allow for mapping traditional window objects to 3D representations which can be rendered with various transformations such as rotations, translations, scaling or color filtering. While such techniques facilitate the perception of information by adapting their shapes and forms, some displays also aim at reducing cognitive overhead by providing limited information in a peripheral way. These "ambient displays "often transform arbitrary information to a reduced, dedicated representation. Ambient displays do not demand exclusive attention and are thus suitable for multi-user and multi-display environments, but naturally lack in their expressive power. Several research activities like e.g. Vogel & Balakrishnan (2004) are already exploring the combination and complementary use of pervasive computing display and interaction techniques such as public ambient displays supporting both public and personal information, taking position cues into account for rendering and supporting multiple input mechanisms such as hand gestures and touch screen input. At the current point in time, however, the exploration of the pervasive computing GUI design space is still at a prototypical state with appropriate enabling technologies and interoperable development tools only beginning to emerge.

In principle, the basic issues of pervasive computing GUI toolkits are similar to those of the TUI toolkits discussed so far. They should facilitate and simplify the development of graphical user interfaces in smart environments, tackling the idiosyncrasies of different, heterogeneous devices and provide an appropriate level of abstraction that allows generating device-adapted, coherent graphical interfaces without having to deal with their concrete implementations. GUI toolkits especially need to cope with different display sizes and orientations, different operating systems and resource constraints on handheld devices, and support the typical input modalities found in pervasive computing displays (R2.3), specifically finger or pen based touch input. Pervasive computing GUIs that are used with dedicated display surfaces such as the horizontal surfaces found on tabletops or the vertical displays of interactive walls should also adapt to the affordances of these surfaces. The fundamental requirements for GUIs on tabletop surfaces were identified by Shen et al. (2004). The most important of these requirements include the arbitrary directional orientation of document placements, the direct manipulation of interaction objects with bare hands (or a stylus device), and the management of user interface components that are either rotatable or rotation sensitive. Hence, a pervasive computing GUI toolkit that supports horizontal surfaces should provide both the rotational functionalities to take the different viewing angles of the users into account and address the need for direct manipulation without mice or keyboards. Vertical displays and PDAs do not share the same viewing angle issues, so rotational functionalities do not need and should not be available without another application-specific reason.

For the development of pervasive entertainment applications it is finally vital to provide sufficiently fast graphical updates for realtime rendering and multimedia effects as well as support for common file formats and graphics objects such as 3D meshes, animations, videos, bitmap graphics, alpha channels, etc (R2.2).

GapiDraw (Viktoria Institute)

GapiDraw is an enabling platform for the development of multimedia applications, especially games, that was presented by Sanneblad & Holmquist (2004). It mainly targets handheld

2. State of the Art

devices such as Palm, Symbian and Windows Mobile, but also provides a port for Windows PCs. The approach of GapiDraw is to provide a C++ API for multimedia programming that is unified across platforms, thereby addressing the lack of standardized programming interfaces across different mobile hardware configurations. With GapiDraw, developers consequently re-use the same code across a variety of devices without focusing on device-specific implementation details. This is an important property that differentiates GapiDraw from the graphic hardware APIs available for mobile devices such as OpenGL ES (www.opengl.org) or Direct3D Mobile (www.microsoft.com/directx) that are not compatible with the versions for PCs and only offer the feature sets that the specific device supports.

The features GapiDraw provides for rendering graphics are closely related to the demands of gaming applications and include rotating, zooming, blitting (including alpha channels) of animations and (masked) bitmaps (R2.2). It does not offer any 3D graphics support, but provides access to the devices' framebuffers as well as to any of the surfaces it defines in memory, so that a 3D rendering module can be integrated on top of GapiDraw. The idiosyncrasies of handheld devices are addressed by the toolkit both in terms of the display orientation (which can be rotated dynamically during runtime), and by the provided input mechanics. In addition to pen based touch input that is mapped to mouse events on stationary PCs, the hardware keys found on common PDAs such as the joystick or the "home" button are associated with corresponding semantic labels that allow for abstracting from a specific device. Naturally, the developer still needs to be aware that there remain cross-platform considerations that he has to deal with such as devices not having a touch display, thus demanding a key based control.

Programming-wise, GapiDraw has two main components, a cross-platform API and an application framework. The API comprises several classes for accessing the display, loading and manipulating images, applying real-time effects, etc. The framework contains only a single base class which wraps many low-level activities such as initiating full screen mode, enabling application switching, capturing and processing messages from the operating system, etc.

Although interoperability with pervasive computing communication platforms is no issue for GapiDraw due to the open C++ API, Sanneblad & Holmquist (2003) also present a related peer-to-peer networking platform specifically designed for wireless ad hoc networks. This "OpenTrek" platform integrates seamlessly with GapiDraw by extending the application framework with several network related functions in a derived application class.

GapiDraw is a relatively low-level development platform that does not provide elaborated functionality for creating graphical user interfaces apart from raw pen/ key input and surface blitting. User interface components such as the widgets, controls, windows found in other toolkits are missing, although they could be implemented on top of it.

Therefore, GapiDraw provides a solid development platform for mobile devices that makes optimal use of the capabilities of resource constrained PDAs and cellphones, the affordances of other display devices in pervasive computing environments such as tabletop surfaces or large vertical displays are however not addressed (!R2.3).

BEACH (Fraunhofer IPSI, i-Land)

The previously discussed BEACH software framework (Tandler 2003) does not only provide a communication and coordination infrastructure, but also contributes modules for creating

33

user interfaces that integrate interaction techniques related to the heterogeneous devices populating pervasive computing environments. The sophisticated and complex architecture of BEACH distinguishes between different software layers that represent different conceptual levels ranging from general-purpose core functionality at the bottom to highly task- and domain-specific functionality at the top. On each of these layers, different models that separate different basic concerns such as a user interface model or an application model are located. This matrix of compartments and layers facilitates the development of adaptable software. For instance, a change in the environment model such as the software being executed on a horizontal instead of a vertical display surface might cause adaptations in the user interface model, but leaves data and application models unchanged (R2.3).

Regarding the concrete support for user interface development, BEACH provides both common user interface components such as windows, buttons, edit fields, etc. and also contributes extensive support for incremental gesture recognition, scribbling, and specialized interaction techniques such as magnetic card clusters adhering to the Metaplan® metaphors or augmented mind maps (Prante et al. 2002). Most importantly, the user interface model takes the properties of different types of display properties into account. The window objects created with BEACH can be "thrown" on large surfaces such as the DynaWall Roomware component, where traditional drag and drop interaction is not feasible due to the long physical distances on the surface. On horizontal surfaces, BEACH allows for rotating interaction objects 90° degree wise to address the different viewing angles of collaborating users. Consequently, a "passing" metaphor is implemented that combines pushing and rotating interaction objects from one user to another with the objects auto-orienting to the respective target user.

BEACH is implemented in SmallTalk 80 which allows for both a clean object oriented design and a comfortable development and debugging of BEACH applications, because of SmallTalk's integration of the development tools in the applications themselves. However, interoperability with non-BEACH applications is currently only marginally provided and there are severe performance issues, especially on constrained devices (!R2.2). Although a PDA application exists that shares information objects with BEACH (Magerkurth & Prante 2001), PDAs, there is no support for heavily constrained devices such as PDAs or mobile phones for which there is no SmallTalk runtime environment available.

The most important contribution of BEACH remains the automatic adaptation of interaction objects to the properties of the respective interaction devices which unburdens the developer from anticipating changes in the physical setup of devices. While the interaction metaphors BEACH provides are especially tailored to pervasive computing display surfaces, parts of the respective implementations are currently at a research prototype state (e.g. the 90° rotation constraints and the lack in performance, which is especially an issue for pervasive entertainment applications). While development toolkits generally focus on high interoperability with other middleware solutions, the extensive framework approach of BEACH demands applications to be specifically targeted towards this particular platform and therefore aggravates the adaptation of an existing technology base.

DiamondSpin (MERL)

DiamondSpin (Shen et al. 2004) is a Java toolkit that is especially geared towards facilitating the creation of multi-user interfaces with graphically adapted interaction objects on horizontal surfaces. Similar to the combination of BEACH and the Roomware components, it was developed in the context of the DiamondTouch tabletop input hardware (Dietz & Leigh 2003) which allows multiple users to interact simultaneously on a tabletop. In DiamondTouch, individual touch location information is determined independently for each user through the use of a capacitive touch technology. The goal of the DiamondTouch hardware and the DiamondSpin software combination is to support small group collaboration on a horizontal display interface where users maintain eye contact while interacting with the information objects on the tabletop. Without the DiamondTouch hardware, DiamondSpin loses its simultaneous multi-user touch interface, but is still capable of rendering graphical information objects adapted to the requirements of tabletop surfaces.

At its core, DiamondSpin provides a polar to Cartesian transformation engine based on Java 2D and JAI (Java Advanced Imaging). This allows arbitrary positioning and orientation of graphical objects on a tabletop surface, so that the viewing angles of the users can be taken into account when displaying information. The transformation engine is capable of mapping information objects to various polygonal tabletop layouts, of which rectangular and circular shapes are the most commonly needed in typical pervasive computing setups. Due to the nature of a polar coordinate system that has one meaningful central position and each graphical object being aware of it, it is straightforward to implement tabletop-specific interactions that surpass the 90° rotations of BEACH. Interaction metaphors supported by DiamondSpin include the "passing" metaphor of BEACH augmented with a stepless change in orientation as well as several "magnetizations", which are constraints on the objects' orientations and positions, and auto-layout functions for graphical objects.

The API consists of a number of Java classes with a central container class representing the workspace that comprises the graphical objects on the table surface. Several GUI components such as frames, panels, and menu bars are available that are subclassed from their respective Swing counterparts. This allows for creating simple DiamondSpin GUIs in a similar fashion as traditional Swing interfaces, but with the benefit of the transformations provided by the toolkit. Apart from the basic GUI components, no other interaction objects seem to be available. Consequently, the provided sample applications mostly deal with the collection and layout of photographs or other images.

Because of the implementation based on the Java language DiamondSpin is sufficiently extensible and portable for heterogeneous pervasive computing environments. At its current state, the sole support for plain bitmaps as interaction objects (referred to as "documents") is hardly sufficient for creating entertainment applications. No sophisticated rendering effects apart from object orientation and scaling are available (!R2.2). While the toolkit provides support for tabletops with appropriate 2D object rotations, it does not adapt to other pervasive computing interaction devices such as vertical displays as BEACH does (!R2.3).

Conclusions

The currently available GUI toolkits suitable for pervasive computing environments focus on different aspects of user interfaces. While all of them meet the requirement of facilitating and simplifying the development of GUIs for heterogeneous devices, none of them is appropriate for addressing the idiosyncrasies of horizontal and vertical displays of varying dimensions as well as mobile devices (R2.3). While GapiDraw provides a rather low-level abstraction of mobile and stationary devices with various advanced realtime rendering and multimedia effects (R2.2), it is clearly focused on PDAs and does not account for higher level viewing angle, rotational or distance issues of horizontal or vertical displays. Both BEACH and DiamondSpin are geared towards these types of pervasive computing interaction devices, DiamondSpin focusing more on tables, BEACH on both tables and walls, but with serious drawbacks regarding multimedia effects. To provide a coherent interaction experience across devices concepts or ideally even code of the different solutions should be shared. However, at an implementation level the differences in supported programming languages (C++, Smalltalk, Java) aggravate this in a similar way as on a conceptual level, where different GUI paradigms (MVC, widgets) and the framework nature of each solution work against effective interoperability. What is needed is an integrated solution that addresses the idiosyncrasies of all pervasive computing GUI devices. Since GUIs are only one aspect of pervasive computing user interfaces, an integrated solution should furthermore allow for the integration of tangible and graphical interfaces alike and combine them with a dedicated communication and coordination infrastructure. This dissertation provides such an integrated contribution in the home entertainment domain that is discussed in the forthcoming three chapters.

2.5. Summary

This chapter reviewed the state of the art in three distinct research fields that are relevant for the application domain of hybrid games, namely smart environments projects and the respective middleware that drives these environments as well as tangible and graphical user interfaces. The smart environments projects build up the frame and boundaries in which the gaming applications take place, whereas tangible and graphical user interfaces provide the interface building blocks to be integrated by the smart environments middleware and to bridge the gap between the human users and the overall information system. These three research fields are not the only disciplines relevant for hybrid games. Certainly, the specific elements of video games and game research in general are at least as relevant for the emerging field of hybrid games. Game research related issues were, however omitted from this chapter, because these commonly do not deal with technically relevant requirments. Also, from a research discipline perspective hybrid gaming is not yet well defined and the respective issues from that field are still subject to investigation. Consequently, the application domain of hybrid games is subject to its own dedicated chapter that reviews the gaming related models out of which hybrid games as a concept developed. Likewise, a formative and exploratory evaluation of that concept is also discussed in the next chapter. This means that the computer science constraints and requirments in order to lay the foundation for hybrid games were reviewed and discussed in this chapter, but the concrete realization from a gaming perspective and the game related classification is subject to the next chapter.

The technical requirements for the respective research fields discussed here were mostly elicited from requirements published in prior art and applied to current contributions in each field. The number of requirements for each field differed according to the importance of the individual field for the overall goal of the dissertation and the focus of the contributed hardware and software platform. In this respect, graphical user interfaces are, for instance, less central than tangible user interfaces, as both the magnitude of contributed physical interaction devices outweighs the GUI contributions as well as the concept of hybrid games depends stronger on physical interaction than traditional GUIs.

The central question of whether existing contributions in the discussed state of the art meet the elicited requirements can finally be answered in a unified way for all three research fields, as the individual conclusions to these sections have revealed: None of the existing approaches alone is sufficient to meet all relevant requirments, as different contributions clearly set different focal points. This unfortunate situation often occurs with information systems and the solution usually comes down to either a.) adopting an existing solution and bear the respective shortcomings, or b.) building upon and augmenting an existing system or standard, or c.) creating something new from scratch that explicitly addresses all relevant requirments. The choice between different flavors and variants of these fundamental solutions is obviously dependent on many factors such as cost, market structure, skills and resources, organizational constraints, etc. For this dissertation, a pragmatic approach was taken so that existing contributions were picked up and integrated or augemented whenever possible and otherwise created from scratch as to optimize the cost / utiltity ratio. As it will be shown in the forthcoming chapters, certain existing tangible user interfaces such as the iBracelet that directly met the required functionality and offered appropriate means of integration were merely added to the platform as is, effectively following the first solution of direct integration. An example for augmenting an existing system is for instance the GapiDraw graphics platform that was utilized as a basic platform for high performance rendering, but augmented with lacking functionality. Finally, the hybrid gaming software platform itself largely followed the last approach of building it from scratch, because of the mutlitide of respective requirements and the unavailability of an appropriate platform to build upon. This cost-efficient flexible choice of solution alternatives aims at meeting all the requirements elicited in this chapter while keeping the effort and cost in balance. Later chapters will reveal in how far this approach was successful.

3. The Application Domain of Hybrid Games

In the previous chapter, the state of the art in pervasive computing middleware, as well as tangible and graphical user interface support for pervasive computing environments was discussed. This chapter reviews the application domain that is addressed with the respective hardware and software platform contributed by this dissertation. As noted in the previous chapter, the degree of complexity in interaction devices is usually connected to their specificity. Simple interaction devices such as buttons or sliders are also general purpose devices that are largely independent of a specific application domain, whereas the characteristics of the application domain become relevant and dictate the design of complex, more specialized user interfaces. Therefore, a discussion and analysis of the application domain is a precondition for the development of concrete interaction devices that are informed by the characteristics of the domain.

The application domain that frames the platform discussed in the succeeding chapters is that of home entertainment, more specifically games. Computer games are already a major driving force for the innovation in many fields of computer science, such as network technologies or computer graphics. While traditional games such as Chess or Go have been popular for thousands of years, the advent of computing technology even catalyzed their success with unique features impossible to realize without a digital representation. For the first time, computer games have allowed the players to immerse into a virtual game world, where the effects of game actions were only limited by the imagination of the programmers. When computers became more powerful, rich audio and visual presentations as well as more complex simulations enhanced the gaming experiences and turned the computer games industry into a mass market. Today, computer games generate revenues similar to average Hollywood film productions.

3.1. Constituents of Hybrid Games

In order to access the scope and constituents of the application domain, the nature of games is analyzed in terms of their foundations and their transition from a non-technical activity over digital entertainment to games that utilize pervasive computing technologies. The following sections discuss the definitions of games and the respective implications for the development of a conceptual model that defines the specifics of hybrid games.

Traditional Games

As quoted from Hinske at al. (2007), "Salen and Zimmermann (2004) describe a game as "an activity with some rules engaged in for an outcome" and they further define a game as a "system in which players engage in an artificial conflict, defined by rules, that result in a quantifiable outcome". The key elements in this description, and this definition, respectively, are:

- Activity with rules and an outcome,
- System,
- Artificial conflict, and
- Quantifiable outcome.

Rules are seen as an (artificial) conflict or competition, and a measurable outcome as central elements of games. Additionally, Salen and Zimmermann stress another interesting aspect: A

3. The Application Domain of Hybrid Games

game is also a (social) system. Salen and Zimmermann differentiate between three systems: Formal systems, which are closed and where rules play an important role, experiential systems, which can either be open or closed and where the emphasis is on playing (no rules per se), and contextual systems, which are open and of cultural nature.

In this context, a game, in contrast to playing, is a closed system (everything is usually determined and set in the beginning and cannot or at least should not be changed during the ongoing game) with rules being the central element that converts and open system into a closed one (cf. Figure 2). Although the range and strictness of applying the rules can vary very much; however, usually acting outside the rules is considered "cheating". Obviously, *rules* are a major element that turns play into a game.

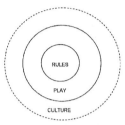

Figure 2: The relation between rules, play and culture

This aspect of "some sort of boundaries" in a game is also similarly described by Walther (2003). According to him, in gaming "the distinctions that guide the form of play are not enough. In addition, one observes - and responds to - the very criteria of a specific game. At least, one has to be aware of these criteria in order to advance and, preferably, win the game."

He continues: "Thus, the organization of gaming lies in a third order complexity which, in logico-formalistic terms, can be explained as follows: First, a fundamental distinction occurs. Either one is in or one is out. [...] Next, a second transgression takes place. [...] The suppleness of play stems from the fact that it is open to the repetitive fabrication of rules. The flexibility of games is precisely that they are autonomous in respect to rules; instead, they are open for tactics. [...] Finally, the movement towards rule is a result of a form within a form within a form, i.e. a third-order complexity, a temporal displacement of two transcending acts - that of constituting the contingent modality of play and that of fixating the principles of a game's structure." This is visualized in Figure 3.

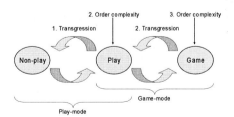

Figure 3: Transgression and complexity in play and game

39

3. The Application Domain of Hybrid Games

Following the two definitions, we can state that the social dimension is central to both playing and games, but that games differ from mere playing by their complex systematic nature that defines rules and boundaries in which goal-directed activities are performed.

Other authors follow these definitions. For instance, Craig Lindley (2003) gives a compatible definition of games: A game is "a goal-directed and competitive activity conducted within a framework of agreed rules". The elements listed by him coincide with the elements already found:

- Goal-directed,
- Competitive, and
- Framework of agreed rules.

Similar to Lindley, Klabbers (2003) defines a game as "a contest (play) among adversaries (players) operating under constraints (rules) for an objective (winning, victory or payoff)". According to him, the difference between play and game are "constraints (rules)" and "an objective".

Juul's definition of game is built on six points (Juul 2003):

- Games are rule-based,
- Games have variable, quantifiable outcomes,
- In games, value is assigned to possible outcomes,
- The player invests effort in order to influence the outcome,
- Player is emotionally attached to outcome, and
- It is optional whether a game has real-life consequences.

Finally, a slightly different approach is taken by Costikyan (2007). He sees a game as "a form of art in which participants, termed players, make decisions in order to manage resources through game tokens in the pursuit of a goal". Although the consideration of a game as a form of art is very interesting, it is probably beyond the scope of this discussion, whereas the other elements go in line with the already identified ones. Table 2 lists the amalgamated elements of a game:

Table 2: The six essential elements of a game.

Element	Synonyms
Rules	Framework of agreed rules, constraints, rule-based
Competition	Competitive play, artificial conflict, competitive activity, contest among adversaries
Goals	Pursuit of a goal, goal-directed, objective
Outcome	Unit of scoring, quantifiable outcome, variable and quantifiable outcome
Decisions	Manage resources
Emotional Attachment	Value assigned to outcome, effort invested for influencing outcome

Digital Games

The six essential elements of games defined above are invariant among the media used to realize these games. A fundamental step in the technological evolution of game media is the emergence of home computers and video games. This technological evolution leads to the question of the special qualities of digital media that can support gaming experiences not possible in other game forms. Salen and Zimmermann (2004) identify four "traits" of digital media that represent the qualities that appear most robustly in digital games.

Immediate but Narrow Interactivity

One of the most important qualities of digital technology is that it can offer immediate, interactive feedback. Designing systems of actions and outcomes, where the game responds seamlessly to a player's input, is a common element in digital games. Digital technology thus offers real-time game play that shifts and reacts dynamically to player decisions.

A common misconception about digital games is that they offer players a broad and expressive range of interaction, that a computer can mimic any medium and provide any kind of experience. However, the kind of interaction that a participant can have with a computer is quite narrow. Interaction with a home computer is generally restricted to mouse and keyboard input, and screen and speaker output. Comparing the activities of clicking, dragging, and typing with the range of possible non-computer game interactions, they are obviously very few and narrow.

Information Manipulation

Digital games often include and utilize great amounts of data including text, images, video, audio, animations, 3D content, and other forms of stored data. Computer games certainly drive forward the data-rendering capabilities of computers more than any other genre of consumer software, as high-end computers, specially configured for the best display of 3D graphics and audio, are commonly marketed as "gamer" machines.

Graphics and audio are not the only kind of information that a digital game manipulates, as every aspect of a digital game such as the underlying rules, mechanisms for handling player interactivity, memory management, etc. can be regarded as information. Digital games manipulate this information in ways that non-digital games generally cannot. For instance, in a typical board game it is necessary for at least one of the players to learn the rules and understand them fully before a game begins. On the other hand, with a digital game it is possible to learn the rules of the game as it is being played.

Digital games make it also possible to hide information from players and revealing it in different ways. Many real-time strategy games and also one of the proof-of-concept prototypes of Hybrid Games discussed in a later chapter make use of a "fog of war" mechanic: the game is played on a large map, and the territory and actions of a player's opponents are initially hidden and only revealed as the player's units explore the game map. Depending on the context, the computer application this communicates different aspects of its knowledge to the players. As it will be pointed out, this interplay of a digital representation of the game space and the exchange of information with the social space of the players is also a central component of hybrid games.

41

Automated Complex Systems

The most obvious characteristic of digital games is that they can automate complicated procedures and facilitate the play of games that would be too complicated in a non-computerized context. In most non-digital games, players have to move the game forward at every step, by manipulating pieces or behaving according to explicit instructions outlined by the rules. In a digital game, the program can automate these procedures and move the game forward without direct input from a player. As Magerkurth et al. (2004) point out, this both contributes to a relief of the players from mundane tasks and also allows for more complex and believable game relations. For instance, when miniatures wargamers get together to stage their battles with tiny lead figures, they follow complex rules that determine the movement, lines of sight, and combat resolution of their armies. There are certainly limits on the degree of complexity that can be handled by humans, whereas this kind of complexity can be handled well by a digital application. Consequently, wargames created for play on computers generally take into account many more dynamic variables than their non-digital counterparts.

Networked Communication

A final characteristic that most digital games possess is that they can facilitate communication between remote players. There are many forms of digitally mediated communication, such as email and text chat or even real-time video and audio communication.

It is obvious that all multiplayer games, digital or non-digital, are contexts for communication among players. However, digital games offer the ability to communicate over long distances and to share a range of social spaces with many other participants. Although communication input and output are limited by the narrow input and output of digital media, communication in a digital game does not have to be restricted to text. For example, an ego-shooter deathmatch gathers a small number of players together in a single communicative game space. And although text chat is one way that the players interact, their primary form of communication takes place through the decisions they make about their player's movement and weapon attacks and the perception of actions from other players. Game play itself is thus a form of social communication.

Naturally, networked communication, even over long distances, occurs also in traditional games. For instance, the postal system was used as a medium for game play in play-by-mail games or role-playing games that take place entirely through written correspondence. Nevertheless, most traditional games employ communication via traditional face-to-face situations in which part of the enjoyment comes from the close social interaction, whereas the networking capabilities of computers have fostered the development of distributed games, in which the communicative channels are less rich, but that allow for joint experiences among distributed players.

Games Utilizing Pervasive Computing Technologies

The emergence of pervasive computing technologies allows for addressing some of the deficits that the introduction of digital games had over traditional games. For instance, the immediate but narrow interactivity of digital games implies that there is simply less freedom in interactions as with traditional games. Likewise, the automation in the complex systems defined inside the computer tends to lead to more rigid and less flexible rules as those that are negotiated and constantly re-evaluated between players in a co-located social situation.

Pervasive computing has the potential to bridge the gap between traditional and digital gaming applications. As cited from Hinske et al. (2007), "the central vision is to bring the

3. The Application Domain of Hybrid Games

computers into the world, and embed and weave them into the fabric of our surrounding in such a way that they are indistinguishable from it (Weiser 1991). By doing so, we can add a virtual layer to the physical world. This aspect is also referred to as "Augmented Reality", which in contrast to "Virtual Reality" describes the paradigm of bringing the computer into the world, instead of bringing the world into the computer. Figure 4 shows Paul Milgram's Virtuality Continuum which is based on the classic taxonomy by Milgram and Kishino (1994).

Figure 4: The Virtuality Continuum

The Real Environment is the physical world we live in. A Virtual Environment is an artificially generated world that is either based on someone's imagination and fantasy, on the real environment (a projection, called "Augmented Virtuality"), or on a combination of both. The beauty of such Virtual Environments is that, on the one hand, there is no limit as far as the imagination and fantasy of the creators and the users are concerned; and, on the other hand, the possible number of virtual worlds (in contrast to the real world) is potentially infinite.

In addition, Stapleton et al. (2002) introduced the model of compelling mixed reality, which adds the component *imagination* (which in turn can be the basis for *a* virtual world) to real and virtual environments:

Figure 5: Compelling Mixed Reality

Mixed Reality describes a reality somewhere on the continuous spectrum between the real and the virtual environments. Mixed Reality is combination of two worlds, the real and the virtual. This combination is also referred to as a hybrid world. The proportion of real and virtual components is dynamic and usually difficult to determine, but the major advancement over purely digital and over traditional games is the integration of both worlds which opens up a large space of possibilities to create novel interaction experiences. As Kampmann (2005) similarly to Magerkurth et al. (2005) notes, these games that utilize pervasive computing technology and integrate both worlds can be categorized as follows:

Mobile Games

A mobile game is a game that takes changing relative or absolute position/location into account in the game rules. Strictly speaking this excludes games for which mobile devices merely provide a delivery channel where key features of mobility are not relevant to the game mechanics. Therefore, one could distinguish between mobile interfaced games and mobile embedded games. As noted in the introductory chapter, especially the mobile games market is predicted to grow significantly within the next years due to the increasing performance of mobile phones. Mitchell et al. (2003) present such a mobile game that utilizes mobile IPv6 and discuss the related challenges such as fluctuating connectivity, network QoS, and host mobility issues.

Location-based Games

A location-based game is a game that includes relative or absolute, but static position/location in the game rules. This moves the focus of the game more towards the specific characteristics of the places and spaces the game is deployed. Falk et al. (2001) present a respective mobile game system called "Pirates!" in which players move around in the physical domain and experience location dependent mini-games on mobile computers, triggered by RFID proximity.

Augmented Reality Games

Augmented reality (AR) games and mixed reality games are an approach to the creation of game spaces that seek to integrate virtual and physical elements within a comprehensibly experienced perceptual game world. Augmented Reality is a variation on virtual reality that draws virtual objects into a physical world environment. Users see their view augmented with 3D objects registered such that they appear to exist in real space. Although augmented reality can be created with a range of different technologies, the most common way is to use a head-mounted display that augments a camera image with virtual information. "Mind-Warping" is an early influential AR game (Starner et al. 2000) that adheres to such a computer vision approach.

Hybrid Games

A hybrid game uses the computational and communications infrastructure embedded within a smart home environment to augment traditional games such as board or tabletop with information technology. The term "hybrid" refers to the equal integration of physical, social, and virtual dimensions. The result is a new gaming genre that blends elements from all of the three dimensions using pervasive computing technology. In contrast to mobile and location-based games, the locations of players are usually not part of the gameplay. Mandryk & Maranan (2002) discuss such a hybrid board game called "False Prophets".

The remainder of this dissertation focuses on hybrid games as the entertainment genre that especially matches the characteristics and constraints of smart homes due to their concentration on small-scale environments.

Figure 6: Multimodal stimulation in a Hybrid Game

44

3. The Application Domain of Hybrid Games

In contrast to mobile or location-based games, hybrid games are typically deployed within a single room that provides a number of tangible and graphical user interfaces. Illustrated in Figure 6, the atmosphere in the room is also frequently adapted to the current state of the game application by altering illumination, sound, and ambient displays. As noted in the previous chapter, the user interface orchestration is therefore especially important for this kind of entertainment application. Streitz et al. (2005 a) identify the unique qualities of experience and perception that define hybrid games from the user's perspective. These qualities are reviewed in the next section.

Qualities of Experience and Perception

The fundamental approach of hybrid games is to capture the experience of traditional co-located games and augment it unobtrusively with calm, pervasive technology, thus realizing Weiser's often quoted vision of the most profound, disappearing technologies that "weave themselves into the fabric of our everyday life, until they are indistinguishable from it" (Weiser 1991). The following specific qualities can be identified that specifically relate to the experiences with hybrid games.

Social Quality

Players meet face-to-face for playing hybrid games and exploit rich means of communication including non-verbal hints such as mimics or gestures. Social dynamics can emerge much more easily than in traditional computer entertainment, where the notion of a player is only conveyed through a computer display.

Haptic Quality

Similar to board games, the primary interfaces in hybrid games are tangible artifacts such as smart playing pieces or game boards. The haptic quality of these artifacts provides natural interaction means. Additionally, many physical pieces are nice to touch, to look at, to assemble, or to collect.

Multimodal Stimulation

Multimodal stimulation adds to the immersion of the gaming experience and can effectively be realized with a pervasive computing infrastructure that connects various output devices. Changing the environment of the players to reflect the status of the game can vastly enhance the atmosphere of the gaming experience. The modes to stimulate are manifold, ambient light or sound or even creating wind with a simple fan can add to the multimodal stimulation of the players (see Figure 7).

Real-world Parameters

In the same way as the gaming experience can be stimulated by altering physical aspects such as light or sound, these real world properties can also provide an input for the virtual parts of a game. For instance, the noise level in a room might influence the efficiency of a virtual spy that try to eavesdrop a conversation. Or the light in a room might affect how well digital flowers bloom.

Virtual Attributes of Physical Artifacts

Arbitrary virtual properties that differ from game to game can be assigned to physical artifacts. In one game, an artifact might be associated with attributes such as intelligence or dexterity, in another game, certain behaviors or alignments might be put into the artifact's digital representation providing for context aware enrichments. Even dedicated GUI artifacts might be used to peek into the physical artifact and to modify its virtual state.

These qualities briefly characterize the typical user experiences with hybrid games in order to give an informal introduction to the application domain; a systematic conceptual model is presented in the next section that can be used as a basis to derive design recommendations for the development of hybrid games.

3.2. A Conceptual Model

Conceptual models help understanding the experiences with gaming applications and open up a design space to explore. After a short recap of the existing models in the body of digital games research and their implications and scope, a model of hybrid games is presented that specifically takes the properties of the virtual, the physical and the social dimensions into account.

Previous Models

Three related conceptual models of gaming applications can be identified in the research of digital games. Game Experience (Sutton-Smith, 1986), Player Roles (Sutton-Smith, 1991), and Atomic Actions (Kampmann, 2005) each focus on specific aspects of games and contribute to the development of the integrated hybrid games model.

Game Experience (1986)

Sutton-Smith (1986) presents an early model that is based on the psychological processes by which games are experienced. Although Sutton-Smith specifically addresses traditional video games, his model is relevant to other kinds of games as well. He identifies five elements of game experiences:

- Visual scanning: visual perception, especially scanning the entire screen at once.
- Auditory discriminations: listening for game events and signals.
- Motor responses: physical actions a player takes with the game controls.
- Concentration: intense focus on play.
- Perceptual patterns of learning: coming to know the structure of the game itself.

Sutton-Smith offers a precise description of the elements that constitute the experience of play within a digital game. Visual scanning and auditory discrimination represent the sensorial activities of the player, motor responses represent the player's physical actions, and the other two elements (concentration and perceptual patterns of learning) represent cognitive mechanisms internal to the player that link these inputs and outputs.

Although Sutton-Smith's five categories help describing the experience of early, single player console games, they are certainly not inclusive of all games. A game might be invented, for example, that involves smell-based sensory input. And even before the development of hybrid games, there were already many games that involved social communication between players, which Sutton-Smith's model does not take into account.

The model's main contribution therefore lies in the description of relationships between input, output, and internal player mechanisms. This three-part model is a useful general structure for understanding how players experience a game. The way that a player perceives a game and takes action in it is always specific to a particular design. But these details are contained within a larger system of experience that always includes sensory input, player output, and internal player cognition in one form or the other. All three components of this model can be considered in isolation, but they only generate meaningful play as part of a larger designed system. Even though Sutton-Smith does not regard the entire width of the physical domain, he already identifies the importance of tangible interaction in computer games, but the lack of social factors ultimately make the model unusable for hybrid games.

Player Roles (1991)

While the social domain was missing in Sutton-Smith's earlier model, it is specifically addressed in his later "Player Roles" model (1991). The rationale of the model is that players constantly play roles that may permanently change during the course of a game. Whenever a player enters the system of a game, that player is given a role to play. The term "role" does not mean that a player becomes a character in a story, but that each player is associated with a role in the social network of a game. Within this system of social relationships there are a wide variety of roles that players can assume, such as enemy, or team leader, partner, patron, etc. Roles are not fixed and may change many times within the course of a game. For example, in a three-player competitive game with one winner, at any moment one player might take the role of a temporary or permanent ally to one of the other players, or an enemy to one or two of the other players. As the game proceeds and the balance of power shifts, these roles can quickly change, finally reaching a potential end when one player takes the role of the winner and the other two lose.

As Sutton-Smith notes, games are complex emergent systems. The relationships between objects in the system - between players - is in a constant state of redefinition. For instance, in a game in which players work together to attain a common goal ("cooperation"), players take on the social role of comrades who must use teamwork to play well together. If there was a single enemy hidden among the group of friends, however, the relationships between players take on a completely different tone, and the game is infused with an air of deceit. A related point is the opposition of an actor and a counteractor. In Sutton-Smith's model, the roles of actor and counteractor are both equally important in constructing the experience of play. The actual play activity is a function of the two player roles. The activity of Chase, for instance, occurs when one player (the chaser) attempts to catch another player (the chased), who in turn attempts to elude the chaser. If the chased player decided not to run anymore, to give up the role of eluding the chaser, the chase play would end.

Sutton-Smith's model is useful in understanding play as a function of player roles. It provides a first approach to analyze the existing social play in a game. The important contribution of the model is the implied notion of information flow that alters according to the changes in the relationships between players. When friends become enemies, their role changes dictate how information is shared between them. Sharing information or other resources is only sensible in a cooperative situation, but not in a competitive one. Hence, in hybrid games, the partitioning of the social space should be reflected also in the physical and virtual domains, so that the relationships in the social space are effectively supported. For instance, when the social relationships of two players change from a cooperative nature to a competitive nature, it must be ensured that information that was previously shared in the virtual domain, becomes separated according to the new social roles. This leads to the notion of different degrees of private and public information that will be introduced with the forthcoming hybrid games model.

Atomic Actions (2005)

Atomic Actions is an attempt by Kampmann (2005) to describe and analyze the formalisms of pervasive games which, as noted above, can be regarded as a broader category that includes,

3. The Application Domain of Hybrid Games

but is not limited to hybrid games. In Kampmann's view pervasive games consist of atomic entities that merge into a molecular structure exhibiting emergent features during the actual gameplay. The model introduces four axes of pervasive games (mobility, distribution, persistence, and transmediality). It also discusses the role of spaces by differentiating between tangible space, information embedded space, and accessibility space. Regarding the connection of pervasive games to general pervasive computing applications, Kampmann identifies two essential qualities that relate strongly to pervasive games, namely

1. the explicitness of computational tasks, and
2. the importance of physical space.

The former quality implies that actions are carried out beyond the traditional desktop PC oriented environment with pervasive computing shifting the users' attention from data manipulation to simulated and natural interactions with things and physical objects. This interweaves with the second aspect of pervasive computing as objects obeying the laws of physics are open to (digital) manipulation and thus take on a double meaning: they are objects within the outside (non-game) world, but can also be objects within a game world. This aspect also relates to the aforementioned experience quality of physical artifacts having respective virtual attributes. The four axes that the model defines relate to:

Distribution
Pervasive computing devices are frequently mobile or embedded in the environment and linked to an increasingly ubiquitous network infrastructure composed of wired and wireless components. This combination of embedded computing, dynamic networking, and discrete information sharing affects and strengthens the distributed nature of pervasive computing applications.

Mobility
New challenges of pervasive computing further include mobility, i.e. computing mobility, network mobility, and user mobility. Particularly relevant for the field of mobile pervasive games is the growth in 3G technologies.

Persistence
The persistence factor in pervasive games is based upon the notion of temporality. Persistence means total availability all the time, i.e. a game is not limited to a certain group of players interacting at a particular point in time, but potentially persists even when the players are absent.

Transmediality
Transmediality refers to the integration of different media and interaction devices that a pervasive game consists of. In contrast to traditional digital games that only use standard displays for output, pervasive games utilize a multitude of different media and devices interchangeably and complementarily.

These four axes open up the design space for pervasive games with each game consisting of elements distributed on these axes. Combining distribution, mobility, persistence, and transmediality thus entails the field of potentials for developing pervasive games. Furthermore, Kampmann also introduces the notion of tangible and information spaces that represent physical and virtual worlds as well as the accessibility space that mediates between the two worlds.

48

3. The Application Domain of Hybrid Games

Tangibility Space

One of the most crucial aspects in pervasive games obviously is the player's interaction with the physical reality. This tangibility space is defined by Kampmann as not just the sum of the surrounding environment and the vast amount of objects it possesses, but also as a specific organization of this space.

Distributed Information Space

Since pervasive gaming involves the blending of physical and virtual spaces, the tangibility space is facilitated by and projected onto an information embedded space. This information space hence is the digital representation of the tangibility space.

Accessibility Space

Finally, the accessibility space is defined as the interface between the embedded information and tangibility in the pervasive game universe.

Kampmann addresses the important issues of distribution, mobility, and transmediality and also acknowledges correctly the relations between virtual and physical spaces, but fails to realize the importance of social roles or relationships. As discussed in the Player Roles model, a social reality is a most important factor for gaming applications, especially if they take place in the real world which consists of both physical and social dimensions.

The Hybrid Games Model

Taking the contributions and limitations from the previous models into account, it becomes clear that no single previous model is appropriate for hybrid games. In contrast to traditional computer entertainment, hybrid gaming applications define game elements from the physical and the social domains as integral parts of the gaming experience. While the Player Roles Model is mainly concerned with the social domain, and the Game Experience model is derived from single player computer games, the Atomic Actions model is specifically geared towards pervasive games and contributes the notion of physically distributed interaction devices, but also neglects the social qualities of pervasive games. Therefore, a specific hybrid games model is presented here which focuses on the spaces ("domains") that make up a hybrid game and the interfaces between them. The rationale behind this is that by defining domains and the flow that information can take between them, it is possible to deduct design recommendations which are presented in this chapter and are applied to the sample realizations of hybrid games discussed in a later chapter.

The model includes three domains that share game elements and that are connected via dedicated interfaces.

First, there is a virtual domain as in traditional computer gaming applications that stores game data, applies rules to the current game state, and possibly includes a proactive game instance that acts as an autonomous confederate or enemy to the human players.

Second, there is the social domain that includes the individual players and their shared knowledge of the game. Some of the information between the players might not be known to the virtual domain, but still have an important impact on the progress of the game. For instance, the contextual information that player X shares an animosity with player Y might not be reflected in the virtual domain, but still plays an important role in the decisions and actions made by the group.

3. The Application Domain of Hybrid Games

The third domain is the physical world in which the players reside. Real-world physical artifacts might be used to let players interact with each other and with the virtual domain, as well as properties of the real world might be influenced by and also actively influence the other domains.

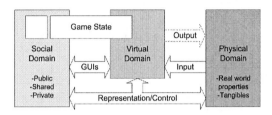

Figure 7: The three Domains of Hybrid Games

As Figure 7 illustrates, the three domains are connected to each other and the issue in developing hybrid games is now to find the optimal distribution of game elements among these domains. Some elements clearly belong into one domain or the other, but in many cases it is a matter of deliberate choice. In the following sections, each of the domains are discussed regarding their scope and function in hybrid gaming applications.

The Virtual Domain

The predominant domain in traditional computer games is virtual, i.e. the entire game takes place inside a micro-controlled system. A digital game logic sets up and maintains a virtual game world that is perceived and controlled through a graphical user interface. The virtual domain hosts part of the game state information. According to the typology of Pearce (1997) game state information can be

- known to all players: In Chess, this would consist of the rules of the game, board layout, and piece movement parameters.
- known to only one player: In Gin, this would be the cards in a player's hand.
- known to the game only: In Gin, this would be unused cards in deck. In Space Invaders, this would be the paths and frequency of alien space ships.

The virtual domain is where game state information known to the game only resides which can be made available to the players via shared ("known to all players") or individual ("known to only one player") communication media. In a traditional computer game, each player uses a GUI to access a segment of the game state that is relevant for him in the given game context. In an augmented hybrid game, segments of the game state can also be outside the computer, e.g. in the physical domain, and a GUI becomes only one of several means to modify and retrieve game information within the virtual domain.

Apart form pure information management, the virtual domain can also actively process game events and thus model functions of traditional, non-digital games such as uncertainty generation and rule execution. As it will be pointed out, there are dangers involved with transferring game elements that were originally social or physical in nature into the virtual domain. But the usage of computing functionality definitely introduces beneficial effects both to enhance existing deficits of traditional media as e.g. in board or tabletop games and to create entirely new experiences. Some of these benefits identified in Mandryk & Maranan (2002) and in Magerkurth et al. (2004) are listed below:

Realistic Rules, Believable Game Relations

More complex traditional games are often prone to using simplified or unrealistic relations between game objects. This is due to the requirement of keeping the game play fluent enough and not wasting time with gathering too many relevant parameters from handbooks or performing complex calculations manually. By modeling parts of the game logic in a software application, more realistic object relations can be achieved that do not disturb the game flow and lead to more plausible effects of game actions.

Persistency and Session Management

Many traditional board games take longer than the typical two or three hour period of a single session. With a growing complexity, achieving persistency of the game world becomes an issue which includes recording game events and possibly the creation of a corresponding game history. This can automatically and implicitly be realized in computer applications minimizing the unpopular paperwork that e.g. is associated with many role playing games and conflict simulations.

Rich Audio and Video Presentations

The static game media of traditional tabletop games pale against the audio-visual feasts of contemporary computer games. With the emergence of smart computing environments such as the AMBIENTE lab at Fraunhofer IPSI (Streitz et al. 2001) an even more immersive multimodal stimulation can be realized with the entire environment including walls and tables being integrated in a joint output mechanism. The static nature of traditional physical media such as game boards profits by the computer's capability of providing highly dynamic visualizations that can change during the course of game events.

Relief from Mundane Tasks

Repetitive activities that do not directly contribute to the enjoyable playing experience are part of many games. Most of these can be eliminated by letting the computer shuffle cards or build up game boards. Additionally, the pre-processing of role playing adventures and tabletop campaigns can be facilitated by providing the game master with software tools to design dungeons, traps, treasures, etc.

The Social Domain

Face-to-face group settings with natural means of interaction between players inevitably create social situations. By the use of directed speech, gestures, and mimics, a social domain emerges in which parts of the game state can reside that are only partially (or not at all) reflected in the virtual segments of the game state. For instance, in games with a strong emphasis on cooperation and competition, diplomacy and alliances will be key elements of the gaming experience, but they might entirely be of social nature without the virtual domain necessarily being aware of them. Virtual interfaces such as private GUIs might be used for clandestine negotiations, but apart from the communications functionality, the virtual domain would still be unaware of the players' state of the diplomacy. Nevertheless, game state information could also be shared among both domains, e.g. a social alliance could result in virtually forging a pact to allow controlling the partner's troops or sharing virtual resources.

Obviously, while multiple users can share a single physical space, each of those users also has a unique cognitive space. A user's cognitive space is composed of many factors, such as individual thought processes, impressions, perspectives, plans, goals, and concerns that are specific to that individual. Given any set of cognitive factors, in interacting with the physical and social environment, a user can have a set of plans and actions that are different from those that would come up as a result of another set of cognitive conditions (section quoted from Badre 2002).

Due to the existence of individual cognitive spaces, an important aspect of the social domain is the notion of private, shared, and public information. When cooperation is important in a game, individual information will be made public in order to maximize the group's efficacy. Complementarily, competitive gaming situations cause individual information to be kept private, so that no competitive advantages may be lost. In intermediate situations, some in formation might be shared to only some of the other players and held back or faked towards others. While the virtual domain might not necessarily be aware of players sharing information between each other, the distinction between public and private interfaces across both domains is essential to enable public, private, and shared information in the social domain. Therefore, both private and public output channels from the virtual domain should be available to foster social dynamics. Whenever game information is transferred from a virtual segment of the game state via a private interface, it is up to the player to decide whether to make public, share, fake, or hide the information in the social domain. Likewise, it is up to the social skills of the other players to believe, to doubt, or to mistrust the given information and then act accordingly.

The Physical Domain

According to Badre (2002), the physical domain consists of the world around us. It is the actual physical environment in which users function, perform, and make and execute decisions relative to an application. The physical environment can have a direct impact on how the user interacts with the gaming application. Users take action with a perspective and a mental model that is partially biased by their physical environment. The elements of the physical space that can affect the user's interaction with the game include the following:

- Physical objects
- Real-world properties
- Tangible Interfaces

Physical Objects

In the context of hybrid games, mainly two aspects of physical objects and their interrelationships are relevant for gaming applications. First, there are real world properties such as illumination, noise level, the players' positions, or even time (although the latter is also represented in the virtual domain) that provide context information. Second, there are special physical or tangible interfaces that effectively mediate between the virtual and the social domain.

Real World Properties

The integration of real world properties can add to the immersiveness of a gaming experience, especially when atmospheric properties such as background audio or the illumination level are utilized. For instance, one could think of a vampire game where the light conditions at the game table directly relate to the danger of being attacked by the undead. Or a spy game, where real world noise makes it difficult to overhear a conversation between non-player-characters in the virtual domain. When it comes to letting the virtual game logic consider real world properties, there are numerous ways of integrating different kinds of modalities via

3. The Application Domain of Hybrid Games

dedicated sensing technology, e.g. through distributed sensor particles (cf. Beigl & Gellersen, 2003). The challenges here are clearly more related to making optimal use of the real world data than gathering it and transferring it to the digital game logic. The way back from the virtual to the physical domain is harder to realize than vice versa. Naturally, a computer has only limited means of changing the real world around us. However, creating atmospheric audio or changing the illumination level through an electronic dimmer are only two feasible examples. Even by simply utilizing network controlled hardware interfaces such as power sockets, many real world context generating devices can be regulated.

Tangible Interfaces

For a socially supportive gaming experience to emerge, user interfaces to the virtual domain are required which do not bend the players back to technology centered interaction styles that focus the attention on the computer itself (Cohen & McGee 2004). To create human-centered interaction styles, tangible interfaces such as physical game boards fuse state representations with means of state manipulations. As Ullmer and Ishii (2001) outline, an ideal tangible interface does not differentiate between input and output as a GUI does, because by manipulating a physical state, this state already is its own representation. Tangible interfaces are thus much more direct and natural to use than a GUI, whenever a possible virtual representation matches the physical representation of the interface. This holds true for spatial relationships such as the position of pieces, but also for associative relationships that link physical states or tokens to virtual information. As an example, opening a chest in an augmented computer game can simply be achieved by opening a physical model of the chest on a table surface. Moving and turning the chest corresponds to moving and turning the physical control. Any physical action that is imposed on the control also updates its representation, i.e. the chest obviously is and remains open or turned.

A typical tangible interface is of public nature, i.e. each player should normally be able to perceive and alter the physical state of an interface component such as the position of a playing piece. Therefore, the tangible interfaces' representations are equally relevant for both the social and the virtual domain. The transfer to the social domain is achieved by the group members simply looking at (or touching) the interface, whereas the virtual domain has to utilize appropriate sensors to become aware of the physical states.

Similar to purely social game elements that have no virtual representation, not all physical states have to be transferred to the virtual domain, either. The shape or color of a playing piece might, for instance, have a meaning to the group, whereas the computer only understands its position and identity. Likewise, a representation might in fact be more complex in the virtual than in the physical domain. For example, the virtual game entity belonging to a physical playing piece might have a multitude of virtual attributes such as strength, intelligence, or hit points that are conveyed to the social domain via GUIs and not through the physical representations. The game state itself is, however, not represented in the physical domain. This is because each game relevant property of the physical domain is either transferred to and thus represented in the social domain (players see the color of a playing piece) or in the virtual domain (the computer senses the position of a playing piece). Due to the mediating nature of the physical domain, it thus consists entirely of game state information that is either duplicated/ redundant or irrelevant. Therefore, no unique segments of the game state can exist in it.

Implications of the Model

In this section it is outlined how to apply the model to the design of hybrid computer games. It is discussed which kinds of games are suitable for a hybrid platform setup and how to design game elements that take advantage of the capabilities offered by a hybrid platform.

Scope

A fundamental issue regarding the applicability of the proposed model is the scope of game types that can be realized.

First, games need to be suitable for multiplayer use. The more predominant the multiplayer portion is, the easier it will be to create a strong social situation. Second, games should not entirely rely on real-time GUIs that demand unshared, permanent attention such as e.g. in space combat simulators or jump n'run games. However, neither GUIs per se nor real-time gameplay are problematic, whereas only their combination hinders human centered interaction forms and thus works against the social domain. Naturally, games that deal mostly with information that is hard to convey via physical interfaces will make more use of GUIs than games that borrow elements from the physical world, such as Sim City, Panzer General, or puzzle games. Whenever physical and virtual properties of the same game element complement each other, GUIs and physical interfaces will make up for an ideal combination.

While turn-based games are proven to be suitable for social groups (think board or tabletop games), there is no reason not to make use of real-time gameplay. Due to the time-multiplexing problem of mouse driven UIs, well designed tangible interfaces are in fact much faster to use than many plain GUIs. Care must be taken, though, to keep the pace of the game manageable for group interaction.

Design Issues

Developing games for hybrid setups requires certain considerations that go beyond traditional computer game design. First and foremost, there are multiple domains to take into account, and care must be taken to distribute game elements along these domains. The question arises how this helps realizing games that profit by the different computing devices and still preserve the social dynamics of a group setting. There are several crucial issues to observe when designing the user experience.

Appropriate Choice of Domains

When merging computing functionality and physical media it is especially tempting to move a lot of game elements into the virtual domain, because the computer as a multi-purpose tool is seemingly well suited for a vast array of different tasks.

For instance, in traditional computer games, random number generation for achieving a variable game flow is typically and easily performed by the computer. However, when we introduce physical and social game domains, it might be sensible in certain game situations to adopt techniques from the real world, e.g. creating random numbers via the physical rolling of dice. For most players, the act of rolling dice is a highly social activity involving skillful rolling techniques which are permanently supervised by the other players to prevent cheating. It all depends on the social dynamics of a game situation whether "too lucky" dice rolling is tolerated, appreciated, or condemned. We thus have to weigh the advantage of unobtrusively creating randomness in the virtual domain against potentially exciting social effects when the physical dice interface is seemingly manipulated by one of the players.

3. The Application Domain of Hybrid Games

Another example for overestimating the virtual domain is the movement and actions of so called Non-Player-Characters (NPCs) in role playing games. While the advancements in the field of artificial intelligence make the computer controlled actions of such NPCs more and more believable in computer games, they still pale against the richness of the social interaction with a human game master or storyteller. Depending on the concrete game, there is of course room for both human and AI controlled NPCs even in the same game.

On the other hand, putting too much action into the social domain might incumber the creation of interfaces between both domains and lead to gaming styles that are essentially identical to e.g. traditional tabletop role playing games that work very well without any computer support.

An example for the importance of the physical domain is the representation of money in games of economy such as Monopoly™. During early tests of a variation of this classic board game for hybrid setups, in which money was represented virtually alone, users immediately objected that one of the main features of the original game was the touch and feel of paper money and that the loss of it was not acceptable. Therefore, the additional implementation overhead of providing a tangible money interface must be weighed against the potential loss of experience quality for the users.

Private and Public Interaction

Whenever cooperation and competition meet in a game, the notion of public vs. private information, communication, and negotiation becomes a highly interesting field of research (see Greenberg et al., 1998). When players are forced to cooperate to be successful, but only one player can win, social dilemmas and the need for clandestine communication arise as an addition to the open face-to-face interactions. Conspiracies may be forged in secrecy, while the open diplomacy at the game table may speak a different language. Thus, a hybrid games system should support private communication channels. A related interesting concept of hybrid games is the distribution of private and public aspects of game events that should be facilitated among different interaction devices. Figure 8 shows four characters involved in a fierce battle.

Figure 8: Public and private information

One player, Wolfgang, hits an enemy golem who shrieks for all to hear. On the game board, a small blood symbol is drawn around the golem that is obvious for each player, too. What only Wolfgang sees, however, is the exact location and the amount of damage he inflicted on his private interaction device (Figure 8). Thus, the same game event has different manifestations in the public and the private dimensions.

3. The Application Domain of Hybrid Games

Rules and Game Mechanics

The issue of balancing private and public interaction in a hybrid game is closely linked with the implementation and supervision of game rules. In principle, rules can be implemented in the virtual domain, as it is the case in traditional computer games. Likewise, rules can also be implemented in the social domain, so that they are agreed upon and enforced by the human participants, but not necessarily be known to the computer.

In order to fully understand the formal operation of a game and implement rules according to the implications of the hybrid games model, we need to complexify the understanding of game rules. Salen and Zimmerman (2004) identify three kinds of rules that they demonstrate with the traditional game of Tic-Tac-Toe. The authors define a three-part system for analyzing what game rules are and how they operate.

Constituative Rules

The constituative rules of a game are the underlying formal structures that exist "below the surface" of the rules presented to players. These formal structures are logical and mathematical. In the case of Tic-Tac-Toe, the constituative rules are the underlying logic such as:

- Two players alternate making a unique selection from a grid array of 3 by 3 units.
- The first player to select three units in a horizontal, vertical, or diagonal row is the winner.
- If no player can make a selection and there is no winner, then the game ends in a draw

Operational Rules

Operational rules are the "rules of play" of a game representing what is normally regarded as rules: the guidelines players require in order to play. The operational rules are usually synonymous with the written-out "rules" that accompany board games and other non-digital games. In analogy with non-digital games, there are many different sets of operational rules that could be formulated from any given set of constituative rules. A set of operational rules for a the Tic-Tac-Toe game, designed for two human players on a computer, might include:

- A game begins with an empty 3 by 3 grid on the screen.
- The screen displays an X or an O to one side of the grid to indicate which player will move next. The first player is always X.
- etc...

Implicit Rules

Implicit rules are the "unwritten rules" of a game. These rules concern social norms, etiquette, good sportsmanship, and other implied rules of proper game behavior. The number of implicit rules of Tic-Tac-Toe is vast and cannot be completely listed. The implicit rules of Tic-Tac-Toe are similar to the implicit rules of other turn-based games such as Chess. However, implicit rules can change from game to game and from context to context. For example, one might let a young child "take back" a foolish move in a game of Chess, but one probably would not let an opponent do the same in a hotly contested professional match.

For the development of hybrid games it is crucial to decide how and where to model the respective rules. For operational rules, a language is provided and discussed in a later section that allows for a certain degree of flexibility and adaptivity in order to facilitate a digital representation of the rules. Nevertheless, operational rules could as well be implemented in the social domain and not be accessible from the virtual domain. It is also the nature of implicit rules that they are usually taken for granted. But it might still be possible to alter the implicit rules of computer interaction for a hybrid game. For example, a computer logic might convey different or even contradicting information about the same aspect to different players via private communication channels and thereby manipulate implicit rules. Finally it should be noted that rules, especially consituative rules, might even be represented in the physical domain. For instance, the grid array size of 3 by 3 units from the Tic-Tac-Toe example might be defined and enforced by the physical layout of the respective game board.

3.3. Formative Evaluation

Since hybrid gaming is a novel application domain for pervasive computing technologies, it is important to align the concept with the expectations and desires of its potential users. It is only worth developing a hybrid games platform, if it is reasonable that a future market will adopt the concept and these types of applications will be successful, once available to a broader public. Therefore, it still has to be investigated, if future users of such technologies will adopt their full potential or if contemporary forms of entertainment and gaming are already sufficient. From a user interface perspective, we can clearly perceive that computer games focus the users' attention mainly on the computer screen or 2D/3D virtual environments, and players are bound to using keyboards, mice and game pads while gaming, thereby constraining interaction. By bringing more physical movement, ambient and multimodal stimulation, and social interaction into games, we might be able to utilize the benefit of computing systems while at the same time make the games accessible for ordinary people including elders, who were not socialized with playing computer games and who, consequently, do not participate significantly in contemporary computer entertainment.

Hence, in addition to the *internal validity*, i.e. that what is developed is actually a hybrid games platform and not something else, it is equally important to ensure the *external validity*, i.e. that in order to meet public demands for future entertainment platforms, the hybrid games approach is a promising one. In retrospect, the recent emergence of hybrid entertainment technologies in the mainstream market such as the Sony EyeToy, the Nintendo Wii controller, or the Philips AmbX system, might be considered an external validation, however, when the initial analysis and design of the platform began, these systems were not yet available and it was therefore necessary to conduct a requirements analysis with potential users.

As discussed in Röcker & Magerkurth (2007), a formative multi-method evaluation was conducted that was part of an empirical cross-cultural study at six different sites in five European countries in the context of the EU IST-IP project Amigo, Ambient Intelligence for the Networked Home Environment (http://www.amigo-project.org). While the overall goal of this evaluation was to elicit feedback from a target user population on general concepts for intelligent home environments, only the entertainment related aspects of the evaluation are relevant in the context of the development of a hybrid games platform. Therefore, the study's feedback gathered from potential users on the usefulness and attractiveness of different game concepts for smart home environments is now briefly discussed. The excerpts from the study presented here, investigate, if there is a demand for future home entertainment technologies that emphasize the physical realities of the players, and if yes, how such technologies will have to be designed in order to have an impact with different target groups.

The separation within the formative evaluation between attractiveness and usefulness relates to Hassenzahl's (2003, 2004) model of user–product relationships. It assumes users to construct product attributes by combining the product's features with personal expectations or standards. According to Hassenzahl (2004), the model assumes that two distinct attribute groups, namely pragmatic and hedonic attributes, can describe product characters. Pragmatic attributes are connected to the users' need to achieve behavioral goals. In contrast, hedonic attributes are primarily related to the users' self. For gaming applications, this hedonic quality or attractiveness is certainly a central aspect.

Materials and Methods

In order to get quantitative as well as qualitative feedback about the attractiveness and usefulness of hybrid game elements, the evaluation was subdivided into two parts with distinct methods and measures. For both parts, a scenario-driven approach was chosen to elicit feedback from a target user population.

In the first part, the participants had to evaluate a fictitious scenario regarding its usefulness and attractiveness. In the second part, single aspects of the scenario were discussed in a structured focus group session. A focus group is a form of group interview that is frequently used in social sciences research. Normally, 3 to 10 people are involved, and the discussion is led by a trained facilitator. Participants are selected to provide a representative sample of the target population, which has the advantage of requiring lower sample sizes than with randomly chosen participants (Sharp, Rogers, and Preece 2007).

To collect quantitative feedback on the different concepts, the scenario was visualized and shown to the participants in an exhibition-like setup (cf. Röcker et al. 2005). The participants were asked to rate each scenario element regarding its usefulness and attractiveness and to list the advantages as well as disadvantages of each concept. The stimulus material consisted of respective textual descriptions together with visualizations of the scenarios, with a corresponding text as an introduction.

The scenario involved a family living in a smart home environment that is assisted by ambient intelligence technologies. The scenario elements relevant in the context of the home entertainment domain illustrate the family's son interacting with a fictitious ambient intelligence game system that is capable of adapting the physical environment of the house to the respective situations in the game. A key focus of the scenario lies on the interaction with the game system using physical interaction devices and body movements as well as on the adaptation of the game to include the son's friends and their private game controllers when they join an existing game session. The individual scenario elements that were to be rated individually are shown in Table 3.

Table 3: Scenario elements with functionalities of a future gaming system

Scenario Element	Description
A) The game system asks for parental permission.	Before a game session can be initiated by the family's son, his remote mother's permission is queried via a network connection to her office.
B) It downloads and shows game play lists.	The game is adaptive to the properties of the player (e.g. his age and the available interaction devices) and provides suitable game lists only.
C) It adapts the lights and the sounds of the	After a game was selected, the light and

home to the environment of the game.	sound of the physical environment is altered to provide an optimal multimodal stimulation.
D) It displays a video wall to show the game and other players.	The room utilizes a wall-sized display to visualize game content and to connect the player to potential remote players (the family's grand father in this case)
E) It lets the game player interact with body movements and physical devices.	Interaction with the game system involves non-standard interfaces that relate to well-known interaction metaphors from real-world experience
F) It recognizes friends at the front door and lets them join in the game.	Visitors that do not belong to the family are recognized by their ID badges; known persons with the respective access rights may join the son's game session.
G) It recognizes and integrates the game devices of the friends.	Personal interaction devices of the son's friends are recognized and integrated with the current game session.
H) It downloads the profiles of the friends.	The preferences and playing history of the friends become accessible over the wall-sized display.

Two neighboring rooms were furnished as a reception room with tables and chairs, refreshments, paper, pencils and as an exhibition room showing the visualization of the scenarios (see Figure 9). In the reception room, the participants received a general introduction and a short instruction on the tasks that they had to perform in the exhibition room. The participants were instructed to form small groups with 2 to 4 people. When they entered the exhibition room, each group was instructed to assess the scenario and its elements. After fulfilling these tasks the group moved to the next scenario. The participants were asked to rank the elements for each scenario according to their perceived usefulness and to list advantages and disadvantages of the elements.

Figure 9: Stimulus material (left) and assessment of scenario elements (right).

In addition to the scenario evaluation, a focus group discussion was also conducted in the second part of the evaluation. The goal of the focus group discussion was to obtain qualitative feedback on the concepts described in the scenario and to investigate the expectations and needs for future gaming applications. The discussion was guided by structured questions focusing on the specific aspects of the scenario. The participants first were asked about their current entertainment preferences and then they were asked to develop ideas on how to improve the entertainment experience in the future. The discussion was supported by a metaplan technique. All ideas and comments of the participants were collected on cards, than clustered and labeled by the participants, and finally rated concerning their importance.

Participants and Schedule

The evaluation was conducted with N=10 participants of two different age classes (see Table 4) and lasted ca. three hours. One group consisted of three men and two women aged between 16 and 25 and the other group consisted of two men and three women aged between 32 and 38.

Table 4: Participants of the formative evaluation

Group	Participants	Gender	Age
Group 1	1	male	15
(15 – 25 years)	2	female	24
	3	male	23
	4	female	15
	5	male	25
Group 2	6	male	35
(32 – 38 years)	7	female	32
	8	male	35
	9	female	32
	10	female	37

The overall schedule for the quantitative and qualitative evaluation parts is shown in Table 5. The total time of the evaluation was 180 minutes. The time period before lunch was used for the scenario presentation and the scenario evaluation part using questionnaires from which quantitative results were obtained. In the afternoon, the focus group session took place in which a free discussion should reflect on the participants' preferences and their input on the realization of a respective system.

Table 5: Schedule of the formative evaluation

Duration	Activity
5 min	Arrival, introduction and explanation
10 min	Warming up
15 min	Presentation of scenarios
20 min	Questionnaires
40 min	Lunch break
50 min	Focus group discussion
10 min	Coffee break
20 min	Clustering and rating of the focus group results
10 min	Unwinding, cooling down, debriefing

3. The Application Domain of Hybrid Games

Results

Both quantitative results (rankings of scenario elements) and qualitative results (advantages and disadvantages of the scenario elements, results of the focus group discussion) were obtained and are presented in the following two sections.

Evaluation of the Fictitious Scenario

Usefulness

In the first part of the questionnaire, the participants had to rank the scenario elements regarding their usefulness (1 being the most useful scenario element, 8 the least useful element). Table 6 below gives an overview of the ranking results. SD stands for standard deviation, which is a simple measure of the or dispersion of the data set. The median is the number separating the higher half of the sample from the lower half.

Table 6: Ranking of scenario elements regarding their usefulness

Element	Sum	Average	Median	SD
A	28	2,8	2	2,300
B	53	5,3	4,5	1,829
C	36	3,6	3	2,319
D	51	5,1	5,5	2,558
E	42	4,2	4	2,098
F	64	6,4	6,5	1,430
G	40	4	3,5	2,625
H	43	4,3	4	1,767

The evaluation of the ranking task showed that the standard deviation for most scenario elements is rather high for the usefulness measure. In order to compensate for this variance, the ratings of the first three ranks were accumulated, before prioritizing the scenario elements, which is shown below in Table 7.

Table 7: Prioritization of scenario elements regarding their usefulness

Priority	Scenario Element	Top3
1	A) The game system asks for parental permission. C) It adapts the lights and the sounds of the home to the environment of the game.	70%
2	G) It recognizes and integrates the game devices of the friends.	50%
3	H) It downloads the profiles of the friends.	40%
4	E) It lets the game player interact with body movements and physical devices.	30%
5	D) It displays a video wall to show the game and other players.	20%
6	B) It downloads and shows game play lists. F) It recognizes friends at the front door and lets them join in the game.	10%

3. The Application Domain of Hybrid Games

Attractiveness

In the second part, the participants had to rank the same scenario elements regarding their perceived attractiveness. Again, Table 8 gives an overview of the respective results for attractiveness.

Table 8: Ranking of scenario elements regarding their attractiveness

Element	Sum	Average	Median	SD
A	48	4,8	6	3,155
B	50	5	5,5	2,160
C	25	2,5	2,5	1,354
D	48	4,8	4	2,486
E	37	3,7	4	2,163
F	62	6,2	6	1,549
G	45	4,5	5	2,121
H	45	4,5	5	1,900

The standard deviation is again rather high for the attractiveness measure, so that the ratings of the first three ranks were accumulated again. Similar to the previous part, Table 9 shows the number of participants who rated each scenario element in one of the first three ranks for the attractiveness measure.

Table 9: Prioritization of scenario elements regarding their attractiveness

Priority	Scenario Element	Top3
1	C) It adapts the lights and the sounds of the home to the environment of the game.	90%
2	D) It displays a video wall to show the game and other players.	60%
3	H) It downloads the profiles of the friends.	40%
4	A) The game system asks for parental permission. B) It downloads and shows game play lists. E) It lets the game player interact with body movements and physical devices.	30%
5	G) It recognizes and integrates the game devices of the friends.	20%
6	F) It recognizes friends at the front door and lets them join in the game.	0%

Ranking Results

The ranking of scenario elements concerning their usefulness and attractiveness revealed that the hedonic qualities of the scenario elements are indeed perceived as independent from their pragmatic qualities. For instance, while there is a clear trend to regard the remote inquiry of parental permission as something useful, if the parents are not at home and the son wants to engage in potentially inappropriate gaming activities (priority 1 in usefulness), it is still not universally regarded as something that would make the game system attractive (priority 4 in attractiveness). Conversely, the attractive notion of video walls showing ambient game elements (priority 2 in attractiveness) does only relate to priority 5 in usefulness, as this is not

3. The Application Domain of Hybrid Games

an integral part of the game mechanics. Whenever there is a correlation between the hedonic and the pragmatic evaluation it is, of course, easy to estimate whether the respective scenario element should make it into a prototype realization. While the adaptation of ambient light and sound to the game activities is generally regarded as favorable (priority 1 and 2) for both qualities, the recognition of friends at the front door is generally regarded as unfavorable (priority 6 for both qualities). For the uncorrelated cases it is a matter of balancing both qualities. Before conclusions are drawn here, the open discussion of advantages and disadvantages of the scenario elements is taken into account that followed the initial ranking task.

Discussion of Advantages and Disadvantages
The discussion of advantages and disadvantages mainly reflected the quantitative results from the ranking tasks, i.e. participants mostly related to their own rankings of the scenario elements and provided a rationale for their respective decisions. The feedback on the different scenario elements can be clustered into three domains:

Adaptiveness of the Environment
The idea of adapting light and sound to the current game situation was the concept most often addressed by the participants of both age groups. Adapting the physical environment to the virtual game atmosphere was regarded as one of the major building blocks for an enhanced gaming experience and increased realism. Concepts such as a video wall were generally regarded as the next step after simple light and sound adaptations and each participant agreed that such a feature would make a game more attractive. However, severe concerns were raised about the potential costs of the hardware and about the utility of such a wall display outside the context of a game application. Most participants expressed that they would not want their living rooms to be permanently altered in their physical appearance by adding a large wall display, especially among the older group of participants.

Enhancement of the Social Situation
The concept of extending traditional video games into the real world and thereby enabling rich social interactions between the players was regarded as an attractive feature for new gaming applications. In this context, easy integration mechanisms for additional players and devices were widely appreciated. Being used to the small effort necessary to participate in traditional board games, the integration of players and control devices into current video games, seems to be a major problem for the average user. Nonetheless, the integration of friends' profiles and devices in order to create a better matching game situation were generally appreciated, although fear of cumbersome handling led to a lower perceived usefulness than attractiveness.

Automatic Control and Security Mechanisms
Although the topic of automatic security and control mechanisms was addressed quite often, the expressed opinions regarding the usefulness of such mechanisms varied considerably. Most users, and especially those in the group of older participants that had children, liked the idea of automated age control, and regarded this feature as useful assistance in protecting children from inappropriate game content. In contrast, others feared that such autonomous control mechanisms might lead to a depletion of social contacts and an erosion of parental authority. Although automation was widely appreciated in order to minimize the installation effort for game devices and players, the majority of participants feared that too much automation might lead to a loss of control. Especially functions like the automated access control (scenario element F) raised serve concerns among the participants. Related to that, the boundaries of the game application were generally regarded as something that should be

clearly defined so that anyone knows where the game starts and where it ends. Functionality provided already at the front door consequently evoked consistent opposition and had no attractive aspect to it.

As suspected, the open discussion was consistent with the ranking results, i.e. participants commonly explained and defended their rankings. It became clear that attractiveness was the quality perceived as central to gaming applications, whereas usefulness was perceived as a means to realizing attractiveness. Usefulness also commonly had a confounding factor related to it, namely that participants mixed up the concept of something being useful, if it provides the proposed functionality, versus the difficulty of actually realizing the functionality with technical means. In this respect, the prioritization of scenario elements regarding their usefulness is probably influenced by the technical feasibility in the perception of the participants. The conclusion for the realization of a hybrid games platform that stems from this is that, as along as participants regard a feature as attractive, the estimation of usefulness seems to be of lesser importance, and thus the functionalities regarding ambient adaptation, ambient video presentation, and adaptation to user profiles appear to be of highest priority.

Focus Group Discussion

The third part of the evaluation, the focus group discussion, was largely unstructured and provided opportunities for the participants to stress their own ideas and comments. Since the focus group discussions provided unstructured results, the feedback gained during the focus group discussion is presented as divided into five groups forming clusters of similar topics that came up during the discussion.

Needs and Requirements

Most participants felt satisfied with existing entertainment devices and remarked that it would be hard to convince them of the benefits of a new entertainment system. Most participants were also rather satisfied with traditional board games and therefore quite reserved concerning the need for new entertainment systems. Especially the group of older participants mentioned that new systems have to be really innovative to be of any interest. A simple improvement of existing features would not be enough to convince them. The younger group was more open for innovations, but noted that existing systems cover all their needs. Hence, the acceptance of future entertainment systems will strongly depend on their functional quality. The older participants further remarked that new systems are likely to be interesting in the first moment, but that classical board games might be favored in the long run.

Basic Qualities

The participants cared most about the compatibility, extensibility and usefulness of the system. They clearly wanted a flexible system with upgrade options. Many participants remarked that it would have to be possible to take the system with them if they move into another house. They would only buy a new system, if it offered multiple different functions and a possibility to extend it, so that they would be able to use it for a long time. Both groups generated a cluster labeled "extensibility". This cluster included multiple items claiming options to add new functionality, possibilities to integrate further game parts, as well as an update opportunity for the system. All participants agreed that a future entertainment system should combine various functionalities. Similar to modern game consoles, which offer possibilities to watch DVDs, to communicate and to listen to music, a new entertainment system must also combine various functions related to entertainment. The group with the older participants also remarked that the system should save power. They asked for low power consumption in general as well as an automatic stand-by function which automatically turns off the system, if it is not used for a certain period of time. There was also a common agreement that such systems should not be too expensive. A price comparable to the price of today's games consoles was considered as appropriate.

System Design Goals

All participants agreed that there had to be a simple way to disable automatic control mechanisms such as the parental control. Generally, it was regarded as very important that the user always remained in control of the system and never the other way around. Most participants emphasized that the interaction should be easy, quick and intuitive. A few suggested an interface with speech input and output. This should facilitate intuitive interaction mechanisms for multiple situations beyond mere game play, ranging from the setup of the system, over its configuration to the daily interaction. Another requirement, especially among older participants, was to have service persons to deliver and install the system, to give some basic training on how to configure and use each feature, and to be available afterwards to help if problems occur. Furthermore, the system should not require any maintenance after being installed.

Both groups used traditional tabletop games as a benchmark to judge new entertainment systems. Participants in both groups noted that the game board should remain as a physical object. This requirement was explained with the natural social situation while using tabletop games. The participants claimed that they wanted to play together with their friends, although the system should offer the opportunity to function as an additional player. One participant explained that real game pieces and game boards would enable a haptic experience and generated an atmosphere on their own, which he appreciated very much. Another participant suggested that the system could add sound or special effects to traditional board games or represent the game board in form of a projection. Another topic, which was addressed by many participants, was security and safety. Some participants were concerned about (software) attacks from outside as well as about potential accidents caused by malfunctions of the system.

Content Design Goals

As mentioned above, most participants emphasized the social aspects of playing games. Generally, the system should help fostering a sense of community between users. Participants stated that this should be considered for any application, no matter if it was a game, a communication system or a movie. Games should offer a single-player mode as well as a multi-player mode for differing numbers of available players. The system should be able to replace missing human players as well as an option to control non-player characters. All participants expect that future entertainment systems provide better graphics and a more realistic game world than current systems do. Although this was mentioned as a clear requirement, one participant remarked the ambivalence. On the one hand the participants would appreciate an immersive game world, but on the other hand they fear that this may cause losing contact to reality.

Features

Generally, the participants wanted a useful combination of features realized in independent components. The users should be able to decide on their own, which features they need and then be able to integrate them into the system on their own behalf. It was also noted by most participants that the system should focus on entertainment exclusively. Completely different features of smart home environments, like for example housekeeping functionalities, should not be integrated into the system. Future gaming applications should be able to control the physical environment, e.g. light or sound, in order to adapt the room to the current game situation. The system should also include new technologies, like graphical projections, tangible user interfaces, or speech interfaces. Furthermore, the system should improve traditional board games with additional feedback in form of acoustical and visual effects, and provide an option to simulate additional players. Finally, the applications should represent remote players, who play from a different location, as if they were in the same room.

Conclusions

The three different methods of ranking elements, the discussion of advantages and disadvantages of scenario elements, and the unstructured focus group session provided a rather consistent view, although naturally, the open discussion brought up additional topics that might not be in the strict focus of a gaming system such as the question of service persons delivering the system, or power saving features. Since the evaluation was conducted in the context of an all-inclusive ambient intelligence system that might provide more functionalities than just gaming, participants might also have had a more hollistic view on an entertainment system than just the next generation of a games console, leading to thoughts about moving house, configuration issues and training activities. On the other hand, the order of the different methods certainly led to *priming* and a *mere-exposure-effect*, which was somewhat designated in order to come to a focussed discussion.

Given the nature and goal of an early summative evaluation, it is neither very useful nor always possible to come to a quantitative analysis of this mostly qualitative input. In general, there seems to be an interest in hybrid gaming systems, if certain constraints and requirements are met, whose realizations are partially out of the scope of this dissertation. The demand for providing related entertainment functionality like watching DVDs (that the current generation of games consoles also provides) is certainly an important requirment at a commerzialization stage. Likewise, the price point discussion is of high importance for the potential consumers, but not so much during the current research stage, as prices and availability of novel technologies are known to decrease when entering the mainstream.

What is central for the development and evaluation of a hybrid games platform is to translate the global requirement for a highly innovative, potentially even disruptive, gaming system to a concrete combination of features that users can evaluate with respect to its attractiveness. The summative evaluation already provided hints about which kinds of features or scenario elements would contribute to such an augmented interaction and gaming experience. These features related to the adaptation of ambient parameters, video wall presentations, and the adaptation to user profiles and were consistently named among different methods.

Although it might be possible to derive concrete requirements from these features, this is not done here, as certain scenario elements were already presented to the participants in a fixed way and 1.) have certainly influenced their own idea generation as well as 2.) were already derived from the theoretic model of hybrid games. In order to prevent a tautology, the results of this formative evaluation are not regarded as fixed requirements, but the feature selection of the participants is interpreted as a hint about which combination of features can be seen as an appropriate starting point for delivering a protoypical hybrid games system for the end users to evaluate. This is discussed in chapter 7.

The formative evaluation presented here demonstrates in general that the concept of hybrid gaming is attractive to different user groups. As an open evaluation with a limited participants count it serves its goal as a tool for idea gathering and a coarse identification of the target population's perspective, but of course does not contribute statistical depth.

The quantitative part provides an identification of priorities and directions, while the focus group discussion contributes input to concrete features and design goals. Since the issues of modularity and extensibility were raised by the participants as well as the importance of an intuitive interaction with (graphical) immersiveness on the other hand generally seen as ambivalent, it becomes clear that a platform for experimentation with the concept is needed. It must be possible to flexibly combine different interaction devices and also test varying implementations of concepts.

As discussed in this chapter, the design space for hybrid games is complex and involves virtual, physical, and social dimensions, which implies a need for thorough experimentation with different game element implementations. Consequently, it is necessary to rapidly prototype the various possibilities of appropriate user interfaces that might be realized as tangible media or via more traditional graphical interfaces. To provide an infrastructure of different physical interface components that can be applied to hybrid games in an easily interchangeable way, the next chapter discusses various tangible interface components that are specifically dedicated to hybrid gaming applications.

4. Interaction with User Interface Devices

The most crucial point and challenge for the success of hybrid games is the provision of appropriate interfaces that stimulate the direct interaction between human players and with the information that is relevant in the context of the given task. The goal is to provide the players with a set of interaction devices that support hybrid gaming applications appropriately with unobtrusive and intuitive interfaces fostering direct communication. In this chapter such interaction devices and the appropriate interaction designs are discussed. The entirety of these devices can be flexibly integrated to any hybrid gaming application developed with a dedicated software platform that is presented in the next chapter. The interaction devices presented here hence form the building blocks from which hybrid game applications can be developed.

Regarding the scope of interaction situations, the focus and contributions of this dissertation clearly focus on room-sized environments in which players mainly interact in a face-to-face fashion. Mobile pervasive gaming based on WLAN hotspots or GSM cells (e.g. Chalmers et al. 2005) where players explore larger areas such as entire buildings or city blocks is a related emerging field that has its very own technical issues and challenges for interaction design. For instance, the physical movement of the players in the real world and their delimitation to non-players (Smith et al. 2005) that happen to be in the same place by chance is not regarded as a situation to be dealt with. Furthermore the focus is on explicit interaction (cf. Abowd et al. 2002) either with graphical or tangible interfaces. Implicit interaction and the integration of real world context parameters to hybrid gaming applications is an interesting research field that will gain an increasing amount of attention from the scientific community, but is beyond the scope of this dissertation.

The general HCI framework to which both types of interfaces adhere to is that of "direct manipulation" introduced by Shneiderman (1983). It refers to the manipulation of objects in a way that capitalizes on users' knowledge of how they do so in the physical world, regardless of them actually manipulating tangible or graphical interfaces. As Rogers et al. (2007) point out, direct manipulation interfaces are assumed to enable users to feel that they are directly controlling the digital objects represented by a graphical or tangible interface. User interfaces are thus designed that they can be interacted with in ways that are analogous to how physical objects in the physical world are manipulated. As Shneiderman illustrates, there are many benefits of direct manipulation interfaces. These include among others:

- Helping beginners learn basic functionality rapidly
- Allowing infrequent users to remember how to carry out operations over time
- Preventing the need for error messages
- Showing users immediately how their actions are furthering their goals
- Helping users gain confidence and mastery and feel in control

While both graphical and tangible interfaces can implement direct manipulation, there is a certain tendency towards tangible interface components as they seem to be especially beneficial for gaming applications. A study from Rogers et al. (2002) points out that this kind of physical-digital manipulation encourages creativity and playfulness. In their study exploring color mixing, it was found that children were far more creative, collaborative, and reflective when mixing colors with physical cubes as an interface compared to a corresponding graphical user interface.

4.1. Requirements

Apart from realizing direct manipulation, the interfaces presented in this chapter should also help ensuring both the group situation to remain socially adequate and the transition from and to the virtual domain to be performed effectively. Human attention should remain focused on the social situation of the game and not shift towards the interface to the virtual domain. Consequently, interaction metaphors are proposed that relate to well-proven physical interfaces found in strongly human centered entertainment genres such as tabletop or board games. These physical interfaces should mediate the interaction between the human players and the virtual representation of the game world. For instance, placing and orienting playing pieces that represent a group of dungeon explorers directly on a game table surface is more natural and more direct than doing the same with a traditional graphical user interface in a computer game. In the traditional computer game, the additional layer of indirection imposed by the mouse or joystick prevent the desired unification of representation and control: A spatial embodiment of the system's digital state in the interface (Ullmer & Ishii 2001) is not realized and the user's attention is focused on the indirect graphical interface (Cohen & McGee 2004). This attenuated mental capacity is especially relevant, when players are supposed to perform together and need to synchronize their actions.

With respect to the user requirements study discussed in the previous chapter and their implications for non-hardcore gaming target groups, it is especially important to allow users to pick up the respective user interfaces quickly and encourage their interactions with the gaming platform. Since gaming applications are usually used voluntarily as a leisure activity, it is not acceptable to provide users interfaces that are not easy to learn and master, as perceived frustration is likely to put players off.

Consequently, the first and most important requirement towards appropriate interaction devices discussed above can be summarized as:

> *R4.1: Real-world metaphors – Appropriate interaction devices shall realize direct manipulation and provide analogies to end users' previous interaction experiences*

Since this dissertation contributes specifically to the field of hybrid games, the selection and design of interface devices should be geared towards their appropriateness for realizing specific functionalities within a hybrid gaming context. This can imply a potential generalization to other, broader application domains, but the adequacy for hybrid gaming purposes is of higher relevance than domain-unspecific characteristics of a device.

For instance, for the realization of a game specific user interface to cast magic spells, it is plausible to pick up the metaphor of a magic wand, since potential users are likely to understand the implications of the respective interaction metaphor from their previous body of knowledge (see R4.1). Coincidentally, a wand-like interface is also suitable for realizing a broad range of pointing applications, if equipped with appropriate sensing technologies, and can be used for other gesture applications as well, such as for conducting or similar activities. While such generalizations and transfers to other fields are appreciated, they should only be a side-effect of the specificity to hybrid games. Another user interface device, the Smart Dice Cup that is discussed later in this chapter, similarly picks up a well-known interaction metaphor, namely shaking a dice cup to provide for randomness and variability in a game. Unlike the previous example, there is little room for generalization of this interaction technique as there are both numerous other means of generating variability in other application domains as well as only limited applicability of a shaking-based interaction technique outside of its specific gaming context.

R4.2: Specificity – Appropriate interaction devices shall fulfill purposes specific to gaming applications over a general applicability outside the context of hybrid gaming

User interface devices themselves can be innovative and provide appropriate research opportunities, but it is certainly the entirety of devices and their interplay that allows for evaluating the approach of hybrid gaming by realizing complete gaming applications that form a testbed for social and technical research questions.

Due to the enormous efforts necessary to develop complex applications such as distributed games that cope with changing physical setups, it is outside the scope of this dissertation to provide a multitude of different complete games and their evaluations. Nevertheless, the sum of the user interface building blocks that adhere to real-world metaphors (R4.1) and are specific for their gaming functions (R4.2) must be great enough to form the basis for more than trivial sample games. They must allow for complete game setups of sufficiently complex content that meet the expectations of potential user groups.

Apart from smaller sample applications to outline each interface's capabilities and characteristics, two more complex gaming applications are thus discussed and evaluated in a later chapter that make use of the complete set of provided interaction devices. The respective requirement can be formulated as:

R4.3: Completeness – The entirety of provided interaction devices shall be sufficient to realize complete proof-of-concept games

The final requirement builds upon R4.3, but relates it to the hybrid nature of the application domain. Hybrid games are intended to bridge the gap between the physical and the digital world and utilize real-world interaction metaphors (R4.1). In order to draw conclusions, if this is actually beneficial and really contributes to a better gaming experience that supports social situations and makes games generally more enjoyable, it is important to realize that it must be possible to vary and alternate the concrete realizations of interface devices with other realizations that follow different design rationales. This allows for addressing confounding factors of interface and game characteristics, i.e. the variance of enjoyment between different game sessions must be explicable by game related and interface related factors. Ideally, the exact identical game should be evaluated with different interaction device setups in order to assess the appropriateness of a hybrid gaming interface setup.

If we imagine a continuum of "hybridness" of interaction devices, the realizations discussed in the following sections would be located somewhere in the middle of the continuum. For instance, a roleplaying game might be played with the same set of rules 1.) in a traditional pen & paper way without any computer support as one extreme and 2.) as a screen-centered GUI application in the tradition of a conventional computer game without any dedicated physical interface devices as the other extreme. Depending on the concrete device setup, a hybrid approach would be in between both extremes and – as the hypothesis to be tested – would presumably attribute to a better gaming experience.

R4.4: Alternative realizations – There should be alternative interfaces with different characteristics available that allow for appropriate comparisons

The implication of R4.4 is that a respective software platform is available that allows for flexibly integrating different design alternatives for similar game-specific purposes. This should make it possible to play a game e.g. with only graphical UI components, with physical interaction devices, or with a combination of both. Likewise, it should be technically indifferent, whether a game is played co-located like a traditional tabletop or board game, or whether the individual players (and their respective user interface components) are distributed and connected via the internet. The respective software requirements are outlined in the next chapter.

The following table summarizes the interaction device requirements discussed above.

Table 10: Interaction device requirements

Req.	Description
R4.1	Real-world metaphors: Appropriate interaction devices shall realize direct manipulation and provide analogies to end users' previous interaction experiences
R4.2	Specificity: They shall fulfill purposes specific to gaming applications over a general applicability outside the context of hybrid gaming
R4.3	Completeness: The entirety of provided interaction devices shall be sufficient to realize complete proof-of-concept games
R4.4	Alternative realizations: There should be alternative interfaces with different characteristics available that allow for appropriate comparisons

To meet these requirements, the interaction devices contributed in this dissertation are mostly based on custom-built physical or tangible user interfaces on the one side and adapted graphical user interfaces on the other side. The physical interfaces are aimed to be used exclusively in hybrid gaming applications. Interaction devices such as smart dice boxes or physical game boards are naturally dedicated to entertainment purposes, although a gesture based interaction device could serve as a magic wand in a game and as a conductor's baton in a musical teaching application. The scope of the adapted graphical user interfaces is broader and definitely relevant outside the domain of hybrid gaming. The research on most adapted GUIs presented here stems from earlier work in the AMBIENTE division at Fraunhofer IPSI that had traditionally addressed issues of interaction design in smart and augmented office environments. As pointed out in a previous chapter, the work of the AMBIENTE group was mainly concerned with the invention, development, and evaluation of so-called "Roomware" components that integrate information technology into arbitrary room elements such as tables, walls, or chairs (Streitz et al. 2001). Following the Disappearing Computer paradigm (Streitz et al. 2005), Roomware components typically embed touch sensitive displays that are operated with pens or plain fingers and allow for providing natural and unobtrusive interfaces that facilitate easy access to graphical information without focusing the users' attention to the computer.

The remainder of the chapter is separated into a section on the novel dedicated tangible interfaces developed for hybrid gaming applications and the adapted graphical user interfaces that build upon previous work on Roomware technology.

For each interaction device it is briefly discussed how the respective requirements R4.1, R4.2 and R4.4 are addressed. Since requirement R4.3 does not concern any individual interaction device, it is discussed for all devices at the end of this chapter.

4.2. Custom Tangible Interfaces

The following section introduces four physical interaction devices that contribute to the design of natural interfaces especially suited for hybrid gaming. All of them have been used and tested in the development of several hybrid gaming prototypes that are discussed in a later chapter.

The Gesture Based Interaction Device

Nowadays, mice and keyboards are the common interaction devices for most tasks involving computer systems, although several application areas such as simulations or computer games utilize specialized devices such as steering wheels, joysticks, or gamepads. The interaction devices dedicated to traditional computer entertainment applications normally do not link between the physical and the virtual world in a way that mastering the interface itself is a central and demanding component. Hence, real world skills gained by training the interface are not necessary to achieve an effect in the virtual domain of the game application. Recently, physical gaming interfaces that integrate real world skills have emerged such as the GameTrak boxing / baseball interfaces (http://www.in2games.uk.com) or the Playstation Eye-Toy (http://www.eyetoy.com), both relating to the prior dance pad interfaces such as "Dancing Stage" (http://www.konami.com) that tracked the users steps on a pad augmented with pressure sensors and were consequently used for all kinds of dance tracking applications. The tremendous success of the Eye-Toy (Minkley, 2003), a camera addon for the Sony Playstation that integrates the filmed shape of the player as an action object in the respective video games, is a clear indication that dedicated physical interfaces involving real world skills are an important future trend for hybrid games. Likewise, the tremendous impact of the current generation of Nintendo's WII game console (www.wii.com) with its multitude of controller variations demonstrates this trend as well. This goes in line with Garneau (2001) who points out that both the exertion of physical activity and the application of an ability contribute to the perceived enjoyment of a game.

4. Interaction with User Interface Devices

Figure 10: The gesture based interaction device

The gesture based interaction device (Magerkurth et al. 2006) is an interaction device to allow for novel forms of human computer interaction. It follows the approach of linking the exertion of a physical skill to a respective effect in a virtual application and also allows for other innovative interaction techniques as illustrated below. It consists of a stick augmented with an accelerometer in its head (see Figure 10) that can be swung in a similar way as a conductor's baton or a magic wand. It picks up and digitally converts the radial movements of the stick to discrete acceleration measures.

While the gesture based interaction device was primarily designed for controlling hybrid games, it can also be used as an interface for numerous other applications in ubiquitous computing environments, where it can make up for the lack of standard interaction devices and allow for complex command chains conveyed by 2D gestures. Also, the teaching and training of conductors could effectively be supported by the device, if the parameters gathered from the device were matched with a respective audio output.

Operating modes

There are three possible operating modes of the device, each relating to different usage scenarios and applications.

Gesture Recognition

As illustrated in Figure 11 (left), the primary operating mode of the device is gesture recognition. In a typical hybrid gaming application, the device translates and maps the real world qualities of the user's gestures to a virtual representation that has a certain effect in the game. The more accurate a player is able to perform a set of given gestures, the more successful is his outcome in the virtual world. Applied to a fantasy role playing scenario, one could for instance imagine several different magic spells that each have unique effects and are more or less hard to perform. A simple spell might turn the light on or off and consist of two easy gestures (e.g. a circle or a straight line) to be performed consecutively by the spell caster using her magic wand. A more powerful spell might eradicate all life in a 50 yards diameter and require ten more difficult gestures such as certain characters or words from the alphabet to be performed in a sequence (possibly even in a certain amount of time).

4. Interaction with User Interface Devices

Figure 11: Operating modes of the gesture based interaction device

Hence, the application of the device in the gesture recognition mode ("wand" mode) can match the real world skills in mastering gestures of varying difficulty to a respective virtual proficiency. A computer game wizard is no longer mighty due to some numbers stored in her character database, but because of physical skills acquired by real experiences.

Intensity Measurement

The gesture recognition mode works by matching the features of a set of stored gestures to the current incoming stream of data from the device. Another way of using the gesture based interaction device is by regarding the magnitude of the raw sensor data in order to measure the force of the swinging. By doing so, it is possible to create hybrid games that use the gesture based interaction device like a hammer or a sword instead of a wand or a conductor's baton. A sample game ("SteinSchlag") that utilizes the device in both ways is discussed in a later chapter.

Pointing

The final operating mode requires an RFID antenna built into the device's head. As illustrated in Figure 11 (center) one can equip arbitrary artifacts with RFID tags that can be read and unambiguously identified by the antenna's head as shown in Figure 11 (right). This allows for unobtrusive multimodal interaction styles that follow Bolt's paradigm (Bolt 1980) by naturally specifying source and/ or target artifact of an arbitrary action. Although the current version of the gesture based interaction device does not yet have the RFID integrated inside the head, the respective software for the pointing mode has already been completed (and utilized in a slightly modified version for the iBracelet presented in the next section). Currently, the antenna must be fixed to the outside of the device's head with adhesive tape and will be integrated inside the head during the planned revision discussed below.

Technical Realization

As shown in Figure 11, the current realization of the gesture based interaction device consists of a stick with an accelerometer in its head and an interface for the universal serial bus that converts the analog signals from the accelerometer to the respective digital data.

Figure 12 shows the transverse sections of the stick's head from the side and from the front. The currently used accelerometer is an ADXL311 integrated circuit from Analog Devices (www.analog.com). It delivers a proportional voltage to the current acceleration.

4. Interaction with User Interface Devices

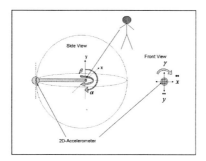

Figure 12: Transverse sections of the stick's head

Stick

Apart from its purpose as an interface for the interaction, the stick is also crucial for the functioning of the device. It is used for transforming the rather small angular movements of the wrist to the amplified radial acceleration of the sensor. The longer the stick is, the higher the amplifications of the angular wrist movements become.

USB Interface

The sensor board in the stick is connected to the USB interface board via a PS/2 (Mini-Sub-D-5) socket. The interface board transforms the received analog signals to digital signals with AD converters that have adjustable thresholds. The voltage ranges that determine the resolutions can be adjusted via respective potentiometers. The interface board software controls the two AD converters and transmits the received signals to the PC via the USB port. When the system is initialized, the software on the interface board is downloaded from the PC in order to facilitate software updates and extensions. For simplicity reasons, the utilized Cypress EZ-USB chip (AN2131SC) is integrated into a standard USB module from Braintechnology (www.braintechnology.de).

PC Software

On the PC side, a dedicated software component, the "Wand Server", is responsible for receiving and processing the digital signals from the interface board. It can either perform gesture recognition on the stream of incoming signals or perform basic intensity measurements. The Wand Server is connected to other software components based on a communication mechanism discussed in a later section. This allows other applications within a hybrid gaming environment to utilize the interpreted signals from the gesture based interaction device.

4. Interaction with User Interface Devices

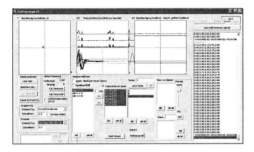

Figure 13: Training new gestures with the ZauberAnalyse application.

Figure 13 shows a related software component ("Zauberanalyse") that visualizes the raw and transformed sensor data. It allows not only to perceive the digital representation of the physical device movements, but also to record and interpret gestures. There are several gesture recognition / similarity measurement algorithms available and all of them operate on groups of homogenous gesture records that serve as referential gestures to the currently interpreted device signals. A similarity measure is calculated for each referential gesture. The referential gesture with the highest similarity to the currently interpreted gesture is associated with the gesture and a respective similarity index is given.

Regarding the gesture recognition, there are several approaches. A popular and lightweight algorithm was already introduced by P. C. Mahalanobis in 1936 (cited from Devroye et al. 1996). It determines the "similarity" of a set of values from an "unknown" sample to a set of values measured from a collection of "known" samples. It is superior to Euclidean distance because it takes distribution of the data points (correlations) into account and is traditionally used to classify observations into different groups (Taguchi & Rajesh 2000). The algorithm is defined as follows:

$$D^2_t(x) = (x - m_t)S^{-1}_t(x - m_t)`$$

D_t is the generalized squared distance of each pixel from the t group
S_t represents the within-group covariance matrix
m_t is the vector of the means of the variables of the t group
X is the vector containing the values of the environmental variables observed at location x

Design Revision

The version of the gesture based interaction device that was presented above is the current implementation as it was used and tested in the context of several hybrid games such as SteinSchlag and Caves&Creatures, both discussed in a later chapter. While the device itself already allows for novel and exciting interaction experiences, there are also several opportunities for augmenting the current realization.

At the moment, the device is connected to a PC via a USB interface and a two meter cable. While the cable is long enough to allow for free form interaction without conveying the perception of being bound to a stationary machine, its usage scenarios are still limited to rather static and close proximity interaction situations such as tabletop games. By eliminating the cable, the device could be used in all kinds of smart spaces such as networked home

76

environments where players move through the entire house or use the device in a pointing and gesture mode to control home appliances such as HiFi systems. Using a similar wireless middleware platform as e.g. the smart dice box discussed below, it is planned to enhance the stick to communicate wirelessly with the environment and thereby augment its usage scenarios.

Furthermore, as alluded to above, the next version of the gesture based interaction device will include the RFID reader in the head of the stick, in contrast to being attached to the outside with adhesive tape. This will require a slightly larger head (or a new reader hardware that has smaller dimensions than the currently used IQ Automation Easy key /R module from www.iqautomation.de).

A third and more complex augmentation involves a redesign of the sensor hardware with a 3D accelerometer that supports 3D gestures. Currently, the device is unaware of translations along the Z axis, i.e. the device can be moved pointing away from the torso of the user without notice. By integrating a new accelerometer that also measures the Z axis, new forms of interaction become an option. The first usage scenario that comes to the reader's mind in the context of hybrid games is of course the possibility for swordplay-like interaction including stabbing. However, many more interactions involving a pointing mechanism become feasible even without an RFID tagged target artifact. In general, a broader range of interesting gestures can be realized with a 3D gesture recognition mechanism. Naturally, the respective gesture recognition software would have to be rewritten to cope with the new dimension, since the currently used 2D distance measurements would not be appropriate anymore. While basic 2D gesture recognition based on e.g. Euclidian or Mahalanobis distance could also be performed on a moderately powerful embedded PC such as in (Beigl & Gellersen 2003), the applicability for 3D gestures would still need to be investigated.

Review of Requirements

The gesture Based Interaction Device clearly affords its interaction design by the usage of sticks in real life that are used for pointing at things or for swinging and hitting. Although the specificity of this general-purpose interface could be questioned, the use of sticks for casting magic spells in games (magic wands) nonetheless fulfills a game specific function. Alternative realizations of spell-casting interfaces from the domain of traditional gaming include rolling physical dice, whereas in computer games there are various means of spell casting interfaces commonly involving random number generation. Table 11 lists the realizations of the respective requirements.

Table 11: Gesture Based Interaction Device requirements

Req.	Realization
R4.1	Magic wand
R4.2	Casting spells
R4.4	Rolling physical dice, random number generation

iBracelet

The pointing at arbitrary tagged artifacts with the gesture based interaction device is an intuitive interaction technique that augments the innate capability of human (and anthropoid) beings to convey information about a specific object by pointing at it with her fingers. By pointing with the stick, the information about the artifact of interest is also shared with the

4. Interaction with User Interface Devices

virtual domain in addition to the social world. A similar interaction technique is the taking of artifacts. It conveys to the social domain the (at least temporary) possession of an artifact. To share this information with the social domain, the author utilized augmented bracelets that are worn at the players' wrists just like ordinary wristbands (see Figure 14).

Figure 14: An RFID augmented iBracelet.

The iBracelet consists of an RFID reader connected to a custom-built radio transmitter that operates below the 900 MHz band. The reader's antenna is wrapped in the incasement of the bracelet and the entire electronics is hidden beneath a plate atop the bracelet. Hence, the iBracelet looks much like an ordinary bracelet that performs its augmented functions unobtrusively.

The device itself was developed by Intel Research, Seattle, as a research grant supporting the work on hybrid and computer-augmented games (Smith et al. 2005). Already the third device built by Intel was donated.

Whenever a tagged object is held in the hand of a person wearing the iBracelet, the reader identifies the tag and this information is sent wirelessly to a small base receiver that is plugged to the USB port of a standard PC. Similar to most other RFID readers, the detected tag IDs are transmitted continuously over a serial connection and also the included USB driver sets up a respective virtual COM port that can be listened to by any application including HyperTerminal that ships with most versions of the Windows operating system. In contrast to some other standard RFID readers such as the Easy key /R or the ProxLine (www.cardcontrol.net), the iBracelet appends its own bracelet ID to any transmitted RFID tag, so that a PC application can always associate artifacts and bracelets accordingly. The respective proxy software the author developed to integrate the iBracelets with the remainder of the device and software infrastructure consequently performs this mapping and allows other software components to subscribe to changes in the artifact-user associations.

Intended Usage

The iBracelets allow for the development of natural interfaces through which a digital application can be informed about associations of artifacts and users, because bracelets and users are permanently associated in a 1:1 relationship, i.e. a user wears a specific bracelet and does not usually take it off or trades it with another user. In order to trade an artifact between users, one simply hands the artifact to the other person, just like she would do in a traditional face-to-face situation without computer support.

4. Interaction with User Interface Devices

In the context of hybrid games the iBracelets are used in a similar way as in other application domains, namely to inform the virtual domain about changes in the temporary possessions of artifacts between the users. For many game related artifacts, this has shown to be especially valuable, since the players do not only deal with copious amounts of similar artifacts such as playing cards or figurines, but mainly with unique objects that need to be temporarily shared among players. The gesture based interaction device, for instance, might be used by multiple players sequentially, e.g. in a battle of wizards, where one wizard at a time casts a spell on her opponents. Another frequently exchanged artifact is the smart dice box that is presented in the next section. Prior to the implicit bracelets interaction such temporary changes in artifact possessions had to be either explicitly communicated to the virtual domain via another interface or dictated by the virtual domain and then supervised in the social domain. In this case, the game application would simply enforce e.g. a turn-taking interaction style and would rely on the players to exchange artifacts as demanded. Apart from the lacking freedom to change game mechanics on the fly (the players might e.g. want to grant someone a free additional turn due to her bad performance), it should be noted, though, that respective social protocols usually work appropriately.

Scope

The iBracelet devices operate in a broad range of interaction situations and can be regarded as a calm, universal technology. At the current state of the realization, however, the following limitations should be considered:

The antenna in the bracelet is not directed towards a specific direction such as the hands and thus the reader might also detect artifacts being near the antenna, no matter if they are taken by the user or not. For the exchange of artifacts between users or for picking up artifacts, the reader works quite reliably. However, in certain more filigree interaction situations such as dealing with (tagged) playing pieces on a game board, the resolution of the device is simply not sufficient to differentiate between artifacts.

Furthermore, the transmission range of the radio module is currently limited to a bit more than a meter, depending on certain obstacles that reflect or divert the signal. While a careful table or room layout certainly helps coping with the limited transmission range, it is still an issue to consider.

Despite these imperfections, the iBracelets already function maturely enough to be deployed in real-life situations. While the form-factor of the devices imposes certain limitations regarding their applicability in certain usage domains such as picking playing pieces, it is the first comparable sensing device that is unobtrusive enough to not be permanently perceived as a piece of technology being disguised in a clumsy case. For devices such as the earlier iGlove (see O'Connor 2004) sentient glove this does not hold true.

For the prototypical games developed, iBracelets can be used to detect other interaction devices as well as tagged figures and playing cards (see Figure 15) which are common for many traditional games. Due to RFID tags glued to the backs of the cards, the event of being played and picked up can be detected by an iBracelet, or, correspondingly by a stationary RFID reader.

4. Interaction with User Interface Devices

Figure 15: Tagged Playing Cards.

Review of Requirements

The iBracelet artifact takes a special role as an interface device, since it realizes only implicit interaction. That means that the device per se does not afford any special usage, but implicitly tracks the usage of other (secondary) physical devices. Although it is very intuitive to put into operation (i.e. wearing it just like any traditional bracelet), the metaphors and game specific-functions of the secondary devices it tracks are more relevant than its own. While the basic functionality of associating physical artifacts with human users is definitely not specific to games, but applicable to any kind of application, enabling the usage of game-specific secondary artifacts such as cards and figures are highly important for gaming applications, nonetheless.

Regarding R4.4 the distinction between the device itself and the secondary artifacts it tracks leads to two levels of alternative realizations. Without means of implicitly tracking physical objects, the social domain would keep track of object associations exclusively, e.g. by means of spatial encodings (an object near a person would be considered by the entirety of human players as belonging to her). In order to synchronize virtual representations of the game state, one would have to explicitly convey this information to the virtual domain by means of other interaction devices. The implication for the use of secondary artifacts is that game specific objects would either be realized and used in an identical way to the RFID-augmented versions tracked by the iBracelet, but lose the implicit synchronization with the virtual domain, or that purely virtual objects, such as graphical representation of playing pieces on a graphical game board would be used, which means that the physical domain would not be involved in the interface at all. Table 12 lists the realizations of the respective requirements.

Table 12: iBracelet requirements

Req.	Realization
R4.1	Bracelet (implicit)
R4.2	Tracking cards, figures, and other artifacts
R4.4	Using implicit social or explicit digital inventories

The Smart Dice Cup

Both interaction devices discussed so far represent suitable interface components for hybrid gaming applications that can be utilized to link physical and virtual domains. While they are not fully dedicated to gaming applications alone and could also be used for several other purposes as well, the following two physical interaction devices are specifically targeted towards typical hybrid games. The device discussed in this section is a heavily augmented version of a traditional dice cup called Smart Dice Cup (Magerkurth & Engelke 2006). The CAD figures and the actual built device are shown in Figure 16.

Figure 16: The Smart Dice Cup

Dice are crucially important components of a wide range of games. They are used for creating variations in the game flow. By rolling dice, an element of chance is introduced to an otherwise static and deterministic flow of game actions. The chance in the dice, however, is not equal to the generation of a random number. Rolling dice involves both a physical act and skill (some people and some dice roll better results than others) as well as a social mechanism to supervise and control the physical act, because cheating is a common phenomenon associated with this particular way of adding variability to games. Hence, rolling dice is a very interesting example of a gaming interface that spans all three domains and is thus particularly suitable for a computer augmented realization.

Design Alternatives

There are several design alternatives when augmenting the physical rolling of dice with information technology in a way that the virtual domain is informed about the outcome of the respective results. The challenges are related to providing a convincing natural interaction experience that ideally resembles the traditional techniques of rolling dice very closely and allows for individual variations and styles in the way the interface is utilized. Furthermore, the transition from the physical to the virtual domain must be absolutely reliable and robust, because an erroneous or failed transmission at a decisive point in the game flow definitely destroys any gaming atmosphere. Finally, regarding economic feasibility, the technology involved should not be completely unrealistic to develop into an economically viable product in the future.

Augmenting the dice with respective sensors

Terrenghi et al. (2005) propose a cube-based interaction device that is equipped with a Smart-Its particle (cf. Beigl and Gellersen 2003) and compasses in order to determine its own orientation. The sensor data is thus interpreted inside the cube and could possibly be communicated to the environment via radio transmission. A similar approach is also discussed in Block et a. (2004). Naturally, it is possible to create dice (which are cubes) using a similar technology. The major benefits of such smart dice are the natural interaction technique that is identical to the traditional rolling of dice and the autonomy of the artifacts. The dice do not rely on any smart environment to be aware of their orientation. In fact, Terrenghi et al. even use the cube in a stand-alone mode with displays integrated in each of the cube's faces to convey its digital state to the real world. The disadvantages are significant, however. First, great care must be taken to balance the interior of the cube so that each of the sides has an

4. Interaction with User Interface Devices

identical chance of being rolled. Second, with current particle technology it is not feasible to build dice with an appropriate size, cf. the diameter of Terrenghi's cube is about 10 cm. Third, since many games require the rolling of multiple dice (as e.g. Yahtzee), the technology is simply too expensive to be integrated into each of the dice.

Using ordinary dice and detect their faces

A first alternative approach to sense the outcome of rolling dice was implemented by the author and his colleague (Magerkurth & Stenzel 2003; Magerkurth & Stenzel 2004). It involved an optical recognition of the dice on the surface of a Roomware game table. While the Roomware technology is discussed in more detail as an augmented and adapted graphical user interface platform in a later section of this chapter, the optical dice recognition is already presented here.

 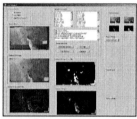

Figure 17: A physical die (left) tracked by the Camera Analyst software (right).

The benefits of optical recognition are immediately plausible. In principle, it is possible to adhere to traditional interaction techniques, in our case the rolling of dice, that neither require modifications to standard interfaces (the dice) nor an adapted interaction design. As shown in Figure 17, a standard dice can be rolled over almost the entire surface of an interactive table and be recognized by a respective software application (the Camera Analyst, see Figure 17 (right)). All that is required for the visual recognition software to work reliably is the diameter of the dice being slightly greater than that of the dice found in most common board games.

The implemented prototype involved an Axis network camera that was mounted over an InteracTable Roomware component (Streitz et al. 2001). The InteracTable features a touch sensitive plasma surface on which dynamically changing game boards are displayed. In exactly the same manner as in traditional tabletop games, players would roll their dice on the surface of the table that substitutes the traditional game boards. In contrast to other augmented tabletop applications (e.g. Shen et al. 2002, Steurer et al. 2003) this setup deliberately did not use top projection from a projector mounted above the table in conjunction with sensing technology embedded in or under the table surface. Apart from the fact that this would aggravate or even thwart the recognition of the dice' faces, the author's approach also has the advantage of robustly providing a high-quality image on the table surface, no matter how the lightning conditions are. Furthermore, unlike top-projection, the game board is not displayed on top of the playing pieces, when it should be beneath them.

The "Camera Analyst" software uses a subset of the functionality found in visual recognition libraries such as the Recognition And Vision Library RAVL (http://ravl.sourceforge.net). It interprets Direct Draw surfaces from the incoming video stream and allows to apply a sequence of configurable image filters to the surfaces as indicated in Figure 17 (right), so that pieces, dice and player's hands are accentuated. Since the image displayed on the table is known to the software, a subtraction of the camera image and the table image would also be an option, however, depending on the pointed lights in the room such a mechanism would fail, if e.g. a desk lamp was pointed to the table surface.

The optical recognition works well in principle and also allows for taking additional parameters such as the players' hands into account, effectively facilitating the rotation of objects on the table towards the respective player's viewing angle, as discussed in a later chapter. The disadvantage of the system, however, was revealed when it was tested with real-world users who would both shake and push the table requiring robust re-calibration mechanisms and who would also frequently bend over the table e.g. to whisper into other players' ears. Since robust optical recognition relies on unobstructed vision, the author finally developed a novel interface that compensated the disadvantages of the discussed alternative approaches.

Developing a novel interface

Due to the size and feasibility problems associated with augmenting individual dice with respective sensor technology, the author decided to integrate multiple dice into one single smart artifact, eliminating the aforementioned problems. In contrast to the passive optical recognition approach, such a smart device is not dependent on any infrastructure and works reliably and robustly in many interaction situations.

The augmentation of a dice cup allows for utilizing a physical manipulation technique (shaking) that influences the virtual outcome; a dice cup is also a well-known interaction device for games that players are used to. The drawback of the approach is that a dice box is not identical to rolling physical dice and some players might not be used to using a dice cup, although with games requiring multiple dice to be rolled simultaneously (such as Yahtzee or several role-playing or tabletop conflict games) it is common to use such a device, in fact, most editions of Yahtzee are shipped with dice cups.

Interaction Design

The interaction was designed to be as similar to a traditional dice cup as possible. To generate random numbers, the device is lifted, shaken, put on a plain surface upside down, and then finally lifted again to see the results. However, in contrast to traditional dice, the sum of the spots is not counted from the physical dice after being tossed on the surface of the table. Instead, the spots are displayed via light emitting diodes (LEDs) on the surface of the dice cup top.

Shaking the device also emits a sound mimicking the sound of shaking a traditional dice cup, although the integrated sound hardware does hardly deliver sound of acceptable quality. Since the smart dice cup is capable of communicating with the environment via radio transmission, it is more preferable to let another sound source outside the device perform the respective audio output.

So far, the interaction design of the Smart Dice Cup reflects the direct manipulation approach with an appropriate analogy to a traditional dice cup appliance. That is, the basic interface of shaking, dropping and turning the device is in analogy to the operation of a traditional dice cup. However, due to the implied complexity of configuring the device and using its more advanced functionality, there is also a conventional button interface with a graphical display integrated in the top surface of the dice cup as shown in Figure 18. The button interface is used for advanced configuration of the device when no other, more sophisticated interface such as a respective GUI application (running on a nearby PC) is available or when single dice are to be "held" or "released", i.e. when they are to be included or excluded from tossing.

Each of the five dice displayed on the surface of the dice cup consists of seven red LEDs that represent the spots of the respective die (see Figure 18). Whenever the device is shaken, the respective light patterns change in accordance to the tossed result. A small green LED is used to indicate whether the respective dice is held or released, i.e. if its face changes when the device is shaken. To toggle between holding and releasing a die, a small button is associated with each die that turns the respective green LED on or off with each press, thus ensuring an intuitive way of changing the individual held states by providing visual feedback and adhering to the Gestalt law of proximity (cf. Flieder & Mödritscher 2006) regarding the button layout.

Figure 18: The Dice Cup user interface.

The graphical display features two lines of eight characters each and is used for any optional interaction with the user beyond the scope of mere dice rolling. It is accompanied by two buttons on the left and right of it labeled "SELECT" and "OK" that allow for simple dialog navigation with "SELECT" cycling through a list of menu options and "OK" confirming the respective choices. As illustrated in Figure 19 the dice cup software currently includes a simple state machine that toggles between several menu states:

Free Play: This is the default state in which the dice cup is used for tossing only.
Game: This state allows to chose one (of currently two) built-in mini games.
Options: The number of players for the built-in games and the sound output can be configured here.
Debug: This state is similar to the Free Play state, but constantly sends debug messages to the graphical display for debugging purposes.

4. Interaction with User Interface Devices

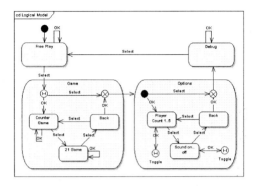

Figure 19: Smart Dice Cup menu states.

The device can be turned off and on and put into a remote controlled mode with a respective three-state-switch above the graphical display. The remote controlled mode allows the device to be controlled from the environment via radio transmission as discussed in the following section.

Operating Modes

The Smart Dice Cup was designed to function both as an autonomous smart artifact that performs its functions independent of the environment and as an interaction device that offers its services to other instances (software applications, smart artifacts etc) in the vicinity.

For the stand alone operating mode, the device's integrated memory and the built-in games offer added value compared to a traditional dice cup. For instance, it replaces pen and paper when games like the aforementioned Yahtzee are played that require the counting of individual results. In fact, a similar game (the Counter Game) is currently implemented on the device, albeit by far simpler than its original.

When the dice cup is brought to a smart environment, it can be put into a remote controlled mode in which it is both able to receive commands from the environment and to convey back information about its own state. As illustrated in Figure 20, an application in the environment can utilize the information from the device and create a respective virtual counterpart.

4. Interaction with User Interface Devices

Figure 20: Virtual counterpart and physical dice cup.

This virtual counterpart interprets and displays the device's radio signals conveying both the orientation/ shaking status measured by accelerometers and the current spots on the virtual dice. To visualize the received dice cup data, a 3D view of the dice cup is rendered illustrating the orientation (whether the device is upside down) and the presumed vertical position. The spots of the dice are visualized as respective bitmaps and an optional sound output of dice being shaken can be generated. The application is furthermore capable of transmitting the received dice data to other software components in a hybrid games setup, so that the dice cup can be exploited as a central tangible input device for any kind of hybrid game.

In the same way as data can be read from the device, the dice cup can also be remotely controlled. All the states from Figure 19 can be set and individual dice can be held or released. Furthermore, additional functions that are not available on the device interface are exposed for the remote software. This includes setting the sides of individual dice and showing messages on the graphical display. It is also possible to change the random number generation on the device with the introduction of so called "luck dice".

Random number generation
The random number generator implemented on the device is a Mersenne Twister (Matsumoto & Nishimura 1998) that is freely available as portable C-code. It has become a popular algorithm, since it passed the relevant, stringent statistical tests and is still comparable to other modern random number generators in terms of speed, hence making it a suitable algorithm for an embedded microcontroller such as the PIC16F876 used with the particle platform integrated inside the dice cup.

The seed of the random number generator is initialized with the data from the integrated accelerometers. This allows for modeling an important aspect of the physical act of rolling

86

4. Interaction with User Interface Devices

dice: Should a person be able to shake a traditional dice cup two times in exactly the same way, she would roll exactly the same results. The corresponding is true for the Smart Dice Cup, although in reality nobody should be capable of doing this with any of the two devices. Depending on the range of respective transformations of the sensor data, one could however investigate in how far the sensor data can be blurred or otherwise modified to allow for perceivable influences of the physical act of shaking and the respective results.

In a remote controlled operating mode, the dice cup allows for tweaking the amount of "luck" a person has by performing additional rolls with respective "luck dice". This is an interesting twist to the traditional realization of luck as a trait, in which a player rolls against an arbitrary luck criterion of differing magnitude. By introducing luck dice, the spots rolled correspond directly to the result instead of being valid only in combination with an external criterion. Each luck dice associated with the rolling of a target die has a 50% chance to affect the result of the target, if it does, a second roll is performed and the higher result becomes the target. The results for 10.000 rolls with no, one, or five luck dice are given in Table 13.

Table 13: Distribution of Smart Dice Cup sides.

10.000 rolls, no luck die		10.000 rolls, 1 luck die		10.000 rolls, 5 luck dice	
Side	# rolls	Side	# rolls	Side	# rolls
1	16651	1	9795	1	474
2	16603	2	12495	2	3262
3	16646	3	15274	3	8870
4	16748	4	18058	4	17279
5	16764	5	20632	5	28261
6	16588	6	23746	6	41854

Likewise, bad luck is implemented by changing sides from bottom to top (1 => 6, 2 => 5 etc).

Technical Realization

The core of the dice cup consists of a Smart-Its particle computer equipped with additional LC displays, LEDs and switches. Such a particle is "a platform for rapid prototyping of Ubiquitous and Pervasive Computing environments, for Ad-Hoc (Sensor) Networks, Wearable Computers, Home Automation and Ambient Intelligence Environments. The platform consists of ready-to-run hardware components, software applications and libraries for the hardware and a set of development tools for rapid prototyping" (http://particle.teco.edu/). Smart-Its is also the name of the respective research project within the European Union's Disappearing Computer Initiative (www.disappearing-computer.net) in which the author's research division also participated leading the Ambient Agoras project (www.ambient-agoras.org).

Beigl and Gellersen (2003) point out that a "defining element of our concept is that we seek to support post hoc attachment of smart technology to common objects" which is realized with the Smart Dice Cup that augments a traditional dice cup bought from a games store.

The Smart-Its particle platform is built around two independent boards, a core board that consists mainly of processing and communication hardware and basic output components and a sensor board containing a separate processing unit, various sensors and actuators. In the case of the dice cup, these were accelerometers, other sensors include light, humidity, temperature, or force/ pressure. The sensor board also runs the user application. The user applications are

4. Interaction with User Interface Devices

programmed in C using a respective application programming interface (API). It provides a straightforward access to the communication stack and the data that the sensors on the sensor board deliver. As an illustration, the following simple sniplet of the Smart Dice Cup code reads out the accelerometers while the device is being shaken.

```
AcclSensorPrepare();
do
{
    time = rf_slotcounter;
    AcclXSensorGetGravity(&ax);
} while (rf_slotcounter!=time);
do
{
    time=rf_slotcounter;
    AcclYSensorGetGravity(&ay);
} while (rf_slotcounter!=time);
sumX=ax/128; //sumX+((ay+32767)>>8);
```

Similar particle platforms developed outside the European Union IST activities include the iStuff components used primarily in conjunction with the iRoom infrastructure (Ballagas et al. 2003) and the Berkely Motes (Akyildiz 2002) that focus more on large-scale networks supporting ad-hoc routing and other capabilities not relevant for small-scale environments hosting co-located hybrid games.

Conclusions

The Smart Dice Cup is the single most important physical building block for hybrid games contributed by this dissertation. Since rolling dice is a central component in many tabletop games, the transition between the physical act of rolling dice and the respective virtual processing is crucial for realizing effective hybrid games. The scope of the device is broader than e.g. the gesture based interaction device while at the same time providing a similarly natural and intuitive user interface. Particularly interesting in terms of the discussion of autonomous vs. dependent smart artifacts is the realization of complementary operating modes, making the device both usable outside of any IT infrastructure as well as integrating itself smoothly into an existing smart environment.

Review of Requirements

The Smart Dice Cup picks up the real-world metaphor of a conventional dice cup and provides an interaction design that resembles the original interface very closely. The device affords shaking in analogy to the conventional artifact and reinforces the user by providing audio feedback that conveys the impression of traditional dice being shaken. The symbolized dice at the bottom of the artifact clearly represent the respective sides of conventional dice and are directly comprehensible. The additional functionality the device provides for configuration and built-in gaming applications does not relate to real-world metaphors, but follows best-practices for small-screen user interfaces (Mauney & Masterton 2008). The Smart Dice Cup adheres to the specificity requirement very closely. In fact, outside the domain of gaming the artifact has no secondary function at all. Alternative realizations obviously include using a conventional dice cup, i.e. rolling dice in a conventional manner without pervasive computing support, and generating random numbers as a function call in a standard computer software. This is summarized in Table 14.

4. Interaction with User Interface Devices

Table 14: Smart Dice Cup requirements

Req.	Realization
R4.1	Conventional dice cup
R4.2	Rolling dice
R4.4	Using a conventional dice cup or purely virtual random number generation

Sentient Game Boards

In a similar vein as the Smart Dice Cup, the final class of custom-built interaction devices investigated relate directly to the domain of board and tabletop games. The interaction design of board games is proven to support social group situations effectively (Mandryk & Maranan 2002) partly due to the horizontal orientation of the display. This facilitates direct face-to-face communication among players. The common turn-taking, slow-paced game styles let the board interface only briefly and infrequently demand exclusive attention from individual players.

The interaction with tangible game boards is also a prototypical example for the *spatial approach* that Ullmer & Ishhi (2001) identify as the primary TUI approach in which physical artifacts within a physical reference frame are directly interpreted and augmented by a virtual application, not involving any additional layer of indirection. Accordingly, the game board is a tangible interface that seamlessly integrates representations and controls and is thus preferable to graphical user interfaces in which spatial relationships are controlled in a different way (via the mouse) than they are represented.

The interaction with a sentient game board that conveys its physical state to a virtual application should be as natural and simple as with a traditional game board. Physical objects should simply be put on a dedicated horizontal area and thereby represent their own positions. Due to the augmentation with information technology, it might be possible to achieve additional benefits to the mere sensing of the physical artifacts. For instance, in contrast to a traditional game board, a smart board might be used as an additional output device and display dynamically changing game boards, if it includes a screen, or convey information via LEDs or other means. Likewise, playing pieces might be equipped with additional functionalities. This includes a simple memory or unique identification capabilities by e.g. integrating RFID tags or even integrating entire particle computers. Some platforms such as the Smart Dust (Kahn et al. 1999) are only a cubic millimeter in diameter, thus allowing for being integrated into small-scale artifacts such as typical playing pieces. Recently, one research group even proposed the integration of relative positioning, communication and computing devices into playing pieces (Krohn et al. 2004) theoretically eliminating the need for smart game boards and realizing highly autonomous pieces. Due to several unresolved issues regarding feasibility, power supply, size, etc. the author however focused on the sentient game board approach. This approach involves multiple potential realizations (as alluded to in Table 15), but they all share the benefit of centralizing the smartness in only one point (the board) in contrast to distributing it among multiple pieces, each being prone to failure and potentially expensive to manufacture.

4. Interaction with User Interface Devices

Table 15: Sentient game board technologies.

	Magnetic Fields	Elec. Resistance	RFID	Optical solutions
Identification	-	+	+	+
Continuous Pos.	+	-	+	+
Discrete States	-	+	-	O
Orientation	+	+	-	O
Memory	-	-	+	-
Output	O	O	O	+
Robustness	+	+	+	-
Ease of handling	+	-	+	+
Inexpensiveness	+	+	O	-
Mobility	+	+	+	-

The technologies investigated here were chosen due to their obvious suitability for spatial tangible user interfaces either because of the experiences in related TUI research projects (Underkoffler & Ishii 1999) or because of their usage in commercial applications such as chess computers that also bridge the gap between physical and virtual domains in tabletop gaming. There already exist detailed comparisons of location systems for Ubiquitous Computing (e.g. Hightower & Borriello 2001), however these focus on larger scale areas either outdoors or indoors and are mostly targeted towards locating human beings and/ or their mobile terminals. A comparison of the specific advantages and disadvantages of the very different approaches in developing game board sensing technologies is now presented with regard to the parameters mostly interesting in the context of hybrid games. These parameters are listed in Table 15. Some of them, such as mobility, the means of using the board as an output device, or the capability of identifying unique states to which a piece can be set (e.g. opening or closing a chest) are beneficial features not necessarily important for all hybrid games, whereas parameters such as robustness or ease of handling are absolute requirements that must be fulfilled in any case for a feasible implementation. Hence, not all relevant parameters are of equal gravity and the respective technologies are discussed in detail with their implications and scopes within the next sections.

Magnetic Fields

Magnetic game objects can be sensed very inexpensively by magnetic field sensors built into a game board (the right part of Figure 21 shows the interior of the author's magnetic sensor board). These simple reed sensors are triggered, whenever a magnetic field of a certain strength is sensed. Building a respective game board thus comes down to finding the matching relation between the strength of the magnets integrated in the playing pieces and the sensitivity of the reed sensors.

4. Interaction with User Interface Devices

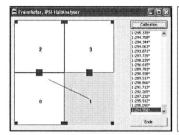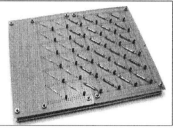

Figure 21: A Magnetic reed sensor board

While a position recognition based on a grid of reed sensors works robustly, such sensors can not be used to determine an object's identification, i.e. objects would have to be identified by the strength of their magnets, however, as the field strength decreases with the distance to the sensor, variations in positioning would result in different field strengths at the sensors. This lack of object identification capabilities is, of course, a severe drawback to the technology.

As an augmentation to the simple and inexpensive reed sensors, Hall effect sensors can be applied that measure magnetic fields perpendicular to the Hall element, i.e. a single magnetic object results in differing sensor magnitudes depending on its orientation. Thus, the orientation of playing pieces can be sensed in addition to their positions. This allows for interesting new game elements as e.g. in spy games, where players can try to sneak past guards that face to a different direction unable to "see" them. A respective software component to determine the orientation of a piece is shown in Figure 21 (left).

While the sensor technology can not easily be integrated into a common display to show game boards and serve as a rich output channel, light emitting diodes can form a cheap and effective alternative channel from the virtual to the physical domain. They allow conveying information about spatial ranges, territories, and most importantly the placements of objects, i.e. the virtual domain can effectively communicate desired object positions through LEDs.

If economic factors play a role (and they do within any commercial exploitation!), magnetic field sensors might be a good choice. In fact, practically all electric chess boards available make use of magnetic reed sensors. To tackle the missing object identification, the virtual domain must however rely on certain assumptions constraining the use of the game board. For instance, no two objects must be removed from the board at the same time. Also, the virtual domain must have some means of conveying to the players where a certain object should be placed, as noted above, this can be achieved with simple LEDs (see Figure 21 right).

Electric Resistance

One of the benefits of magnetic field sensors is their wireless operating mode. It is sufficient to put or hold a piece near a sensor in order to detect it. This advantage cannot be realized with any solution involving electric current. However, when electricity flows through playing pieces, varying resistors built into them allow for a cheap, robust and fine-grained identification of an arbitrary amount of pieces. The real beauty of electric current however lies in the extreme simplicity of providing playing pieces with discrete states that change within individual pieces. For instance, as shown in the author's prototype board in Figure 22 (right), the state of the topmost playing piece (which is a chest) is currently open. By closing it, the

91

virtual representation of the physical piece in Figure 22 (left) would change from an open to a closed state. Similarly, continuous state changes such as pieces' orientations are possible. The wizard and the blue creature are facing towards distinct directions as visualized in the virtual counterpart application. By turning the physical objects, the virtual representations would rotate accordingly. Such discrete and continuous state changes are simply implemented by integrating switches and potentiometers into the pieces that alter the objects' resistances. By looking closely at the bottom of the wizard in Figure 22 one can even see that the piece is in fact a potentiometer with a hand-modeled lump of FIMO attached to it. Likewise, the chest contains a push button switch that closes its circuit when the lid is pressed down.

Figure 22: Virtual counterpart and physical game board.

Apart from the disadvantage of the necessary physical contact of the pieces, the technology offers significant advantages over magnetic solutions including object identification and the unique feature of having discrete object states. Otherwise, its features are comparable to magnetic solutions, both are cheap, can interoperate with simple output mechanisms such as LEDs, mobile boards can be realized, and they work robustly enough. The disadvantage of using sockets of any kind and the related problem of corrosion however weigh heavily. To tackle with the inconvenience of forcing players to ensure an electric current through the board, other projects have also explored utilizing the resistance of the human body (Dietz & Leigh 2001), which, however, introduces problems with the robustness of physiological measures.

RFID

A very robust albeit slightly expensive enabling technology is the radio frequency identification (RFID) that has recently gained a lot of commercial and scientific momentum. The internet of things and the department stores of the future are only two examples of the envisioned ubiquitous use of RFID tags as tokens mediating between physical artifacts and their virtual counterparts. Accordingly, arbitrary game objects can be tagged with small (cheap) RFID transponders and detected by appropriate (expensive) antennas. When these antennas are integrated in a game board, discrete positions and object identities can be detected wirelessly. Furthermore, most transponders can also store a few bytes of state information. This allows for equipping playing pieces with a simple memory that is invariant among game boards and applications. This memory is insofar not identical to the state information the electric current variants provide, since the physical state of the object cannot affect its virtual state, e.g. a door cannot be physically opened or closed and propagate this state change to the virtual domain. Unfortunately, RFID does not provide the other additional features discussed so far such as supporting physical states (which are more important for a TUI than object memory) or allowing object orientations to be sensed. Nevertheless, RFID combines the advantages of providing object identification with an easy handling that works robustly in a broad range of interaction situations. The integrated memory and the globally unique tag ID furthermore support the development of games that share individual pieces among different game instances. One might, for example, buy a single piece and let it develop throughout multiple games.

Since RFID does not impose any serious disadvantages such as a lack of identification or a cumbersome handling to sentient game boards, it is a good choice at least for research platforms in which production costs are less central than in commercial applications. Consequently, the author uses RFID game boards for some of the examples presented in a later chapter. Additionally, the InteracTable Roomware component that is used for graphical game boards also contains an RFID antenna that detects physical tokens placed on the table surface. Although the single antenna cannot provide a spatial mapping, it is used to initiate and terminate game sessions in a natural way by simply placing a tag on the table to begin, and removing it to end and save a game session. This way, the players avoid dealing with mouse or keyboard to get a game going and make use of the metaphor of placing a physical board on the table to begin and remove it to end a game.

Other game related projects have successfully integrated RFID tags in playing cards (Römer & Domnitcheva 2002), as wearable tags in children's games (Konkel et al. 2004), or as a smart jigsaw puzzle (Bohn 2004).

Visual Recognition

A final approach to sensing playing pieces, but also other game objects, involves the recognition of a camera image. The general advantage of cameras is that they can recognize arbitrary artifacts or persons. For instance, not only the playing pieces, but also dice and even the hands of players reaching over a table can be detected. The latter is useful for determining on which side of the table a player is actually standing. The hybrid games software platform discussed in the next chapter can integrate this information in order to rotate and scale information objects to the player currently taking her turn.

Depending on the resolution and quality of the camera, an optical recognition approach is generally able to perform some kind of object identification. However, unless adapted playing pieces with distinct shapes or colors are used, the reliability and robustness of the object identification is naturally lower than that of other technologies e.g. relying on RFID that is not affected by varying lightning conditions, obstructions, unintended movements of camera or target (or both), etc. Since cameras can be set apart from the actual game board, it is trivial to make use of horizontal computer screens as a basis for the game board, thus allowing for a dynamically changing game board display that contributes to the attractiveness and the immersion of the game. This combination of a rich output channel and an optical recognition was also picked up by the author's Roomware realization of a game board discussed in the next section.

It is only a minor disadvantage of the optical recognition approach that it is hardly mobile, since in addition to the board, the respective camera needs to be moved and then fixed and calibrated again. A more severe drawback is the general susceptibility to the various disturbing factors mentioned above. This can affect the respective interaction styles, since players might need to pay attention not to lean over the board or shake the board during a game session.

4. Interaction with User Interface Devices

Review of Requirements

Similar to the Smart Dice Cup, sentient game boards directly pick up real-world interaction metaphors and provide an analogous interaction design. Controlling conventional game boards is mostly identical to controlling sentient game boards, however the later provide an interface from the physical to the social and the virtual domains. The specificity and scope of sentient game boards is restricted to gaming applications with little or no use outside the entertainment domain. Alternative realizations include un-augmented, conventional game boards without a link into the virtual domain as well as traditional graphical user interfaces that do not have a physical component. Table 16 summarizes how the respective requirements are met.

Table 16: Sentient game boards requirements

Req.	Realization
R4.1	Conventional game board
R4.2	Spatially relating game figures
R4.4	Using a conventional game board or a graphical user interface

Conclusions

Dice, playing pieces, and game boards are the most prominent physical building blocks, from which tabletop games are constructed. Computer augmented tabletop games pick up these physical interaction devices and their respective interaction techniques to preserve the social group situations found in traditional board game systems. From the technologies discussed to realize the link between the physical and virtual domains of a game board those seem most promising that reflect the advantages of traditional game board media, namely robustness and ease of use. Even though e.g. solutions involving electric current flowing through pieces allow for mapping interesting physical properties such as rotational angles or other arbitrary states, it is the ease of use that finally prevents the distraction problem (Cohen & McGee 2004) that hinders natural group interaction. Therefore, solutions robustly and intuitively providing object identification and positioning without any constraints are preferable to build augmented game boards. These include RFID technologies and to a certain degree also optical recognition. While the former approach is practically unbreakable (the author even baked tags at 110 degrees Celsius in an oven during the production of playing pieces without affecting their performance), the latter approach is especially suitable for smart environments with mostly static room element architectures, in which undesired movements of game boards or cameras are less likely to happen than in mobile and dynamic environments. The realization of such a camera based game board involving a graphical display is discussed in the next section on adapted graphical interfaces.

4.3. Roomware Interfaces

Traditional graphical interfaces differ from the physical interaction devices discussed so far. As Ishii & Ullmer (1997) strikingly exemplify, the abacus is not an input device, because it makes no distinction between input and output. This distinction is, however, fundamental in graphical interfaces that distinguish between input controls (mice, keyboards) and output devices such as displays for the visual representations. As discussed before, the unification of control and representation in tangible interfaces make them preferable over graphical interfaces in group situations. However, certain types of information such as numbers or

4. Interaction with User Interface Devices

graphics or even some kinds of spatial or associative information are less suited for physical interfaces. Therefore, the careful complementary use of graphical interfaces is sometimes inevitable. The challenge is to design the respective interactions in such a way that they do not demand exclusive attention and distract from the social group dynamics.

In the domain of hybrid games, two specific uses for graphical interfaces can be identified:

1.) Since typical tangible interfaces are of public nature (e.g. the physical positions of playing pieces on a smart game board can be perceived by everybody), it is necessary to also provide additional private communication channels between the virtual domain and the players or between players, respectively. Otherwise any distinction between public and private game data in the social domain cannot be exploited by a virtual game instance, thus hindering the support of games with simultaneous competitive and cooperative nature.

2.) Rich video output can add to the immersion of any gaming application. A multimodal stimulation of the players can easily be supported by an ambient display that does not require any input and attributes to setting up an atmosphere according to the current situation in the game. For instance, a wall-size display such as the DynaWall Roomware component can change its display calmly in the background and convey a respective mood to the group.

Roomware Technology

Most of the graphical interfaces utilized for hybrid games were developed in the tradition of earlier work on i-LAND, the interactive landscape for creativity and innovation (Streitz et al. 2001), consisting of several Roomware components, e.g., interactive walls and tables and computer-augmented chairs and desks. As pointed out in a previous chapter, a special software infrastructure was also developed that supports cooperative work and synchronous sharing of hypermedia information (Tandler 2004). Especially, two devices from the second generation of Roomware components (Streitz et al. 2002), the InteracTable and the DynaWall, were investigated in the context of hybrid gaming applications. Both of these devices integrate displays into everyday room elements. The room elements themselves still provide the affordances of ordinary, unaugmented artifacts, i.e. one can still sit at a table and put objects on it. But whenever there is a demand for additional computing functionality, the Roomware devices are capable of providing it. Their graphical interfaces are adapted to the requirements of groups interacting in natural ways. There is no indirection imposed by mice or similar interaction devices. Instead, touch sensitive surfaces allow for direct information manipulation via fingers or pens and integrated RFID antennas facilitate the sensing of arbitrary smart objects near Roomware components.

4. Interaction with User Interface Devices

Figure 23: Gaming in hybrid Roomware environments

Figure 23 shows the setup of Roomware components in the lab of the AMBIENTE division at Fraunhofer IPSI. In the background, the DynaWall component displays public ambient information while the smart InteracTable shows the actual game board. As with traditional board games, participants take positions around the table to interact with each other and to jointly modify the state of the game board on the table surface.

Game Table

The game table provides the game board which is displayed on its surface. It offers a tangible interface with ordinary playing pieces that are tracked by an overhead camera. As illustrated in Figure 24 (left), the boards can be visually attractive and highly dynamic, e.g. the open door in the top area of the figure can also be closed, rendering the hallway above in darkness. In addition to the physical playing pieces (which are augmented by virtual counterparts), purely virtual game objects can be displayed on the game board. Although these virtual objects are not tangible except for touching them on the table surface, they might fulfill important functions within a game and add to the user experience e.g. by having audible properties such as doors that creak.

While the tangible playing pieces allow for a natural interaction with the spatial relationships of the game objects, the adapted graphical user interface also facilitates an interaction style similar to the tangible interface. By simply touching information objects with the fingers, they can be manipulated according to the rules of the game.

Figure 24: The InteracTable Game Table.

96

4. Interaction with User Interface Devices

As shown in Figure 24 (center and right), the integrated RFID antenna detects physical tokens placed on the table surface. These are used to initiate and terminate game sessions by simply placing a tag on the table to begin, and removing it to end and save a game session. This way, the players avoid dealing with mouse or keyboard to get a game going and instead pick up the metaphor of placing a physical game board on the table before the game commences.

Wall Display

The wall display is used for conveying game relevant public information that each player can view at any time. It consists of the DynaWall, which is a Roomware component with a rear-projected, touch sensitive interaction space for computer-supported cooperative work. It is divided into three separate segments that are connected and act as one joint large surface. On the wall display, arbitrary media such as videos or animations can be played which are triggered either by a player or by the logic of the hybrid gaming application. Apart from giving game relevant information, the wall can also be used as an atmospheric display that e.g. alters the general mood in the environment by changing the illumination level or reflecting the current game situation in an abstract way, for example by showing an illustration of a dungeon wall when the players explore a respective location. Normally, the wall display functions as an output device and is not used for input, even though it integrates touch sensitive screens. Due to its size, the wall is circa three meters wide, it would be inefficient to directly manipulate information objects on its surface by using fingers or pens. Even though dedicated interfaces were developed to remote control the wall via other interaction devices (e.g. Magerkurth & Stenzel 2003), this has so far not been explored in the context of hybrid gaming applications. The wall display is shown behind the game table in Figure 23.

Private Graphical Interfaces

Both of the Roomware components presented above are of public nature, due to their prominent size and location within the laboratory. To also support the display and interaction with private data, the author investigated standard personal digital assistants (PDA) and an augmented form of a PDA that also includes an RFID reader to interact with other smart artifacts by simply pointing at them.

Personal Digital Assistants (PDAs)

PDAs are mostly private artifacts that each player can bring and integrate with a hybrid game system. Hence, PDAs are primarily used to view or administer private data or enter private commands. For many board and tabletop games, the player's PDA can conceptually be defined as a medium for accessing the virtual parts of a physical playing piece, i.e. the physical playing piece is augmented with a virtual counterpart that can be accessed via the player's PDA. Consequently, a hybrid game entity emerges that has physical properties such as its position on the game board as well as game dependent virtual properties such as character attributes (health, strength, etc) or an inventory of carried objects (see Figure 25).

Another important function of the PDAs for games involving both competition and cooperation (cf. Zagal et al. 2000), e.g. any Diplomacy type game and most treasure hunting dungeon romps, is private communication between players. Any player may send short messages to other players via the PDA. This provides the simple advantage over other communication channels that even if the act of writing a message might or might not be hidden from other players, the message's addressee, and not just the message itself, becomes covered.

4. Interaction with User Interface Devices

Currently, standard Compaq IPAQ 3950 and Toshiba e740 Pocket-PCs with integrated 802.11b cards are used to connect to a game session and perform the functions described above. Additionally, so called Viewport-Devices can be used to access virtual properties of individual playing pieces by just pointing the device at them.

Figure 25: PDA viewing virtual properties of a physical object.

Viewport Devices

To allow for similarly natural interaction styles as with the Gesture Based Interaction Device, PDAs can be augmented with RFID readers to identify and act upon physical objects pointed at with the PDA.

Hence, Viewport devices are special private interfaces that integrate both a physical interface and a GUI in one device (see Figure 26). The Viewport consists of a PDA equipped both with 802.11b and an RFID antenna that detects physical objects such as playing pieces tagged with appropriate transponders. It was developed in the EU-IST project Ambient Agoras (Streitz et al. 2003). The Viewport is geared towards natural interaction styles.

Figure 26: Viewport devices

Figure 26 (left) shows a Viewport displaying information about a tagged object that belongs to the owner of the Viewport. Figure 26 (right) shows the same Viewport displaying information about an object belonging to a different player. Obviously, the information transmitted from the virtual domain consists of a varying degree of detail (concrete stats versus a cursory description). In this context, the interesting part of the Viewport device lies in the combination of its public physical and private virtual interface. While the social domain

4. Interaction with User Interface Devices

gets to know that objects are investigated or manipulated, the concrete action performed is not made public. This allows for highly interesting social situations as alluded to in Figure 27.

Figure 27: Tagged artifacts and their virtual counterparts in the Viewport

By pointing at a physical model with a Viewport, a player searches a statue for a hidden treasure. Due to his high skills, he indeed finds a diamond ring he wants to keep and hide from the other players. However, the public nature of the Viewport's physical interface causes awareness about the preceding action among the others, and thus evokes the necessity to explain them the action he just performed.

4.4. Conclusions

This chapter introduced various interaction devices of different complexity and different purposes within a hybrid gaming application. Some of the individual devices can be used in very different contexts such as a gesture based interaction device might be a magic wand as well as a pointing stick. Similar to one device fulfilling multiple potential purposes, also multiple potential devices might be used for a single purpose. For instance, the 2D spatial mapping of game objects might be achieved by various physical game boards as well as a traditional GUI. Therefore, to facilitate the prototyping of hybrid games, it is essential to be able to both associate devices to different applications and to exchange devices for individual applications easily and flexibly. The software platform presented in the next chapter fulfills this purpose. It allows utilizing the different interaction devices discussed so far as dynamic building blocks for distributed pervasive computing applications. In order to exploit its full potential of dynamically integrating different interaction devices during a game session, it is vital that R4.3 is fulfilled, i.e. that a complete game setup can be formed by different interaction devices and that it is possible to play a game with different realizations of interaction devices, such as only GUI components, physical interaction devices, or a combination of both.

The proof-of-concept prototype "Caves and Creatures" that is discussed in more detail in chapter 6.fulfills R4.3 and is used in a respective summative evaluation discussed in chapter 7. Within the prototype, the respective game elements make up the core of the application and can be completely realized by the interaction devices presented in this chapter. Likewise, potential alternative realizations can be used such as purely virtual interface components or a completely physical realization without any support from the virtual domain. In the next chapter, it will be discussed how the platform deals with the integration of different interface components and how consistency between concurrent instances of functionally similar user interfaces is provided.

99

5. A Software Platform for Hybrid Gaming Applications

The development of hybrid gaming applications involves the integration of physical, social and virtual aspects, thus introducing a new dimension of complexity to the entertainment applications of the pre-pervasive computing era. To develop conceptual models and carry out formative evaluation studies testing novel application designs, it is crucial to be able to quickly prototype and tweak both game rules and mechanics as well as the involved user interfaces and interaction devices discussed in the previous chapter. As Lee et al. (2004) note, the design of physical interfaces with high-fidelity functioning prototypes is prohibitively expensive, if not supported by a dedicated user interface toolkit.

This chapter introduces a software platform that dynamically integrates multiple different interaction devices from the application domain of hybrid games such as smart game boards or dice cups. This platform is named STARS after its origins as a user interface toolkit for horizontal surfaces. STARS is a German acronym for "Spieltisch-Anreicherungs-System" that translates to "Game Table Augmentation system". After its Roomware centered beginning in 2002 it has evolved into a sophisticated distributed infrastructure for user interfaces including tangible and graphical components. It forms the basis for the hybrid game prototypes presented in the following chapter. The platform is divided into several subsystems that each tackle different aspects in the development of hybrid games (see Figure 28).

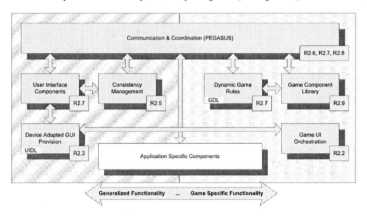

Figure 28: Subsystems of the STARS Platform

As the figure illustrates, parts of the provided functionalities are specific to hybrid gaming applications (those in the right part of the figure), while others (namely those in the left part) are relevant to other pervasive computing fields as well. The rationale behind this distinction is that certain contributions such as the integration and consistency management between user interface components are simply agnostic to the application domain, whereas others, such as a language for defining game rules are specific to games. As hybrid games are embedded in the research on various pervasive computing fields, it is clear that both generalized and game specific functionality is required to realize them. The figure also indicates the relevance of specific subsystems to the requirements elicited in chapter 2. This is also recapitulated in the following Table 17:

Table 17: Relevant software platform requirements

Req.	Label	Related Subsystem
R2.2	Rich multimedia	Game UI Orchestration
R2.3	Display idiosyncrasies	Device Adapted GUI Provision
R2.5	Domain Consistency	Consistency Management
R2.6	Decoupled communication	Communication and Coordination
R2.7	Runtime adaptability	Communication and Coordination, Dynamic Game Rules, User Interface Components
R2.8	Extensibility and robustness	Communication and Coordination
R2.9	Modeling of shared information	Game Component Library

How the respective requirements are addressed in the relevant subsystems is detailed in the subsystems description. In the following section, these main components of STARS are presented in a high level overview, before being discussed in more depth afterwards.

Communication and Coordination

Since applications for pervasive computing environments are commonly distributed in order to reflect the physical distribution of users in the real world and adapt to changes in these real world spaces, the first requirement for any software infrastructure is an appropriate communication and coordination system that allows the respective components to synchronize their states. This fundamental functionality is addressed with the PEGASUS communication subsystem that enables distributed applications to communicate and share information with a publish/ subscribe interaction scheme allowing for a complete decoupling of the participants and the support for physical reconfiguration during runtime. In order to reflect the component based approach of the platform, shared information in the PEGASUS subsystem can be organized in hierarchical data trees with branches representing the data of individual components. Applications running on the STARS platform are distributed and encapsulated in distinct software components that can be physically located on any Windows, Linux or Java based computer or handheld device in the environment communicating via the PEGASUS subsystem.

User Interface Components

Similar to widget components that developers of traditional WIMP software simply drag into their applications from the GUI builder of their development environment, STARS provides support for modular user interface components that wrap both tangible and graphical interfaces and can be exposed to any application. The individual data trees of these UI components are exposed via the PEGASUS subsystem to allow interested parties to subscribe to their state changes. The architecture of user interface components, of which some are readily available for using in arbitrary hybrid gaming prototypes, is discussed in the respective section.

Consistency Management

An important aspect of distributed user interface components is the management of the information that is shared among components. For instance, if a single game board is accessed from different locations via two tangible interfaces, these might be in conflicting states and might not represent the exact same information. In order to resolve conflicts and ensure consistency several consistency modes can be configured in order to cope with conflicting states.

Device Adapted GUI Provision

Given the heterogeneous nature of pervasive computing interaction devices including horizontal (tabletop) displays, vertical wall displays, and mobile devices such as PDAs or mobile phones, it is crucial to provide device adapted, but coherent graphical user interfaces that address the respective interaction issues of each display type. The GUI subsystem provides the required functionality for user interface components to create device adapted graphical interfaces for the domain of interactive entertainment applications that handle animated 3D graphics and multimedia effects. It also contributes a simple user interface definition language built on top of PEGASUS that allows for specifying and modifying user interfaces on any client in real time, even while a game is in progress.

Game UI Orchestration

When a multitude of user interface components is available to a game application for which the association of devices and users are dynamic, it becomes crucial to coordinate them in a way that the orchestration of user interfaces reflects the requirements of the interaction situation. For instance, when multiple graphical displays are available to a certain user with differing resolutions and degrees of privacy, it might be more suitable to display information on a small, private device such as a mobile phone in one situation, whereas the large public display might be preferable in another situation, where the perceptual qualities of the display are more important than the desired privacy of the respective information. This UI orchestration is especially relevant for games that draw some of the desired immersiveness from stimulating different modalities such as sound, visuals or potentially even more channels like tactile input or illumination to ensure a rich multimedia experience. In order to free the developer of a hybrid gaming application from anticipating a concrete setup of interaction devices and interfaces allowing for a neutral formulation of interaction requirements, it is important to provide the otherwise anonymously communicating and un-synchronized user interface components with a reasoning component that assists in finding the optimal configuration of components for a given interaction situation.

Dynamic Game Rules

While the adaptive configuration of user interface components is a central requirement for enabling distributed applications that dynamically integrate and remove components during runtime, it is equally important for a gaming application to facilitate the adaptation of game rules and mechanics to the flow of the game, thus allowing the game to be tweaked to individual preferences and "house rules". Based on the PEGASUS subsystem, a respective game rule description language is discussed that facilitates the dynamic alteration of game rules of distributed hybrid games.

Game Component Library

In order to facilitate a rapid development of hybrid games for less experienced developers or even end users it is crucial to provide the game rule description language with concepts and objects form the gaming domain, so that the effort for the modeling of facts shared among many games is greatly reduced. For instance, the notion of players, variability generators (i.e. dice), or playing pieces are common to most games and are thus available for the game developer, so that in fact a domain specific language is provided for the domain of hybrid games.

Application Specific Components

Applications developed for the STARS platform strictly separate user interfaces and interaction devices from the application logic. Communication with the various user interface components is realized by the anonymous PEGASUS bus that allows for changing the physical configuration of a game during runtime. STARS also administrates the individual game rule descriptions with a rule language developed on top of PEGASUS, so that rules can be altered during runtime and also be shared among multiple application components. As with the user interfaces, developers only need to publish and/ or subscribe to UI or game rule information and are not required to anticipate certain component constellations. Much of the additional complexities introduced by the virtual and social dimensions of pervasive computing can effectively be reduced by this decoupled interaction of components. Application specific components can utilize the provided subsystems in order to focus on realizing specific functionality while not having to address underlying communication or coordination issues.

The individual subsystems that facilitate the development of hybrid gaming applications are discussed in more detail in the subsequent sections. Proof-of-concept prototypes that demonstrate their practical relevance are referred to and discussed in more detail in the next chapter.

5.1. Communication and Coordination

The PEGASUS subsystem provides the functionality to let heterogeneous devices connected in an ad-hoc manner share information and synchronize distributed data objects (Magerkurth et al. 2006). It is designed as a lightweight communication solution which is capable of integrating also resource-constrained devices such as mobile phones or PDAs powered by diverse operating systems and providing wired or wireless communication protocols (see Figure 29).

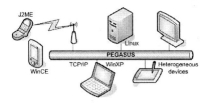

Figure 29: Communication via the PEGASUS Subsystem

5. A Software Platform for Hybrid Gaming Applications

PEGASUS is designed as a coordination language following the distinction of Gelernter & Carriero (1992) between computation languages and coordination languages. Accordingly, by providing a separate coordination language orthogonal to the actual computations, two key features can be achieved, 1.) portability and 2.) heterogeneity. Applications can be portable because of providing a coordination mechanism independent of the computation language and, consequently, heterogeneous compositions of applications based on different hardware or operating systems can be integrated. Providing one single general-purpose coordination language (instead of many specialized ones) is furthermore economical, which is – given the complexity of heterogeneous pervasive computing environments – an important factor for distributed application development.

Johanson & Fox (2002) define the requirements for coordination languages specifically addressing distributed software components in pervasive computing environments. These include 1.) applicability to a broad range of different types of ubiquitous computing applications, 2.) portability across installations, 3.) support for a wide range of devices, and 4.) robustness to transient failures, so that experimentation with new devices does not destabilize an existing system.

The need for applicability to a broad range of applications is not specifically addressed in PEGASUS, since it is geared to hybrid gaming applications that typically involve only a limited number of software and hardware components not demanding e.g. high performance. However, portability across installations is a major concern for hybrid games where the developer typically cannot foresee the setup available at the consumer's place. Accordingly, PEGASUS realizes an anonymous communication scheme based on a publish / subscribe mechanism where individual software components do not directly interact and do not need to know each other, so that individual components can be interchanged arbitrarily thus enabling installation independent applications (R2.6). The support for a wide range of devices is also a key issue, because hybrid games typically integrate a multitude of heterogonous interaction devices that come in various shapes and sizes, running on different hardware platforms (R2.7). This heterogeneity also involves resource constrained computing devices such as mobile phones or particle platforms, hence motivating an additional requirement for a lightweight implementation. Robustness (R2.8) is addressed with a distributed architecture not requiring a central server component. Single components can crash or disintegrate at any time without affecting the overall stability of the system.

The main design considerations based on the requirements for pervasive computing coordination languages are discussed in the following sections, before the actual system architecture is presented.

Distribution and Dynamic Device Integration

As hybrid gaming applications are comprised by a distributed set of heterogeneous interaction devices that exchange information among each other, the issue of centralized versus direct communication immediately becomes relevant.

Whenever distributed devices need to exchange information, these devices could either be in communication to a central machine or act as standalone devices that directly communicate with each other. Both models provide complete and proven solutions, however, as Brumitt et al. (2000) point out, networked standalone devices are the most likely future of pervasive computing and forms the basis for most intelligent environments projects such as Metaglue (Coen et al. 2000), EasyLiving (Brumitt et al. 2000) or iROS (Johanson & Fox 2002). This is due to the robustness and flexibility of non-centralized communication. PEGASUS does not rely on a central server component, but allows communicating entities to directly exchange information. This allows for the realization of distributed applications that are highly dynamic regarding the integration and disintegration of communicating entities. Physical interaction devices and their corresponding software proxies can be added and removed at any time with their state information being synchronized over the anonymous, decoupled PEGASUS communication bus. In the same way, the application logic can be distributed among communicating entities so that the disintegration of any single central server component does not necessarily have fatal consequences.

A semi-centralized approach that is famous for its notion of code mobility is the Java Jini platform (Harihar & Kurkovsky 2005). Here, so called Jini federations are created of autonomous, co-operating entities that offer services and consume services of other members of the federation. Through the use of one or more lookup services other services can be advertised and consumed which results in transferring actual Java code to the service consumer. This Java "code mobility" has the great advantage of truly providing ubiquitous access to a service, as issues of device drivers, different operating systems etc. are disregarded. Also, Jini is communication protocol independent, which makes it likewise attractive. The major downside, however, is that Jini relies on the Java platform which is not as ubiquitous in the domain of resource-constrained smart items as necessary for wide adoption, especially since it requires a full Standard Edition virtual machine for operation. As a communication infrastructure it is not fully distributed, as the lookup service must be available for the system to operate. However, multiple lookup services can exist in parallel so that from a robustness and a scalability perspective Jini is still preferable over fully centralized architectures.

Other communication infrastructures such as the Event Heap of iROS (Johanson & Fox 2002) or BEACH/ COAST (Tandler 2004) are based on central server components which is sensible for less dynamic and more infrastructure centric environments like the interactive workspaces and meeting rooms of these projects. One can assume the constant availability of a central server in an office building, however with hybrid games in home environments this might not be the case.

Most flexible in terms of device integration and operating system independence and also conceptually similar to PEGASUS are the UPnP protocols (Shirehjini 2005). Like PEGASUS they allow for configurations with or without central server components that are referred to as "Residential Gateways" in UPnP terminology. In principle, UPnP allows for peer to peer networking without any configuration utilizing network information from DHCP and DNS servers which naturally restricts the UPnP scope to IP networks. In contrast to this, PEGASUS allows for arbitrary networks with specialized "Gateway" components that provide endpoint communication over other protocols such as RS-232. UPnP also defines web-based UI functionalities that allow for browser-based configuration of devices even with emerging standards such as CE-HTML that are specifically geared towards consumer electronics devices. In general it shows that UPnP has a strong focus on consumer electronics device integration. While many of the included protocols are optional, the standard is still quite heavyweight as e.g. device control requires a complete SOAP (Simple Object Access Protocol, XML) stack. Also, the notion of personal space, or private and public information, is not addressed with UPnP, although it is common that in a home setting there exist e.g. media that are strictly private such as photo collections. Admittedly, in the STARS platform this modeling of the shared space is also not part of the low-level communication subsystem, but is conceptually part of the game component library. This relates to the biggest conceptual difference between UPnP and PEGASUS which also lies in the intended usage scenarios. While UPnP is mainly a consumer electronics device control system, PEGASUS aims at providing access to shared data structures from multiple devices, in which the data persists independent of the actual devices, because the entirety of shared data structures comprises a game application for which devices merely provide means of altering or displaying aspects of the shared information space. This focus on devices versus data is reflected in the event-centered vs. data centered architecture. UPnP realizes eventing via the General Event Notification Architecture (GENA) which does not provide temporal decoupling, as from a device control perspective it does not make sense to propagate events about or to devices that are currently absent. In PEGASUS, however, the shared data space allows for a complete decoupling, as elaborated in the next section.

Decoupled Communication

For the design of a distributed pervasive computing coordination infrastructure, the choice of an appropriate communication model is most crucial, because of its implications for scalability and flexibility. The decoupling of communication between participants is the primary design goal in order to address the highly dynamic nature of pervasive computing PEGASUS consequently adheres to a publish/ subscribe interaction scheme in order to realize a loose coupling of participating components. As Eugster et al. (2003) point out, the advantage of the publish/ subscribe interaction style over the majority of similar schemes such as shared spaces, message queuing, or remote procedure calls lies in the full decoupling on all three relevant dimensions, namely space, time, and synchronization:

Space Decoupling

The development of component based architectures that support the reconfiguration and exchange of components after deployment and during runtime is greatly facilitated, if interacting parties do not have to know each other. Publishers and subscribers communicate indirectly through an event service. Publishers publish events through the service and subscribers receive their notifications from the service. Neither publishers nor subscribers hold references to each other and they are likewise unaware of the number of participants on both the subscriber and publisher side.

Time Decoupling

Given the dynamic nature of pervasive computing environments in which users and devices might appear and disappear arbitrarily, it is important that interacting parties do not need to take part in an interaction at the same time. Hence, when the event service is timely decoupled, the publisher might publish events regardless of the subscriber's connection state. Likewise, the subscriber can be notified about events, when the publisher is already disconnected.

Synchronization Decoupling

The production of events does not need to block the publishers and complementarily, subscribers can also get notified of events in an asynchronous way, for instance through a callback or through respective message processing threads. This ensures that concurrent activities are not hampered by the interaction of the participants.

The combination of all three decoupling dimensions determines the advantage of the publish/ subscribe interaction scheme. As Huang & Garcia-Molina (2001) note, it reduces coordination and synchronization between the different entities, so that the resulting infrastructure becomes

5. A Software Platform for Hybrid Gaming Applications

well adapted to all kinds of distributed spaces that are asynchronous by nature. Of the other established communication paradigms, none realizes a similar degree of decoupling. For instance, remote procedure calls (RPC) are both coupled in time and space, because of their synchronicity. Notifications eliminate the synchronization coupling, but the space coupling remains. Only, shared spaces, including the tuple space model that e.g. is used in the Event Heap of iROS (Johanson & Fox 2002) is closely related to publish/ subscribe, also providing time and space decoupling and partially also synchronization decoupling.

Subscription Scheme

In order to save communication resources in a publish/ subscribe system it is important to specify which particular events a communicating entity is interested in, so that subscribers do not have to receive all events that are published. The most basic publish/ subscribe scheme is based on topics or subjects that are identified by keywords (e.g. Altherr et al. 1999). These topic-based publish/ subscribe systems are intuitive to understand, but offer only flat addressing, so that hierarchies to orchestrate topics (Eugster et al. 2003) were proposed that permit the organization of topics with respect to containment relationships. Hence, one can subscribe to a topic and implicitly also subscribe to all the subtopic of that particular node. While this is an improvement over the standard topic-based scheme, it shares its static nature, in which events are classified according to a predefined external criterion. A content-based publish/ subscribe scheme, however, allows to classify events according to arbitrary internal attributes of the respective data structures that carry the events (Cugola et al. 2001). In a content-based scheme, the consumers use a subscription language to subscribe to a selection of events by specifying respective filters. These filters usually define constraints comprised of properties and comparison operators to identify valid events. More complex filters can be created by logically combining these single predicates.

Static topic-based publish/ subscribe systems are naturally easier to implement than content-based schemes. While they are less expressive, they also have a smaller performance overhead than content-based systems. Due to the small-scale nature of typical hybrid gaming applications that involve only a limited number of communicating entities in a home environment, the higher overhead of more sophisticated content-based protocols is uncritical.

Therefore, PEGASUS follows a content-based approach that allows filtering events based on the evaluation of predicates that can be dynamically altered during runtime. Events are stored as distributed data trees / XML structures that are also hierarchical in nature, so that the communication scheme of PEGASUS can be seen as a combination of hierarchical and content-based systems. Accordingly, PEGASUS introduces the notion of Functional Objects that get triggered on freely configurable changes within distributed data trees. A Functional Object subscribes to an arbitrary tree or sub-tree and is triggered on the evaluation of predicates that relate to changes in the subscribed tree. This is explained in more detail in the respective section of the system architecture.

System Architecture

The PEGASUS system architecture comprises functionality on three layers of abstraction. As illustrated in Figure 30 these include

1.) the Basic Tools Layer that provides low level functions for dealing with data trees, network transfer, and XML parsing

107

5. A Software Platform for Hybrid Gaming Applications

2.) the Network Data Layer that abstracts access to shared information via Accessor objects
3.) the Functional Object Layer that provides various Functional Objects that implement multiple event handlers triggering arbitrary actions within the respective Functional Objects.

Each participating component must implement most of the functionality from all three layers. PEGASUS was designed to be compatible with any ANSI C++ compiler that is capable of compiling the stdlib and the TinyXML library (http://sourceforge.net/projects/tinyxml). It has been ported to Visual C++ 2005 and Visual C++ 2008 under Windows and has also been successfully compiled and tested with gcc 3.3 under Linux and Windows. A Java port is already available for J2SE and J2ME and is used on cellular phones or PDAs supporting MIDLETS version 2. The C++ version can either be statically linked to respective applications or used as a 260k DLL under Windows.

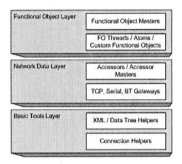

Figure 30: PEGASUS subsystem layers

The functionalities on each of the layers are now discussed in more detail.

Basic Tools Layer

The Basic Tools Layer comprises various lightweight XML-related library functions in which a document class represents the data tree. There are several methods for accessing the data structures via paths. Furthermore, various network related functions for establishing connections between multiple PEGASUS software components and transferring data between them are provided at this layer. With the Basic Tools Layer available, a user could load a data tree out of an XML file, establish a connection and transmit parts of the data tree to another PEGASUS instance via different communication methods such as a socket, a serial line, or a Bluetooth connection.

Network Data Layer

The second layer is the Network Data Layer. It is responsible for the abstraction of access to shared information across PEGASUS instances. It mainly defines three classes of objects that closely work together (see Figure 31).

First, there is the Accessor object that is capable of holding a tree structure either loaded from a file or referenced from a part of a tree of another Accessor. Every Accessor can reference one Accessor and can serve multiple others. An Accessor Master, which is derived from the Accessor class and can also hold data itself, takes control and track of the dependencies among Accessors and thus the creation and destruction of the individual Accessors. The

108

Accessor Master is also responsible for triggering Accessors to update their data in order for information to be synchronized correctly between Accessors. Every Accessor object is configured via a configuration structure that is represented as a data tree and interpreted by the Accessor Master. It minimally includes a unique name for the Accessor to be referenced and either a filename for the XML data or an Accessor/path combination for referencing data from another Accessor. During the initialization of the Accessor, it synchronizes itself according to its configuration. On a change of his referenced data, e.g. from another Accessor instance, the Accessor receives a notification. Similarly, the Accessor can inform other objects of its own change. Accessors hence provide the capability of representing and synchronizing arbitrary data trees among distributed software components based on the PEGASUS subsystem. In order not to waste communication resources and transfer the appropriate amount of data on synchronization, every referenced tree can naturally be a branch or sub-tree of another tree, so that any individual Accessor just accesses the respective information of interest provided that the trees are appropriately constructed.

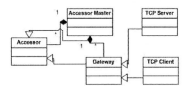

Figure 31: The Network Data Layer

The final important class at the Network Data Layer is the Gateway Accessor. It is also derived from the Accessor class and basically passes information from published Accessors to a corresponding Gateway inside a different PEGASUS instance from which other Accessors can access the corresponding data. Using this mechanism, two or more instances can refer to the same data, even when they reside on different devices with different operating systems. As the Gateway wraps the entire functionality of cross process data transfer, adapters for various communication protocols can be added by deriving from the Gateway class. At the current point in time, connections via TCP/IP sockets, represented by a TCP Server- and a TCP Client Gateway are implemented as well as Gateways for Bluetooth and serial communications. Other connection types such as IrDA or HTTP are trivial to integrate by deriving from the Gateway class.

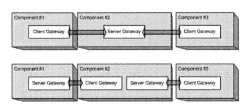

Figure 32: Centralized and cascading configurations

The main difference between Server and Client Gateways relates to the Server Gateway accepting more than one client at a time. Naturally, it is possible to share trees inside a single Server Gateway to which multiple Client Gateways connect and share the trees across clients.

5. A Software Platform for Hybrid Gaming Applications

This resembles a centralized PEGASUS configuration as illustrated in the upper part of Figure 32. Since a single PEGASUS component can implement zero to n Client Gateways as well as zero to n Server Gateways, it is also possible to e.g. add both a server and a client to the same component so that applications with a cascading communication scheme can as well be designed (see the lower part of Figure 32). Upon the startup of a PEGASUS instance, Client Gateways recurrently try connecting to the respective Server Gateway until a connection can be established. Upon the loss of a connection, the client will again recurrently try to reconnect and synchronize any referenced data eventually.

Functional Object Layer

The third layer of the architecture is the actual Functional Object Layer that implements the previously introduced Functional Objects. Functional Objects and their corresponding Functional Object Masters follow a similar management scheme as Accessors and their Accessor Masters. As illustrated in Figure 33, they are derived from their respective counterparts on the Network Data Layer and hence build upon the communication infrastructure of the Accessors requiring only code for the additional functionalities they provide. A Functional Object augments the methods for data access and synchronization that an Accessor provides. More than one input to them can exist, so that different context changes can result in different actions inside the object. The object itself can change data, which in return can result in "calling" actions on other objects, simply by changing the contextual data regarded by them. The transition from one object to another is based on data changes, thus this modification capability has to be available for every object.

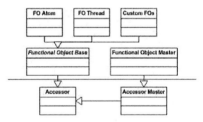

Figure 33: The Functional Object Layer

We define two mechanisms for the contextual evaluation of input data. First, a main condition, called initial condition is evaluated and might initiate a trigger. In most cases, this initial condition is a change in the data the object is interested in. Second, there can be extended verifications which evaluate contextual conditions. They are represented by predicates related to the exact changes in the regarded data. If both conditions are fulfilled, a named trigger will be passed to a dedicated function inside the object.

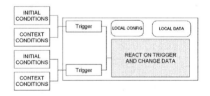

Figure 34: A Functional Object
110

Obviously, this functional object concept relates closely to the object oriented programming approach. Every object has its own data structures and certain methods which can be called on different context changes. The class definition is a hierarchic structure that can be derived from.

With this concept, we can create networks of functional objects that react on data changes appropriately for their defined situations. An advantage of the concept is that a graphical representation of a program can be used for objects and program generation itself, enabling developers to graphically define objects and the related control structures.

They can be informed by other Functional Objects or Accessors of data changes and can evaluate initial and contextual conditions in respect to these changes. This can result in calling a virtual Do()-method of the Functional Object class (which is the actual interface between custom code and the distributed application data) to which the respective data is passed as parameters. The corresponding conditional evaluations are defined in the object's configuration structures and can be changed at runtime. Thereby, Functional Object behavior can be changed dynamically.

As many operations in a contextual change boil down to basic data manipulation, there is a special functional class called FunctionalObjectAtom which is capable of simple data manipulation specified in its configuration tree and executed on a specified trigger. Since objects can call others by simply changing data, it is easy to model a process flow by defining triggers and their corresponding data manipulating operations. By defining additional contextual conditions, basic programming techniques such as state machines, loops, or other control structures can be implemented and changed dynamically by altering the configuration residing in XML trees. This is shown in the next figure.

```
<Functional name="simpleloop" type="atom">
  <data>
    <loopdata counter="0" maxcount="10" step="1"/>
  </data>
    <trigger>
      <loopProcess>
        <initial OnChange="loopdata/counter"/>
        <conditional>
          <bool>
            <lesserequal this="loopdata/counter"
then="@loopdata/max@"/>
          </bool>
        </conditional>
      </loopProcess>
    <on>
      <loopProcess>
        <!--... do processing of the loop here .. !-->
        <add tothis="loopdata/counter" add="@loopdata/step@"/>
      </loopProcess>
    </on>
    </trigger>
</Functional>
```

Figure 35: A simple loop

By setting simpleloop:loopdata/counter to a number below or equal 10 (maxcount) the loop will be initialized and the counter variable will be incremented until it reaches the maxcout value. The <on> section describes the behavior on every change of the counter and finally increments the loopcounter by the specified step size.

To realize asynchronous Functional objects that take an arbitrary amount of time to execute and on that other objects may wait, there is also a second class of Functional objects called FunctionalThreads. These threads are able to process shared data in parallel.

Another example for a control structure is shown in the next figure that is from the UI component for the Smart Dice Cup. The snippet shows a basic state machine for the Smart Dice Cup device that alternates between the two states of waiting and tossing, i.e. when the device is lifted or when it is put on a surface without the particle's accelerometers being triggered.

```
<Functional name="dicebox" type="atom">
  <data>
    <action tossed="0" tossedSum="0" />
    <states state1="0" />
    <in start="0" />
    <out end="0" />
  </data>
  <trigger>
    <start>
      <initial onChange="in/start" />
    </start>
    <tossing>
      <initial onChange="smartit:states/action" />
      <condition>
        <bool type="and">
          <equal this="@smartit:states/action@" with="3" />
          <equaltext this="@states/state1@" with="waiting" />
        </bool>
      </condition>
    </tossing>
    <tossed>
      <initial onChange="smartit:states/action" />
      <condition>
        <bool type="and">
          <equal this="@smartit:states/action@" with="2" />
          <equaltext this="@states/state1@" with="tossing" />
        </bool>
      </condition>
    </tossed>
  </trigger>
```

Figure 36: A state machine

5. A Software Platform for Hybrid Gaming Applications

As shown in Figure 36, there are two distinct states, namely "tossing" and "tossed" that are triggered with respect to the comparison of the Functional Object's own state ("states/state1") with a change in the "smartit:states/action" data that is updated when the respective Device Wrapper receives information from the physical device and alters the UI Component Server data tree (see the section on UI components). The snippet also shows the data block above the state machine definition that a game application usually subscribes to in order to get notified when e.g. the sum of the individual faces of the dice (variable "tossedSum") is updated and, consequently, some sort of game event is triggered. The complete definition of this dice box client can be found for reference in the appendix.

To add more specialized domain-specific behavior to PEGASUS trees, it is possible to extend the language in different ways. In later sections of this chapter, two such domain specific languages (DSL) are presented, the first is called UIDL (User Interface Definition Language) and is used for specifying game related user interfaces for different (mostly mobile) devices. It basically adds specialized tags such as <canvas> or <image> to the XML definitions that are interpreted by respective interpreters. As changes to these specialized tags are propagated through the PEGASUS communication system, it is possible to react on changes to certain parameters like the position of an image or the state of a button in real-time, thus allowing for tweaking interface definitions on a developer PC while the respective target devices update themselves accordingly. The second DSL is called GDL (Game Definition Language) and follows a different approach by embedding scripts into the action attributes of arbitrary subtrees, thus augmenting the inherently declarative nature of PEGASUS and UIDL with imperative elements. An example embedded script could, for instance, look like this:

```
"<WAND_MOVED action='(TEXT PUBLIC)(SETLIGHT
100)(CANVAS/SHOWSCROLL)' />"
```

Just like UIDL or "plain" PEGASUS trees, it is also possible for GDL scripts to be changed during runtime by specialized or generic manipulation tools.

Tool Support

A dedicated client editor called Tree Manipulator is available in order to edit data definitions and provide PEGASUS support tasks. It is able to access arbitrary sub-trees of data, to manipulate this data and to trigger according functions, as well as to log events and to add/ remove/ rename attributes from trees. The Tree Manipulator is realized as a Win32 GUI application built with MFC and consequently runs on Windows only. It offers a large tree control that shows and allows manipulating tree data with respective context menus for task selection. It is shown below in Figure 37.

113

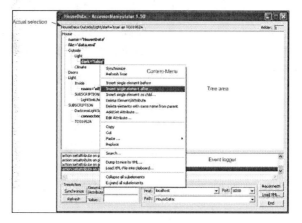

Figure 37: The Tree Manipulator tool

The Tree Manipulator operates as a low-level client sniffing tool in a similar way as the iROS tools (Johanson & Fox 2002) by connecting to any gateway server and to access a corresponding tree or a part of it. Like any other PEGASUS client application it automatically reconnects on restarting gateway servers, so that instances of the Tree Manipulator are usually run all the time. A comprehensive description of the Tree Manipulator's functions can be found in the annex. While the Tree Manipulator could, in principle, be used to define complete applications from scratch, there exist also command line tools for e.g. generating trees out of MindMaps that can be loaded into the Tree Manipulator. For PEGASUS-based domain specific languages such as the Game Definition Language (GDL) or the User Interface Description Language (UIDL) that are discussed in forthcoming sections, it is also possible to develop dedicated graphical editors to simplify development and content adaptation.

5.2. User Interface Components and Consistency Management

To integrate the various tangible and graphical interfaces discussed in the previous chapter, a component based approach is the optimal choice in order to allow for adding, removing, or reconfiguring a setup of interfaces during runtime (R2.7). Each user interface component includes means to access one or more graphical or tangible controls that share the same data model which is made accessible via the PEGASUS communication subsystem. Optionally, components can also be configured regarding the handling of data updates and contradicting state information e.g. from a virtual and a physical control to ensure the consistency of the component's state. Within a PEGASUS application, there exists one global UI component tree, into which all UI components publish information about themselves, so that applications or coordinating components such as the Game UI Orchestration component discussed later can find and access individual user interface components.

5. A Software Platform for Hybrid Gaming Applications

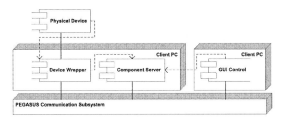

Figure 38: User interface components

User interface components consist of several modules (see Figure 38) that communicate with each other and synchronize their individual data either via PEGASUS or in case of the physical device and the Device Wrapper via a different synchronous protocol. Both tangible and graphical interface modules can co-exist in one component provided that they operate on the same shared data model. This allows for treating user interfaces with graphical and tangible elements as single coherent components with each module accessing a different aspect of the interface. Additionally, graphical and tangible interfaces can be used concurrently, for instance, a tangible game board might be the primary interface to a hybrid game in a smart home environment, whereas a remote player connected over the internet might utilize a graphical game board to participate in the game. The individual modules within a user interface component are now discussed in more detail.

Physical Device and Device Wrapper

Similar to the elements of tangible user interface architectures such as the iStuff components in the iRoom (Ballagas et al. 2003), there exist physical devices that are connected to dedicated software modules wrapping the devices' idiosyncrasies. These Device Wrappers provide interfaces to the devices and function as communication nodes between other modules and the devices. Each physical device needs its own dedicated wrapper to be integrated with the platform. In contrast to the iStuff components that are primarily geared towards wireless communication and Phidgets (Greenberg and Fitchett 2001) that focus on USB cable connections, there is no preferred communication media or transport protocol to the device. So far, both USB and wireless media are supported. A third method of connecting to physical output devices that are not necessarily intended for remote control is the use of Ethernet controlled power sockets for which a Device Wrapper exists as well.

Device Wrappers are associated with the Component Server that propagates state changes of the devices to other components subscribing to the Component Server's exposed data. Theoretically, multiple Device Wrappers can be associated with the component's single Component Server, although this might be semantically questionable, if the physical devices are perceived as distinct and non-related interfaces. It is however reasonable to combine multiple complimentary devices in one component. For instance, the Device Wrappers of two individual potentiometers and a switch might be combined to form a Joystick-like UI component, each providing a distinct part of the component's shared data (X-axis, Y-axis of the stick, and fire button).

GUI Control

Graphical user interface controls are UI modules complementary to the pairs of physical devices and Device Wrappers. They are similarly used to provide user interfaces, but without being physically embodied in a tangible form. Just like Device Wrappers, they synchronize with the Component Server in order to propagate user input to other components or to reflect changes in the component's data to the user through a computationally mediated display. In the latter case, the control needs to be coupled with a view, which is commonly the case, although not a requirement. It is possible to create GUI Controls that do not provide output to the user, thus being insensitive to changes in the shared data. A typical GUI Control adheres to the traditional Desktop PC interaction techniques using a mouse or touch sensitive display to control graphical widgets.

Graphical widgets found in TUI toolkits such as Klemmer et al. (2004) are provided to allow for debugging when the physical device is absent. This is also a sensible use for GUI controls in the STARS platform, but their scope is broader, since graphical and tangible interface modules synchronizing over the same shared data can co-exist. The consistency and integrity between them is handled in the Consistency Manager, which is necessary, since not all real-world devices can actively change their physical state via software. GUI Controls may thus also be used to augment physical devices with virtual user interfaces that are not necessarily co-located with the physical device. Therefore, in an extended home scenario, remote users might interact with a virtual proxy of the physical device through a GUI Control, regardless of the presence or absence of the device. Consequently, multiple instances of a control can be created that, although commonly not aware of each other, synchronize via the Component Server.

Component Server

To expose the state information of the user interface component to other software components the Component Server publishes the component's state information to the PEGASUS subsystem and likewise subscribes to changes in the state data from outside of the component. This serves two purposes. First, other components can access the state of the user interface and receive notifications on state changes through PEGASUS. Second, the component can react on other components requesting changes to the user interface state. Through this mechanism, an application might prohibit certain states that are valid at the UI component scope, but invalid at the application scope. For instance, at the UI component scope, a chessboard is in a valid state, if zero or one piece is on each field and no pieces transgress the boundaries of any field to prevent being associated with more than one field at a time. At the application scope, however, a game of chess has very different constraints on the setup of pieces than a game of Checkers, although both share the same interface.

Next to the exposure of the user interface state to other components, the Component Server is also the central point of integration for all of the modules within the component. In contrast to the other modules, there can be only one Component Server within the UI Component. In fact, the Component Server is equal to the entire component from the platform's point of view, because it is a PEGASUS server that offers the only point of connection to other components.

Since updates to the shared data from individual modules and also other components are centralized in the Component Server, it has to ensure that all interested parties are made aware of such changes and also resolve ambiguities in the state information, for instance, if a physical device has a differing idea on its state than its graphical counterpart. In order to resolve potential ambiguities and ensure the integrity of the component, an optional Consistency Manager module can be used that mediates between conflicting state information.

5. A Software Platform for Hybrid Gaming Applications

Consistency Manager

One of the potential problems of tangible user interfaces is the synchronization of virtual and physical states. In terms of the MCRpd interaction model (Ullmer & Ishii 2004), physical representation is intertwined with the control and computationally coupled with the model. When the control is altered by a user, the physical representation changes and updates the model. Likewise, changes in the model should be reflected in the digital representation and ideally also in the physical representation. The problem, however, is that only very few tangible interfaces are capable of actively changing their physical representations. For instance, a sentient game board might convey the positions of its physical playing pieces to the model; however, the virtual domain might not have the actuators to move the pieces in the real world in order to reflect changes in the model not initiated by the user.

To deal with conflicting information from any of the modules or from an update within another component, the Consistency Manager can be configured to give precedence to the potential sources of the conflict (R2.5).

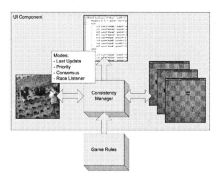

Figure 39: Consistency Manager

As shown in Figure 39 the Consistency Manager mediates between different instances that might attempt to update the data structure in the Component Server. By adding additional information to the currently valid Component Server state and the update candidate information, it allows for different synchronization strategies such as:

- Last Update: This is the default mode. It allows any module to update the component data and the last update consequently becomes valid. As all modules subscribe to data changes, they are capable of adjusting their internal states such as their graphical appearance accordingly.
- Priority: Each module might associate a priority value with its own update candidates, so that other modules are to accept any changes to the component data that is of higher priority than their own priorities. This allows the Consistency Manager to easily implement scenarios such as "physical overwrites digital" or vice versa, by simply assigning respective priorities.
- Race Listener: In order to avoid race conditions while at the same time not impose constraints on the update process, the Consistency Manager can also be configured to intercept seemingly too frequent updates caused by modules that update the tree as a result

117

of being triggered by another update and set a lock attribute that is to be interpreted by subscribing modules.

In addition, two operational flags can also be set in addition to the basic modes of the Consistency Manager.

- Rules resolve: Allows an external component outside the modules of the UI component to update the component data. The typical use case here is for the game itself to check if the state of the UI component is in accordance with the game rules, e.g. if a movement of playing pieces is a correct game turn. If not, the application might reject the last UI component update. By changing the "Rules resolve" flag the Consistency Manager can decouple the UI component from the effects of a game, even if the game has subscribed to the respective UI component.
- Error State: By allowing to set an "error state" to the component data, the Consistency Manager can hint subscribed modules to convey to the user that the component is in an erroneous state which needs to be resolved by manual interception. For GUI modules this is easy to achieve e.g. by respective text messages, but also physical game boards with basic LED output channels are appropriate for this kind of user interaction. This is shown e.g. in Figure 40 (left), where the board conveys the message to the user that he is to move the playing piece to any of the four highlighted positions. [The right part of the figure shows the same board being utilized as an input device for the Caves & Creatures demonstrator at an EU IST conference].

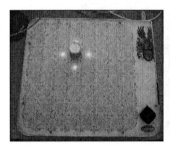

Figure 40: LED output on a game board

In order to facilitate the development of respective GUI Control modules within the UI Component that take into account the specificities of hybrid gaming environments' display types, the platform offers several device adapted GUI provision mechanisms.

5.3. Device Adapted GUI Provision

The display idiosyncrasies (R2.3) of the different display types in pervasive computing environments are addressed with the STARS platform. Apart from desktop PC clients for which no dedicated adaptation is necessary (as they are the "standard"), the focus is on vertical and horizontal displays as well as mobile devices. For vertical vs. horizontal displays, the interaction specificities relate to the individual positions and viewing angles of the users, whereas the issues with common mobile devices relate more to the subtle differences in small-screen dimensions, so that a fine-tuning of the screen layout and real-estate in the device profiles becomes necessary.

Vertical and Horizontal Displays

As discussed in the previous section on user interface components, each component can utilize a GUI control that renders rich multimedia content (see R2.2). Depending on the characteristics of the display, i.e. its position in the environment and its position relative to the users, the graphical output can be automatically adapted. At the application-domain agnostic low-level of GUI adaptation discussed here, the adaptation is passive. This means that each GUI control must be configured by some other entity that adjusts the respective data tree of the GUI control. At the abstraction level of a game application the game UI orchestration subsystem performs this task. It specifically knows about game players and the currently active player in a turn based game to whose position e.g. the horizontal display at a game table adjusts.

For a vertical public display, the static location context is most relevant. Players usually share similar viewing angles to the display as they are usually on the same side of the display, if the display is located on one of the walls of the room. In Figure 41 one of the game board renderers from the game component library is shown for displays located on perpendicular walls.

Figure 41: Vertical display adaptation

As can be seen, the cameras simply follow the physical layout of the displays in so far as they are perpendicularly located as well. Horizontal displays differ significantly from that, as the static location context is mostly irrelevant, since players gather around the horizontal display, each having a unique viewing angle, so that objects displayed on the table surface are perceived differently with respect to the users' relative positions. This means that someone at the left side of a table perceives a different image than someone at the bottom. Furthermore, objects with meaningful orientation such as text can be optimally perceived only from certain angles, so that on a horizontal display there is a distinction between the local orientation of information objects (that can be rotated towards optimizing individual viewing angles) and the global orientation of the information space (that should be static for reflecting world coordinates). Figure 42 shows the same game board renderer as in the previous figure, but this time on a horizontal surface. The left part of the figure shows the display adapted to a player standing south of the table, the right part shows the display adapted to a player standing west. As can be seen, the global orientation of the view remains unchanged ("north remains north"), as the camera moves above the scene pointing at the center of the game board, fixing its roll, however not its yaw (in Tait–Bryan rotations). This results in preserving the global orientation of the game board while optimizing for the viewing angle of the current user.

5. A Software Platform for Hybrid Gaming Applications

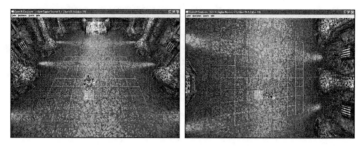

Figure 42: Horizontal display adaptation

In comparison with Figure 41 it can be seen that the text box attached to the playing piece in Figure 42 reflects the static location vs. player position context of vertical vs. horizontal displays. As the text window has no meaningful orientation within the context of the game, e.g. it is not a virtual character looking in a certain direction, it is rotated towards the current player in Figure 42 and consequently rendered south or west of it, although the character always faces south. In contrast, the vertical display in Figure 41 disregards relative player positions and consequently keeps rendering the text box faced to the static viewers, although the virtual character indeed faces to different edges of the screen.

A different implementation of a game board renderer is also shown in Figure 43 which is actually photographed from a Roomware table. As this renderer assumes tangible playing pieces as interaction objects (just like in a traditional board game), the camera can not cycle above the scene like in the horizontal display from Figure 42, as this would invalidate the physical positions of the playing pieces due to the distortion effect of perspective projection. Therefore, simple parallel projection is used to preserve the positions of playing pieces when the display is rotated.

Figure 43: An alternative horizontal game board renderer

The two photographs in Figure 43 show the game table from the south with Figure 43 (left) showing the current player standing south of the display, while the right part shows the western player being active. As the global orientation of the game board remains constant between player changes, the individual information objects are rotated to optimize for the different viewing angles. In addition, this game board renderer also utilizes an alpha channel effect that renders the information objects of other players than the active one as semi-

120

transparent, so that the game board beneath them is accessible to the current player, while the information objects are still barely visible on close distance. To summarize, the problematic issue of positions and viewing angles in traditional tabletop games is tackled by auto-rotation of information objects which is obviously advantageous to abstract, un-oriented game boards and playing pieces that look mostly the same from any viewing angle. Of course, whether the auto-orientation in adapted GUIs works well for a given game depends on the amount of detail of the game objects. When a lot of text is displayed, changing the orientation is usually appreciated by the players. For more primitive game objects, the benefit of rotating objects might be less significant.

Mobile Device Displays

While the orientation issues are prevalent for vertical and even more so horizontal displays that are stationary and usually publicly used within the environment, mobile devices mostly serve a different purpose, namely providing personal access to private data. Here, the richness of the display is less relevant than with large public surfaces, as interaction should not focus on private devices anyway in order to preserve the social dynamics of the co-located game session. What is problematic, however, is the heterogeneity of mobile device platforms with different display dimensions and different operating systems (Windows Mobile, Java, Android, Palm etc). In order to facilitate integrating a large number of mobile devices and adjust their user interfaces, STARS provides a simple XML markup language for the definition of user interfaces called UIDL (user interface definition language). Such markup languages have a very long tradition and numerous dialects such as AAIML, AUIML, XIML, XUL, XAML, UIML, XForms, UsiXML etc. exist that differ in their target domains, expressive power, and level of abstraction.

A detailed review of existing languages is omitted here, since UIDL does not have the expressive power of other established solutions. It does, however, function as a demonstrator and proof-of-concept for the underlying PEGASUS communication subsystem, as it is built on top of PEGASUS and thus inherits its capabilities of synchronizing distributed data structures and thus allows for altering user interface definitions during runtime (R2.7), so that development and testing can take place during the execution of a game on real mobile devices in real time. In this respect, UIDL is similar to the Game Definition Language (GDL) discussed later that equally utilizes the PEGASUS subsystem in order to alter game rules and game mechanics even while a game is being played. In contrast to GDL, it is purely descriptive in so far, as it introduces hierarchical tags and attributes that represent the respective user interface components. GDL, on the other hand, has imperative elements as it also embeds scripts into certain attributes within the XML definitions.

UIDL follows the concept of canvases on which graphical objects can be placed. It defines several related elements such as a <font> (in two flavors, namely built-in system fonts or pixel-precise bitmap fonst), <layer>, <text>, <image>, <rect>, <sprite>, <animation> etc. These elements can be used to build interface descriptions with respective attributes such as e.g. the ones defined for a <layer> element as exemplary shown in Table 18:

Table 18: Example attributes in UIDL

Attributes of a "Layer" element	Description
Type	Sets one of the three types. Can be: "layer|vlayer|hlayer"
X	X position from top left.
Y	Y position from top left.
W	Width of the layer
H	Height of the layer
Visible	Defines if the layer will be displayed and all its underlying layers. Can be [true|false].
Layer	Defines the order of drawing this object in respect to the top layer
ShowDebug	(optional) Can be [true|false]. Shows the rectangle defined by X,Y,W,H.
additional Attributes	For every type there are some additional attributes (omitted here)

The implementation on the client side is based on a respective Java package compatible with the MIDlet 2.0 specification, Applets and desktop Swing applications. Therefore, it can be operated with all Windows Mobile devices, most modern phones (not only smartphones) and in general all devices supporting MIDlets.

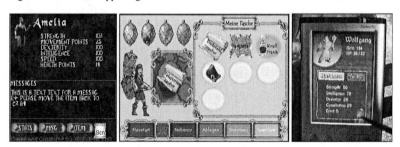

Figure 44: Mobile device user interfaces

Figure 44 demonstrates examples of mobile device displays defined with UIDL. The following snippet (Figure 45) shows the source code of the leftmost example screen on a pocket PC device with the respective resolution of 240*320 pixels.

```
<PrivateCanvas name="PrivateCanvas" file="xml/ui/PrivateGUI.xml">
  <DEV>
    <PocketPC name="PocketPCTemplate" file="xml/ui/PdaClient.xml">
      <Size w="100" h="100" />
      <Pos w="0" h="0" />
      <Color r="0" g="0" b="255" />
      <FullScreen state="on" />
```

5. A Software Platform for Hybrid Gaming Applications

```
<UserKey gameKey="a" userKey="1" />
<UserPtr pressX="213" pressY="233"
pressObj="Layers/Background/Image;" relX="208"
       relY="233" dragX="47" dragY="86" />
  <Fonts default="normalfont">
     <Font type="sys" name="smallfont" size="small" />
     <Font type="sys" name="normalfont" size="normal" />
     <Font type="sys" name="bigfont" size="big" />
     <Font type="irrpixel" name="caves"
img="img/fonts/irr_cavesFontTrans.png"
       startChar="32" endChar="127" cWidth="20" cHeight="20"
xOffset="1" yOffset="1"
       nRows="5" nCols="13" spacing="2" />
  </Fonts>
  <Layers>
     <Background type="layer" x="0" y="0" visible="true">
        <Image type="sprite" x="0" y="0" text="" font="sil"
layer="1"
          img="img/bkg/bkg_240x268.png" visible="true"
action="pressXY" />
        <ProgName type="text" x="1" y="255" text="Caves and
Creatures (c) 2006, IPSI,
          FhG" r="50" g="150" b="128" font="smallfont"
action="pressXY" spacing="2" />
     </Background>
     <PlayerInfo type="layer" x="0" y="2" layer="2"
visible="true">
        <Name type="text" x="50" y="1" text="PlayerName"
r="255" g="0" b="0"
          font="caves" />
        ...
```

Figure 45: UIDL definition of a PocketPC user interface

The client application continuously subscribes to changes in the entire data tree by interfacing it with a Functional Object. It is indifferent, if game related attributes such as the "PlayerName" are set by a different object, e.g. on a PC, or if layout related information such as image positions are updated. In effect, the application updates its display in real time, thus allowing for tweaking layout information from a dedicated user interface builder or a basic editor such as the aforementioned PEGASUS Tree Manipulator.

5.4. Game UI Orchestration

The effective utilization of the mobile, horizontal, vertical, and standard displays available in a game setup might be different depending on the type of information to be communicated, on the degree of privacy of the respective information, on the physical positions of the players, etc. There might be short bursts of information to be communicated clandestinely from one player to another. Or there might be spatial formations of playing pieces to be collaboratively developed on the game board. There might even be fierce discussion not involving the interaction devices at all. For such diverse interaction needs, different media and interaction styles are more suitable than others.

5. A Software Platform for Hybrid Gaming Applications

The STARS platform assists in finding the optimal set of interaction devices by matching the interaction characteristics of each available device with interaction requests a game application might formulate. For instance, if the current game action was to let a player pick an object from a chest, this might either happen privately depending on other players witnessing the action, or publicly. Not having a PDA available for private interaction might result in presenting the dialog spoken over the player's earphones or rendered rotated towards the player's viewing angle on the table surface, so that other players would be hampered perceiving it (as shown before in the game board renderer of Figure 43). The actual devices involved and the corresponding user interfaces in a given game situation are determined by the Game UI Orchestration Manager considering several findings from modality theory (Bernsen 1997), for instance that linguistic input and output is "unsuited for specifying detailed information on spatial manipulation" or that static graphic modes are suitable for representing large amounts of (complex) information.

Game UI Orchestration Manager

The Game UI Orchestration Manager maps interaction request properties from the game definitions to the device properties of the currently connected UI components. Thereby it takes into account hints about certain characteristics a UI component should have. The Game UI Orchestration Manager is the first high-level component discussed here that is specifically geared towards the application domain of hybrid games. As such, it expects interaction requests to be formulated in a subset of the Game Definition Language (GDL) that is discussed in the next section. It transforms these into dialog structures in UIDL, determines the most suitable UI component from the global UI component repository, and publishes them to the appropriate data tree of the respective UI component server, so that the device adapted GUI provision components can render the dialogs accordingly and eventually update any links to game state information, which in turn lets the game logic process this game state update (see Figure 46).

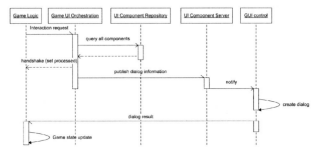

Figure 46: Game UI orchestration

Each UI component server is finally responsible to manage the creation, presentation, and tracking of dialogs. Naturally, the dialog characteristics vary with the properties of the device's interaction modes. What it actually does, depends mostly on the specific device characteristics, e.g. an earphone's only way to display a resource is to read any text/ audio sample included or otherwise fail, whereas a game board renderer has lavish means of conveying a dialog to the users.

5. A Software Platform for Hybrid Gaming Applications

Finding UI Orchestrations

A rule-based system determines how to map an interaction request to one or more UI components. It regards the hints an application provides for the generation of the interface and compares them with the characteristics for every UI component available as well as for combinations of them. A *Suitability Index* is calculated for each combination of components with the highest index being the most suitable. Indices are calculated by weighing every hint about the characteristics of the desired interaction with the attributes of the regarded component. The sums of these weighings make up isolated suitabilities of single modes. Suitability Indices can thus be expressed as:

$$I_m = \operatorname{argmax}_m \{ \Sigma \ (i = 0..\max \text{Attr}) \ \text{Hint}_{mi} * \text{Attr}_{mi} \}$$

Single suitabilities can be further moderated by rules about their combination. The result of each of these calculations is a Suitability Index from which the highest one is chosen.

A Simplified Example

A game developer might request the position and identity of an object to be conveyed clandestinely to a single player, for instance when he has detected a hidden trap some squares ahead on a game board. Given that only the privacy level and the capability of conveying spatial information were relevant, and that an earphone [a] had a privacy capability of 255 and a spatial capability of 50, a PDA [b] had 200/ 150, and a horizontal wall display [c] had 0/ 220, and that no further constraints applied, the isolated suitabilities were as follows for an interaction request with a moderate demand for privacy (100) and a low demand for spatial visualization (40).

$i_a = 255*100+50*40=27500$, $i_b = 200*100+150*40=26000$, $i_c = 0*100+220*40=8800$

Consequently, the data tree of the earphone would be chosen resulting for instance in a "you sense, trap, 4 squares north" audio output. The same service on the PDA would have brought up a map with the trap shown and the "you sense trap" string printed beneath, provided that the request:Spatial hint was higher than 40.

The integration of a Game UI Orchestration Manager is not mandatory for a hybrid gaming application. The GDL defined application logic could also generate UIDL definitions directly and publish them to specific data trees. In fact, game UI orchestration becomes increasingly relevant with a growing number of UI components, so that e.g. more devices than players are available.

5.5. Game Rules and Mechanics

Lundgren & Björk (2004) define game mechanics, as simply any part of the rule system of a game that covers one, and only one, possible kind of interaction that takes place during the game, be it general or specific. A game may consist of several mechanics, and a mechanic may be a part of many games.

In order to allow for flexibility in game play, the Game Definition Language GDL can be used by any hybrid gaming application based on PEGASUS and enables storing all the game play rules and mechanics within PEGASUS trees, allowing alterations to the game without having to recompile any code (R2.7).

5. A Software Platform for Hybrid Gaming Applications

GDL is an XML-based language syntactically similar to many scripting languages with the unique benefits of being based on PEGASUS, allowing for close integration with the hybrid gaming environment. In addition to the previously described UIDL it allows for integrating functions. Functions, defined in a function xml file, consist of a function name, argument names, and a sequence of parenthetically or bracketed expressions describing what actions must be performed. The return type is specified by the xml attribute name. The game engine calls certain pre-defined functions upon events such as the introduction of a new piece, a piece moving, or a card being played. For instance, the xml code:

```
<MOVE action= "(SOUND PUBLIC foobar.wav)"/>
```

defines a function named MOVE. Here MOVE is one of the aforementioned pre-defined function names that is called whenever a piece is moved on the board. SOUND is a built in function that causes a music file to be played over an audio channel. This functions's return type is the default of 'action', meaning that side effects occur. Other possibilities are 'integer', 'bool', and 'string'.

In addition to basic math, string manipulation, Boolean logic, and function calls, GDL provides functions for accessing and manipulation of the PEGASUS objects used by the game. These objects store all the information related to the game, and it is via these objects that the various viewers and devices that make up the hybrid gaming environment interact.

Objects, identified by a globally unique ID (GID), are stored in a global XML tree and have associated attributes which may be strings or integers. These attributes can be read, utilized, manipulated, and set by commands in a GDL function. Returning to the MOVE function, a field can also be updated in the moving object by adding another command after the first:

```
<MOVE action= "(SOUND PUBLIC foobar.wav)
              (UPDATE+ TURN moves 1)"/>
```

Here TURN is a special GID that always accesses the piece whose turn it currently is, and this last line will cause the 'moves' attribute to be incremented by 1.

As GDL commands are stored as plain strings, object string attributes can themselves be lines of code. There is a primitive (DO) that interprets a string attribute as code and executes it. This means that each object can be truly unique, and have unique effects in the game. Extending the MOVE command further, we can now call piece specific move code as follows:

```
<MOVE action= "(SOUND PUBLIC foobar.wav)
              (UPDATE+ TURN moved 1)
              (DO (TURN moving))"/>
```

The last line obtains the string-valued 'moving' attribute of the current piece and executes it as code. In addition, as GDL provides methods for manipulating strings, code stored in attributes can easily be rewritten dynamically during game play. It is even possible for code to modify and delete itself.

As an example, consider an item in the game that can only be used once. With GDL, it is a simple matter to set it up such that after the first use, it can NEVER be used again, because

5. A Software Platform for Hybrid Gaming Applications

the code that would need to be executed no longer exists. GDL code to do that exists in the globalID tree and is shown here:

```
<gid628 use='(actual effects here)
               (UPDATES 628 use "")'/>
```

This code defines an object with global ID 628. The first time it is used in the game, the 'use' attribute is read as code and executed. The first parenthetical command contains the actual effects of the entity in the game, such as playing a sound, or updating an player's character's stats. The second parenthetical command causes the 'use' attribute of the entity with ID=628 to be set to the null string, or cleared. (UPDATES stands for update-string) This results in the entity now having the form:

```
<gid268 use=''/>
```

The next time 628 is used in the game, nothing will occur, as there is no code in the 'use' attribute to execute. In addition to acting as code, strings are also used to make object access simple and stackable. Since an object is just defined via its GID, and the GID is just a string, GIDs can be stored as attributes in an object. This means that an object can have sub-objects, and the GDL allows for them to be accessed and manipulated. For instance, here we have an object, representing a player and its toy:

```
<gid17 name="Player" toy='77' />
```

accessing (17 toy) will return the string 77. This, however, can be used to access the attributes of the toy in a nested manner. If GID 77 exists:

```
<gid77 name="Elmo" cost='One dollar'/>
```

then the cost of the player's toy can be accessed with (17 toy cost) or ((17 toy) cost). These commands will return the cost of whatever toy object 17 is using,. When another object modifies the 'toy' attribute of GID17 during game play, this code will continue to work.

There are also several hybrid-game specific concepts that are built into the GDL, making it easy for developers to write games without knowing the interior mechanics of the system. The concepts of boards, public/private audio and text output, and random number generation are all exposed in simple function calls. This allows a game designer to specify what they wish to happen, without concern for which devices are actually present. It is then the responsibility of the hybrid game environment to make it occur using whatever devices are actually present.

To clarify the concept in a game setting with the typical issue of a player holding a weapon we can now examine a sequence of events, where objects modify each other's attributes in response to actions by the players. The player is defined as

```
<gid100 name="Player1" weapon="" />
```

a weapon the player can hold:

```
<gid201 name="Broad Sword" use="(UPDATES TURN toy 201)"/>
```

127

5. A Software Platform for Hybrid Gaming Applications

and the built in MOVE function can be defined as:

```
<MOVE action="(TEXT PUBLIC
  [CAT (TURN name) 'is holding the '
    (TURN weapon name)])"/>
```

(This causes a string containing the players name and his weapon's name to be displayed)

On the players first turn, the following text is displayed:
"Player1 is holding the"

since the 'weapon' field is initially blank. It is then supposed that the player activates object 201. This can be accomplished by selecting an icon on a screen, playing a card into an RFID reader, or pushing a button. The exact mechanics of object activation are left to the hybrid gaming environment, the game control code itself does not need to care. Once object 201 is activated, it will update the 'weapon' attribute of the turn-taker, who in this case is object 100, to now read:

```
<gid100 name="Player1" weapon="201">
```

On the players next turn, the following text is displayed:
"Player1 is holding the Broad Sword"

This small example demonstrates functionality that object 201 is able to effect game play without any modification to the game code. By more extensively modifying an object's attributes, and with appropriate hooks (like the DO command described above), simple objects such as 201 can cause significant effects in the game.

The entire Caves & Creatures roleplaying game presented in the next chapter is defined in GDL. Its capability of embedding calls to support functions and objects from the specific domain of gaming such as DRINKPOTION or TURN (= currently active player) within arbitrary object definitions allow for concisely defining game behavior. A potion, an amulet, and a location from the Caves & Creatures are shown in Figure 47 as examples:

```
<gid150 name="Potion of Health" use="(DRINKPOTION 150)"
        my_use="(UPDATE+ TURN hp 10)(UPDATE- TURN poisoned)"/>

<gid173 name='Amulet of Command (Intelligence)' use='(WEAR
173)'
        my_use='(UPDATES+ TURN command (173 my_str))'
        my_str='(UPDATE+ TURN intelligence 1)(DOIN TURN 1
                "(UPDATE- TURN intelligence 1)")'
        my_unuse='(UPDATES- TURN command (173 my_str))' />

<gid200 name='Tile of Life' action='(TEXT TURN "Welcome to the
Tile of Life")(UPDATE TURN hp (TURN max_hp))(UPDATES- LOCATION
step_on "(DO (200 action))")(HIDE "(DO (200 action))")'/>
```

Figure 47: Game object definitions in GDL

As can be seen above, the "Potion of Health" can be used by calling a DRINKPOTION function with the object itself as a parameter. DRINKPOTION is defined elsewhere as:

```
<DRINKPOTION action="(DO (POTIONID my_use))(SOUND PUBLIC
battle\drink.wav)(HIDEITEM POTIONID)" arg0="POTIONID" />
```

It obviously plays a gurgling sound file over a public channel (that is determined dynamically by the STARS platform), executes the code that the "Potion of Health" provides itself and lets the potion disappear. By examining the "myuse"-attribute of the "Potion of Health" it is clear that it both increases the player's hp (= hit points) by the amount of 10 and also cures any poisoning that the player might suffer from. The beauty of defining the behavior of the potion as the small snippet "(UPDATE+ TURN hp 10)(UPDATE- TURN poisoned)" directly within the object definition is that it is easy to tweak during game play without having to know how and where the actions take effect in the code.

For instance, the potion might be made stronger by adding a larger number than 10 or the poison curing effect of the potion might be removed by not changing the poisoned variable. Instead, borrowing from the "Amulet of Command" might result in becoming smarter: (UPDATE+ TURN intelligence 1). Looking at the amulet in the example the conceptual difference to a potion becomes clear. Obviously, there is not just a "use"-, but also an "unuse"-case and a function called WEAR is called instead of DRINKPOTION. Without knowing the details of this function it is easy to guess that it "unuses" any other amulet and then calls the "my_use"-code of that specific "Amulet of Command". Finally, the "Tile of Life" obviously makes use of the self-modifying code capabilities of GDL, as it hides its own functionality after being called. That means, once a player steps on this special tile, the tile disappears.

The complete GDL source code of the Caves & Creatures game can be found in the annex, but even from the small code examples presented above, it becomes clear that GDL fulfills its requirements for defining hybrid gaming applications in an appropriate way by being

runtime adaptable (any aspect of the game can be altered during runtime)
distributed and decoupled (as it is based on PEGASUS)
game domain specific (by providing the respective game relevant objects and functions)
agnostic of any concrete system setups and deployments (as there is an inversion-of-control/ observer pattern, i.e. any external components subscribe to changes in the GDL game state)

Furthermore, GDL is also an example for demonstrating how to bridge the gap between declarative and imperative languages.

5.6. Conclusions

In this chapter the software platform STARS was presented that supports the development and execution of hybrid games and allows for integrating the hybrid gaming hardware devices discussed in the previous chapter. The functionality covered by STARS ranges from a rather low level communication infrastructure to couple arbitrary software components to high level subsystems such as dedicated rendering components of game boards or other game data. Parts of the functionality is useful outside the narrow context of hybrid games, as hybrid games naturally share certain requirements with other pervasive computing applications, and other parts are very specific for the application domain, such as the domain specific languages GDL

5. A Software Platform for Hybrid Gaming Applications

and UIDL that address game rule descriptions and gaming user interfaces for heterogenous devices. Taken together, they are supposed to form a complete platform that should be capable of creating and running real hybrid gaming applications that end users should enjoy and value over traditional forms of entertainment.

In order to reach that goal, two next steps are required. The first is using the platform to create running hybrid games that can really be evaluated by end users. The second step is to make sure that these games can not only be created, but are actually enjoyable and accepted by the target audience. The first step is addressed in the following chapter with the discussion of the prototype development.

The second step relates to how to use the platform in an appropriate way. One key idea behind the development of the system was to enrich traditional game forms with computer technology and at the same time take care that the social dynamics of e.g. a board game session remain intact. By integrating too much functionality into the digital parts of the system, players might easily experience interacting more with a computer game in isolation than with each other. They might lose parts of the flexibility that traditional games provide in which rules and mechanics can be completely changed at any time and many processes and regulations exist only by convention between players in the social domain. To preserve such interaction situations, care must be taken not to rigidly enforce certain rules and interaction patterns, but to provide a flexible approach that adapts to the dynamics of a given game situation. A key challenge is thus to build the right games, which is also subject to the next chapter.

6. Proof-of-Concept: Sample Realizations

This chapter presents several proof-of-concept prototypes of hybrid game applications that were developed using the STARS platform. The chapter starts with a smaller example of a demonstrator that utilizes a novel tangible interaction device to control a game application in conjunction with a traditional graphical interface ("SteinSchlag"). A hybrid game for children that solely relies on audio and a tangible board interface ("Candyland") is then discussed along with its implications for a suitable interaction design. Finally, the more elaborated demonstrators "Search for the Amulet" and "Caves & Creatures" are presented that each utilize significant parts of the STARS platform. The main contributions of each prototype are now briefly listed, before the actual demonstrators are discussed in more depth:

SteinSchlag:
- Showcase for the Gesture Based Interaction Device
- Two different game board renderers (2D& 3D) that can be alternated during runtime
- Component architecture based on the PEGASUS subsystem

Candyland:
- Showcase for the Smart Dice Cup
- Integration of a tangible game board as a primary control
- No graphical output
- 2D audio as an alternative interface

Search for the Amulet:
- Utilization of the User Interface Description Language (UIDL)
- Distributed deployment with multiple devices and components
- Implementation of the hybrid gaming conceptual model
- Multimodal stimulation
- Distribution among virtual, social, and physical domains
- Sophisticated application with end user evaluation

Caves & Creatures:
- Highly sophisticated application integrating all available UI components
- Integration of a Roomware environment
- Utilization of both UIDL and GDL
- Commercial quality multimedia and 3D rendering
- Complex game mechanics based on Dungeons & Dragons-like RPGs
- Capability of gradual transition between different degrees of virtuality
- Extensive summative evaluation

While the first two prototypes are regarded as proof-of-concept demonstrators in the strict meaning of the term (i.e. they show that the platform discussed in the previous chapters can actually be used for creating hybrid games), the second two prototypes go beyond the mere demonstration of technical feasibility and are also used for the evaluation of the entire conceptual framework of hybrid games. The respective conceptual evaluation is subject to the next chapter, while the technical proof-of-concept is presented already in this chapter.

6.1. SteinSchlag

SteinSchlag is a simple demonstrator that showcases the interplay between physical and virtual domains in a gaming application. It augments a traditional video game with the Gesture Based Interaction Device ("magic wand") and effectively realizes a hybrid gaming experience that links physical exertion with virtual effects (see Figure 48).

Figure 48. Linking physical exertion to virtual effects

SteinSchlag borrows its game mechanics from a classic video game called Boulder Dash that was extraordinary popular in the early 80ties and has consequently been revived in various modifications and graphical updates until today. The player controls a small avatar that explores and ransacks a cave filled with valuable diamonds. In addition to falling rocks that threaten to bury the avatar, there are also various adversaries that roam the cave and chase the player. Collecting a sufficient amount of diamonds within a certain amount of time triggers a victory condition and lets the player move on to the next stage.

Obviously, the game draws its appeal from the swift reactions of the players and their skilful mastery of the respective input devices, namely joysticks or gamepads. The rationale behind the development of the SteinSchlag demonstrator was to further add to the joyful interaction experience of the tried and tested Boulder Dash game mechanics by integrating a physical activity that is harder to master successfully than the control of a joystick or gamepad. As Garneau points out in his Gamasutra article (Garneau 2001) both the exertion of a physical activity and the application of an ability attribute to the enjoyment of gaming. Since pressing the respective button on a gamepad or moving a joystick is not per se challenging and does not represent an ability in itself, it is plausible to argue that the addition of a physical interaction device that needs to be trained in order to be optimally successful can increase the enjoyment of a gaming application, provided that the overall difficulty of the game does not increase to a degree that causes frustration.

Implementation

SteinSchlag was designed to be first and foremost a demonstrator for the Gesture Based Interaction Device in order to showcase how this controller alters the video gaming experience compared to a traditional game controller such as a joystick or game pad. It is, however, also based on the STARS platform and utilizes the PEGASUS subsystem to synchronize the involved software components. As shown in Figure 49 it runs on a single PC to which the Gesture Based Interaction Device or a traditional controller can be connected (as well as a loudspeaker for the audio output which comes down to playing respective wav files typical for simple arcade games). The game does not utilize any UI orchestration mechanisms

6. Proof-of-Concept: Sample Realizations

and not even complete UI components as discussed in the previous chapter, because these were not yet available when the SteinSchlag application was developed. Instead, the application itself is a monolithic Windows executable that subscribes to the input from the two input controllers' Device Wrappers and publishes its audio output in the respective data tree of the Audio Display.

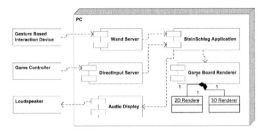

Figure 49. SteinSchlag components

The Game Board Renderer component visualizes the game map on which the avatar moves in order to collect the diamonds. It consists of two distinct renderers that share a single DirectDraw surface handle, so that it is possible to switch between them during the execution of the Game Board Renderer. The two graphical interfaces are shown in Figure 50. Both a tiled 2D view (left figure) is provided for devices with limited rendering capabilities such as legacy PC hardware or Windows CE clients; a 3D view (right figure) is provided for standard PCs.

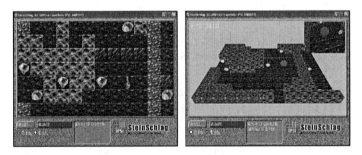

Figure 50. The SteinSchlag graphical user interface in 2D (left) and 3D (right)

The Wand Server and the DirectInput Server share the same subtree in PEGASUS, so that it is possible to use both as input for controlling the avatar concurrently. While the Wand Server is the standard interface for the Gesture Based Interaction Device, the DirectInput Server is a generic interface for any enumerated DirectInput devices. For SteinSchlag, a joystick or game pad would normally be used, but in other contexts other devices would also work, such as a button bar used in conjunction with a DirectInput Server in the consecutively presented "Search for the Amulet" prototype.

133

Interaction Design

The main aspect of the interaction design is the way how the Gesture Based Interaction Device is used. It makes use of two of its operating modes, namely gesture recognition and intensity measurement. Navigating the avatar through the cave is implemented in gesture recognition mode with simple strokes in the respective direction letting the avatar move one tile in that direction. By making a circle gesture the application switches to intensity measurement and the avatar consequently uses a "hammer" in order to remove mud (the player cannot walk through mud) from the game map. The harder the player performs a stroke, the more mud is removed from the game map in the direction the avatar is facing. A slight stroke results in one tile being switched from mud to a free space, a powerful stroke can include up to eight tiles. The issue and challenge for the player is to find the right balance for their strokes, as removing the right number of mud tiles can open otherwise blocked passages to diamonds the player wants to collect, but hitting too hard may remove too many fields and include removing diamonds from the map (which, of course, is of dubious plausibility as the diamond should be too hard for this operation). Once a stroke in intensity measurement mode was performed, the application automatically switches back to the gesture recognition mode in which the avatar is navigated over the map.

As hinted above, SteinSchlag can also be controlled via ordinary PC game controllers apart from the Gesture Based Interaction Device in order to allow for comparisons between the traditional interaction design with a joystick or game pad and the augmented physical interaction with the wand. Here, the navigation mode is realized by moving the controller in the respective direction (or pressing the respective buttons for a game pad instead of a joystick). The hammer operation is simply performed by pressing and holding the joystick button for a certain amount of time similar to the control of the classic video game "Leaderboard", in which the player controls a golf player.

Conclusion

SteinSchlag is a rather basic gaming application that serves the purpose of demonstrating the concept of the Gesture Based Interaction Device quite well by utilizing two of its three operating modes (the RFID pointing mode is not realized with SteinSchlag, but used in the "Caves & Creatures" prototype discussed later). It exploits PEGASUS to a limited degree, although there is a somewhat decoupled communication between the game and its input controllers. The dynamic switching of game board renderers is sound and solid, but our initial findings suggest that it does not contribute much to the actual entertainment experience, probably because both views are functional and neither is especially impressive. From a game play perspective both the augmented control with the wand and the traditional joystick control are sufficiently fun to play with the wand control itself being much harder to learn and master than the traditional control. There were no formal user studies conducted, but the general impression is that the operation with the wand provides a slightly more interesting experience as the interaction itself becomes more salient , complex and the mastery of the device seems to add the factor of exertion and skill to the gaming experience (in the sense of Garneau (2001)). This goes in line with the current success of similar controllers for the Nintendo Wii that also use accelerometers for interaction and have led to several successful gaming titles that are operated with specialized physical controllers such as fishing rods, poles or plastic swords.

6.2. Candyland

The second prototype is based on the concept of creating a hybrid gaming application utilizing tangible interfaces exclusively, so that no LCD screen would be necessary for playing, thus making the application especially appealing for children (or parents, respectively) as a smart toy.

Figure 51. Candyland: A tangible audio game.

Figure 51 shows the physical setup of the Candyland game. The style of the interaction objects (playing pieces and houses) indicates its dedication to children. Depending on the positions of the houses and the playing pieces, different audio samples are played that make up the conversations between Candyland's inhabitants and are damped by houses in a physically adequate way.

Children's Play Rationale

Children all over the world regard playing games as one of the most important activities they adhere to; this holds true for all ages, cultures, and circumstances. If asked why, most children would probably answer that playing is just fun to them. But many psychologists claim playing to be an essential tool for cognitive, social, and emotional development with well-proven benefits for problem solving and tool use (Bruner, 1972), language and thinking (Vygoysky, 1967), self-concept, and personal adjustment (Erikson, 1950). Piaget, a pioneer of child psychology, saw that pretend play was a special element of children's play. He recognized that it promotes children's social, emotional, and intellectual development. Pretense has been viewed as partially responsible for the development of a plethora of skills including symbolic representation, creative and flexible thinking, and self-confidence (Singer, 1973). Additionally it was found that individual differences in the variety and frequency of fantasy play are associated with richer and more complex language skills (Olszewski, 1987), enhanced creativity and imagination (Connolly and Doyle, 1984), and the ability to interact successfully with other children.

Nowadays, technology can influence children's play. Integrating computing devices in children's games gives us the opportunity to create unique experiences that ideally stimulate imaginations and foster creativity and curiosity. However, many parents feel insecure about the effects of computer and video games, as they fear a possible negative impact on their children. Indeed, several violent crimes, including murder, are discussed to be connected with video games that the teenage culprits played excessively (e.g. the Littleton, 1999, or Erfurt, 2002, high school killings). Parents, teachers, and psychologists argue that violent video games offer attractive models for violent behavior. Bandura (1989) shows that children not only learn by acting themselves, but also by observing others, so called "models". If children observe dubious actions to be rewarded in computer games, they learn these actions to be attractive for them.

But even with games that are clearly not violent, parents may feel uneasy about their children playing video games. Especially for younger children, the virtual domain lacks the interaction with real, tangible objects that they can manipulate in a direct way. Direct manipulation implies being free to use the game artifacts in any desired way (e.g. for pretend play) and not being forced to stick to any pre-defined game rules. For instance, a child may take physical playing pieces off a game board and take them out into the car to play a pretend game on a trip with his parents, thus allowing for creative play by being completely free in his ways to interact with the game media.

Additionally, playing video games implies human-computer-human interaction and communication styles. However, playing with real game artifacts is more human centered, because it fosters a direct interaction between children either out of game roles that are projected onto the playing pieces (such as being a king and a princess or mother and child) or in the verbal creation of stories and worlds they play in.

Implementation

A primary concern of the demonstrator is to let interaction and communication take part between the human players, but provide additional benefits through the addition of a virtual dimension. Virtual elements include a simple storytelling functionality that is conveyed through a 2D audio engine that takes the positions of obstacles such as houses into account and a dice cup integration that communicates how far the player should move around. In order to preserve the toy-like interaction the movement range has, however, no further effect. This means that the user free to move the pieces in any way he likes without any punitive game rules being taken into effect.

The hardware of the game consists of a tangible game board which can be covered with various physical game maps and physical playing pieces. An RFID based sensor interface integrated in the game board synchronizes the positions of the physical game objects over the PEGASUS subsystem with the game application itself. While the manipulation of the physical playing pieces makes up the primary input technique for the system, a 2-D audio output is used for conveying information back to the players. This combination ensures an unobtrusive interface in the spirit of the Disappearing Computer paradigm that suits children's interaction and playing styles.

From a system architecture perspective, Candyland follows a similar approach as SteinSchlag. The deployment is shown in Figure 52. Again, it runs on a single PC to which a tangible game board and the Smart Dice Cup can be connected together with loud speakers for the audio output. The audio display is based on OpenAL (www.openal.org) to allow for 2D audio. Just like SteinSchlag, the application itself is a monolithic Windows executable that subscribes to the input from the game board's input controller's Device Wrapper and publishes its audio output in the respective data tree of the Audio Display.

6. Proof-of-Concept: Sample Realizations

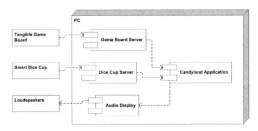

Figure 52. Candyland components

In principle, it would be possible to operate the game with multiple game boards, although this has not been realized due to the rather high effort of creating custom-made playing pieces and houses as appropriate interfaces for children.

Game Mechanics

Candyland represents a small fantasy village inhabited with several imaginative fantasy characters (the Candymaster, Pop & Corn, the Parrot, etc) which, together with the friendly and colorful design of the game map and objects, makes it especially suited for children. The aim of the Candyland village from a gaming perspective is twofold: First, it is an adventure platform that allows children to explore the secrets of the village and its inhabitants. Second, it is meant to help realizing real-world laws of auditive and visual perception (as a justification more geared towards parents).

As an adventure platform, Candyland runs a simple adventure/ storytelling game engine that talks to the children (i.e. plays digitized sound samples) depending on their movements of the playing pieces. For instance, a demo adventure involves saving an important ceremony in the village. To do that, the player has to find out what happened to one of the creatures who strangely disappeared from the village. To solve the mystery, the player must walk along the game map listening to what the inhabitants say or the actions they perform. The inhabitants keep talking to themselves, to each other, or to the child, if she places her playing piece next to an inhabitant. The voices of the inhabitants radiate over several fields on the game board and get louder the nearer the child's playing piece approaches them. Often, this makes it rather difficult to listen to a specific person, if other characters are nearby. There are also houses in which the inhabitants live. They block the sounds the characters emit. The child therefore needs to choose the path of her playing piece on the game board carefully to gather clues and progress with the game.

Each of the characters in Candyland is designed with a strong and distinct personality that is invariant between different adventures. For instance, the grandmother is a friendly and caring character that has accumulated heaps of wisdom during a long live and is thus always good to visit when seeking advice. The child character Torty loves her, but the Candymaster is usually too busy to interact with her intensively. The reasons for providing almost stereotypical characters and relationships between them are to foster both Banduras's learning by observing models and pretend play sensu Piaget. The playing pieces afford being taken from the game board and used just like unaugmented action figures such as Masters of the Universe or Ninja Turtles. This allows for a smooth transition between free and creative forms of play like pretend play and more goal directed play within an adventure at the game board. Both complementary ways of interacting with Candyland can be alternated at any time.

The second goal of Candyland is to provide a model for audio and visual perception suitable for children. Physical laws apply to Candyland in that the speech of its inhabitants is spatially correctly conveyed through a surround sound system depending on their positions. Both line-of-sight and radiation-of-sound algorithms to deal with blocking elements such as houses are available. The children are encouraged to experiment with placing buildings and inhabitants freely on the board and listen to the effects of their spatial manipulations, so that they hopefully develop a sense of physical laws through the exertion of voluntary playful activities.

Conclusion

The Candyland prototype aims at providing a storytelling platform specifically geared towards children. As such, it is not unique, but embedded in related research projects. The "Breakfast in the Coloured Farm" game (Kanjo et al. 2002) shares a similar vision as Candyland. Playing pieces are moved on a game board with sound and vision being provided on a PC monitor. Game elements are recognized through a set of three cameras. While Candyland provides a more robust and affordable hardware setup, Coloured Farm uses a more advanced, but instable link between virtual and physical worlds. ActiMates Barney™ (Strommen 1999) is an animated plush doll that can interact with PC-based software using an internal radio receiver. It has four touch sensors and a light sensor with motors enabling the movement of his arms and head. Additionally, a loudspeaker emits voice samples. The doll is used as a toy providing small games (like singing a song together) as well as a for learning applications, where he gives hints and instructions. Barney is a single player toy with limited interaction abilities, as the interaction is based on touching specific parts of the toy. Nonetheless, it resembles Candyland's approach of providing a toy system that has some interactive features instead of a game with strict and static rules that are enforced by the application.

While both systems include the use of a PC screen, this is not the case for Candyland. As Fontijn and Mendels (2005) demonstrate with their StoryToy storytelling environment graphical displays are not necessary for enjoyable child play. Like Candyland, StoryToy uses an audio replay engine in conjunction with a tactile user interface based on a sensor network. The tactile interface consists of an animal farm with a multitude of animals as actors. Also, no computer display is necessary to enjoy the various stories and games that come with the animal farm. The authors conducted a study to test the toy on children between the ages of two to six. The study demonstrated that audio feedback alone already creates an enjoyable level of interactivity, in addition to the traditional free play that the toy provides. Given the reluctance of many parents to expose their young children to computer displays, it appears to be a promising approach to use unobtrusive audio signals as a primary interface instead of traditional interaction with graphical user interfaces. This finding from StoryToy also serves as a justification for the corresponding design decision in Candyland.

From a technical perspective, the Candyland prototype is at a similar level as the SteinSchlag application in exploiting the STARS platform. While PEGASUS is used for inter-component communication, no further features such as dedicated game board renderers are showcased in Candyland, although both an augmented game board and the Smart Dice Cup are utilized. Compared to the integration of these custom tangible interface components in SteinSchlag only the game board plays an equally central role, as the Smart Dice Cup has a more peripheral role for the gaming experience.

6.3. Search for the Amulet

"Search for the Amulet" is a research prototype of a complete hybrid game that uses the STARS software platform and a combination of dedicated interaction devices to both evaluate the appropriateness of the STARS platform and to explore hybrid gaming concepts such as multimodal stimulation or the distribution of game elements along virtual, social, and physical domains.

Figure 53. Search for the Amulet

The prototype is aimed at providing a simple, yet challenging game that average visitors in an open house or exhibition situation could grasp immediately. Consequently, it was shown at several public occasions on which it was also evaluated using a questionnaire. The setup is shown in Figure 53. The game play revolves around several players moving over a map and searching for items that can be traded between players. Different events aggravate this task and virtual characters try to play off the human players against each other.

Implementation

In contrast to the previous prototypes, the Amulet game is deployed on two standard Windows PCs, a server and a client. The server PC holds the central game application that implements the game logic and integrates the physical interaction devices via dedicated device servers, including a tangible game board as well as a lamp and a fan for multimodal stimulation. The public display process that performs the graphical output that is shared among the players also resides on the server. The client GUI applications are deployed on a respective client PC. In the first version of the game demonstrator, the private displays were attached to physical button bars that realized user input to the private displays. This allowed for a more direct interaction than using mice, since it effectively eliminates the layer of indirection that mice / GUI interaction imposes. The second version of the game included touch sensitive displays for the private GUI clients that allowed users to directly touch the respective areas on the screens, thus eliminating the need for the physical button bars and their software servers.

The distinction between a server PC and a client PC is somewhat artificial, the actual reason for using two devices comes down to obtaining a sufficient number of USB ports and graphics cards as well as to demonstrate the distributed nature of the PEGASUS subsystem. Consequently, depending on the number of players that participate in a game session, the software components on the client PC might also be run on the server PC. The deployment is illustrated in Figure 54.

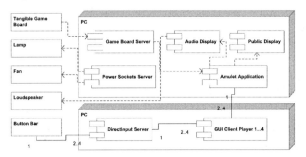

Figure 54. Amulet components

Since each player requires her own private display, the issue of graphic boards available determines if a dedicated client PC is necessary or not. A two player game can run on a single machine, since three graphical displays (one public and two private displays) can easily be connected to a single PC with appropriate graphics card(s).

Amulet is also the first prototype that utilizes UIDL definitions for modeling the graphical user interfaces. In Figure 56 it can be seen quite well that the screen is composed of various graphical elements. The utilization of UIDL allows for replacing the private monitors connected to a PC with using the displays of arbitrary mobile devices such as PDAs or mobile phones. The private GUI clients in Amulet have been tested to work with Windows Mobile PDAs as well with minimal effort of adjusting the graphical layout (as the stationary displays feature twice the resolution of the PDAs, i.e. QVGA vs. VGA). Due to the intended target audience of Amulet at public exhibitions mobile devices were ultimately decided not be used in order to prevent theft, thus going for the deployment on two PCs.

Game Design

There were four fundamental design goals formulated that informed the detailed design of the game application. These goals relate to several aspects of the hybrid games conceptual model and are considered in the evaluation of the game that is presented in the next chapter. The design goals were:

1. Supporting the Social Domain

The application should realize the premier property of a hybrid game, namely to support the richness of human interaction as e.g. in many traditional tabletop games. The interaction should first and foremost take place directly between the human players and not be moderated by computer displays and other devices alone.

2. Representation and Control

To achieve the goal of supporting the social domain, the interaction with the virtual parts of the game should be based on interfaces that unify representation and control (Ullmer & Ishii 2000), thus reducing mental load and leaving more capacities for the social domain. The game should consequently be controlled via tangible user interfaces and keep the interaction with standard graphical interfaces at a minimal level.

3. Multimodal Stimulation

To facilitate a quick immersion into the game world, the game should utilize multiple modalities for input and output. Apart from the immersive aspect, multimodal stimulation should also attribute to supporting the social domain by allowing for peripheral reception of game information in contrast to active interaction with a graphical user interface.

4. Effective Use of the Virtual Domain

A virtual game instance should be able to communicate with individual players and influence the flow of the game effectively by conveying private and public game information to the players. For instance, it should communicate or hold back private information depending on the success of the player compared to other players. By doing this, advantages and disadvantages of individual players could be equalized within certain bounds to help keeping the game challenging.

Detailed Game Mechanics

The game is played by two to four players that take turns by moving tangible playing pieces over a physical game board. To address design goal #2 (representation and control), the interaction in the game focuses on this physical game board on which a map of 8 * 8 fields is shown. The map is divided into different areas such as mountains, forests, hills, or deserts. The board has integrated RFID antennas that sense the positions and identities of smart playing pieces which are equipped with corresponding RFID tags. Consequently, the game board links virtual and physical domains by permanently updating a virtual representation of the map with the state of the physical pieces.

The players move their playing pieces over the map to search for shards of broken amulets and other items hidden on the map. Each playing piece has unique advantages and disadvantages to the other pieces. For instance, one piece ("Betty Bärenstark") can carry an increased amount of items due to her strength, while another character is very good at trading items and a third ("Gisela Glückspilz") is blessed with being lucky, which is taken into account by the virtual game logic e.g. with random events (see Figure 55). When applicable, these individual features of the characters are also reflected in their physical representations, so that e.g. a strong character is represented by a heavy playing piece.

Figure 55. Characters of the Amulet demonstrator

Once a player collects all the shards of a single amulet, she wins. Several events and also virtual characters aggravate this endeavor. For instance, a wicked kobold moves around the virtual representation of the game board and talks to the players from time to time, e.g. telling one player what items the other player has collected so far or stealing items from one player and selling them to the other. The concrete actions a computer controlled virtual character takes is influenced by the individual scores of the players, so that the virtual domain attributes to keeping the game challenging even for advantageous players (cf. design goal #4). The game events are communicated to the players either via public or private displays. There is a large public display to present game relevant public information to the players. The public display for instance shows which player currently takes her turn and how many moves she is allowed to make during this turn. Furthermore, the public display is used for showing the global state of the game, e.g. it shows information about the current weather conditions on the game board (the weather influences several factors in the game, such as the range of moves a player can make during a turn or the probability of certain events such as being stuck in the mud during rainfall).

Complementary to the large public display, each player also has a small display (see Figure 56) that shows private information the other player is not allowed to perceive, such as the content of her bag or the effects of private events (meeting with virtual non-player characters, being caught in a trap, etc). Both types of displays naturally show graphical user interfaces that might interfere with the goal of stimulating interaction between human players than between humans and computers. Therefore, great care was taken to minimize the intrusive effects of the graphical displays by showing only the minimal amount of information necessary, by not using mice or other indirect interaction devices to interact with the GUIs, and by also conveying information on other additional channels when applicable as described in the next paragraph.

Figure 56. Private Amulet display

To underline the interplay between physical and virtual world, the game board is not the only interface that realizes the flow of information from the physical to the virtual domain. The virtual domain also possesses interfaces through which virtual parameters are transported back to the physical world. For instance, as the current weather is a central game element that influences the players' movement and the probability of certain game events, it is also represented in the physical domain to add to the perceived immersion among the players. Apart from displaying the respective information on the public display, the game application can also alter physical light, wind, and sound from the virtual domain to achieve a multimodal stimulation (cf. design goal #3). It is not uncommon for a computer program to feature acoustic channels to the physical domain of its users, nevertheless, the acoustic representation of game information (e.g. birds singing when the weather is good or rolling thunder when a thunderstorm is coming up) is an effective means of immersive stimulation that reaches out from the virtual to the physical domain.

The game additionally integrates a lamp and a fan as physical output devices that are connected via network controlled power sockets. During sunny weather, the lamp shines directly on the game board, whereas windy weather in the virtual world starts up the fan and thereby creates real wind in the physical domain. Thus, the weather conditions are stimulative on multiple sensual modalities and effectively reduce GUI interaction time by conveying relevant information in an ambient, unobtrusive matter.

To ensure the game play to profit by the provision of direct face-to-face interaction between the players, trading items between the players is a central element of the game, since one player might have found an item the opponent is in need of and vice versa. It requires a great deal of negotiation and pretence skills to convince the other player to give away her shards without arousing suspicion that exactly these shards might mean sudden victory for the opponent. Such a *Poker*-like game element can only work effectively in a real face-to-face interaction situation (cf. design goal #1), because in computer mediated communication the necessary contextual clues are not transmitted equally resulting in a less rich communication channel (Barkhi et al. 1999).

Regarding design goal #4, the primary role of the virtual domain is not to mediate communication between the players, but to distribute private information from the virtual game logic to the individual players in order to regulate the flow of the game. This was realized with virtual characters that wander over the game board and occasionally appear on the private displays of the players to interact with them depending on the current state of the game. Accordingly, they might offer helping to find items, hinting about the items of the opponents or even steal from the players (and later approach the opponents to sell them the stolen items).

Conclusion

The technical contributions of the Amulet game are not the central aspect of the demonstrator. The game is indeed more complex than the previously discussed prototypes, it is distributed among different machines, it integrates more physical interaction devices than the previous demonstrators and it introduces the application of UIDL to allow for rapid tweaking of the user interfaces and adaptation to different display sizes and mobile device types (although this was not part of the deployment with public test users). However, these are only incremental improvements.

The actual contribution of the Amulet demonstrator is the game design that seeks to translate central aspects of the hybrid games conceptual model into a working game application and thus open up opportunities for a first evaluation of the model. The appropriate use of the virtual, social, and physical domains, the integration of tangible user interfaces and the multimodal stimulation were formulated as concrete design goals that were accordingly implemented in the detailed game mechanics.

As the game is geared towards short playing durations, observations and test sessions are relatively inexpensive to conduct. Accordingly, the user experiences could be evaluated for multiple subjects on several occasions, when the demonstrator was exhibited on public events such as an open house day or a scientific symposium. A respective questionnaire was created for the game which is covered in the next chapter.

6.4. Caves & Creatures

To demonstrate and explore the benefits of flexibly integrating various interaction devices to a complex hybrid gaming application, a "Dungeons & Dragons" style tabletop role playing game called "Caves & Creatures" was developed. This type of game was chosen, because it offers the chance to implement it with varying degrees of pervasiveness. The spectrum ranges from a traditional tabletop role playing game without any computer support at all to a purely virtual computer game that utilizes standard graphical user interfaces, mice and keyboards exclusively. In-between these extremes, it is possible to replace traditional or GUI components, respectively, with tangible user interfaces that retain the interaction metaphors known from the real world (e.g. shaking dice, using a magic wand), but that establish the link to the virtual domain by being unobtrusively augmented with sentient information technology. The "Caves & Creatures" prototype is so far the most elaborated hybrid game based on the STARS platform. It utilizes practically all tangible user interfaces discussed beforehand and also makes use of all software features of the STARS platform. It has also been deployed to a Roomware environment in order to make use of the available ambient displays for effective multimodal stimulation. Figure 57 (left) shows a frame from a TV documentary that featured the game in action, while Figure 57 (right) illustrates several game components such as two game board renderers, virtual dice, a game logger etc. running on a client PC.

Figure 57. Caves & Creatures

As can be seen on the figure, interfaces used by the game include smart playing cards, game pieces and a game board, bracelets, a dice cup, a magic wand, personal devices such as PDAs as well as large public displays and a lamp for ambient illumination. The utilized devices serve purposes appropriate for tabletop role playing games, such as, for instance, the game integrates RFID augmented playing cards that represent items, weapons, armor, spells to be found, worn, used, cast, and traded between players. The physical game board with RFID augmented pieces can be used for positioning and moving game characters. The smart dice cup implements the rolling of dice and gestures performed with a magic wand determine the success of magic spells, etc.

As each function in the game can be substituted by several software components that relate to different interaction metaphors and different emphases on virtual or physical aspects, the game makes up an appropriate test bed for evaluating the concept of hybrid games as such. For instance, as it is technically irrelevant, if a physical game board as in Figure 57 (left), a 3D rendered display of the board (Figure 57 right, top left area), or a simple 2D GUI control

6. Proof-of-Concept: Sample Realizations

(Figure 57 right, bottom right area) is used to control the movements of the pieces, it is possible to play the game with only virtual UI components, with physical interaction devices, or with a combination of both. Likewise, it is technically indifferent, whether the game is played co-located like a traditional tabletop or board game, or whether the individual players (and their respective user interface components) are distributed and connected via the internet. This potential for evaluating the same game with different configurations and deployments will be further elaborated in the next chapter.

Implementation

Caves & Creatures is implemented in a similar fashion as the previous Amulet prototype using the STARS platform, but realizes a full exploitation of the platform by not only using the UIDL for defining user interfaces (an example of a Caves & Creatures GUI definition was already given in chapter 5), but also the entire game definition and game rules are defined using the Game Definition Language GDL, so that the potential of decoupling game definitions from concrete physical setups could finally be realized.

The game has been deployed in different configurations, partly utilizing Roomware interfaces such as the DynaWall for public or ambient information and the InteracTable as a tangible game board using optical camera recognition. As the game was showcased on several external events, a lean and rather mobile deployment configuration is shown in Figure 58 that does not utilize a Roomware infrastructure.

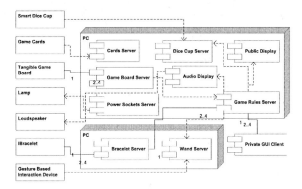

Figure 58. Caves & Creatures components

As the figure shows, the game integrates most of the components already introduced for the previous prototypes demonstrating that components are actually re-usable between different gaming applications. In contrast to the previous prototypes, Caves & Creatures features multiple game board renderers that provide nearly commercial quality multimedia and 3D graphics, so that an evaluation of the user experience would not be confounded by the players' expectations towards off-the-shelf video games.

For technical testing purposes, the game has also been distributed between two sites with corresponding synchronized public displays and game boards, which, however, was not exploited from a game play perspective, as the game design supports mostly face-to-face interaction and does not translate well to sending text messages or other means of narrow communication channels.

Game Design

Caves & Creatures is designed as a traditional turn-based tabletop miniatures/ roleplaying game. That means, players take turns and move their playing pieces over a game board in order to collect items, weapons, armor, treasures, etc. and use these items along with the specific skills that their characters possess in order to fight against other characters (see Figure 59, please note the RFID tags in the bases of the miniatures). Success in battle leads to character advancement and an improvement of skills. Another central element of these types of games relates to interactive storytelling. Groups of players wander around in an adventure setting and jointly advance the plot by solving riddles and engaging in the interactive storytelling situations. In order to immerse into the storytelling scenario it is crucial to create an appropriate atmosphere that commonly takes some time in order to get into.

Figure 59. Caves & Creatures playing pieces

For that reason, the storytelling aspect of the game is deliberately neglected in favor of shorter game sessions where the players' aim is not to advance a story together, but to engage in battles and slay as many other characters as possible. This focus on a 'skirmish' operation allows for evaluating the game with a within-subjects design, i.e. players can replay the game several times with certain variations in the independent variables and without the danger of strong confounding factors related to different interactive story progressions that might interfere with their appreciation of other factors.

The game design as such is very open and the game rules defined in the virtual domain only relate to the effects that different game objects have among each other depending on the actions performed on them. Typical rules define how combat situations take place, how many moves a character might make in a given turn, how flanking effects apply (i.e. when multiple characters jointly attack a target and receive respective bonuses), what effect magic spells and potions have, etc. No rules are prescribed regarding higher level processes and the actual interaction between players. That means that e.g. coalitions or alliances between players, trading of items or gear, negotiations etc. are all agreed upon in the social domain and are subject to change by social protocols exclusively.

While the overall game mechanics are flexible due to being negotiated in the social domain (it would, for instance, be easily possible to focus on storytelling and adventure elements using a

6. Proof-of-Concept: Sample Realizations

human game master instead of purely skirmish play), the concrete set of basic game rules regarding combat, gear and skills that is defined in the virtual domain can correspondingly be adapted during a game session allowing for house rules and rule variations. This is achieved by utilizing the Game Definition Language GDL for the entire game definition.

Game Rules

The general principle of the Caves & Creatures rule definitions have already been discussed in the previous chapter within the GDL section, for instance how items are consumed and how self-modification is used for easily modeling the depletion and consumption of spells, potions, etc. While the entire rules can be found in the annex, some aspects are exemplarily shown here.

In order to provide for a very simple user interaction, the primary controls and "main loop" of the game revolve around the notion of tapping a figure on the game board (either physically with a real miniature or by clicking the mouse on the respective field in a GUI component). As can be seen in the following GDL snippet, tapping an enemy miniature triggers a fight, if the target is a "legal target", whereas double tapping one's own miniature ends one's active turn.

```
<TAP action='(TTARG)[IF (LEGALTARGET)(FIGHT)(TEXT PUBLIC
&quot;Not a legal target&quot;)]' />
<TTARG action="(SOUND PUBLIC battle\tap.wav)(TAPTARG)" />
<TAPTAP action="(SOUND PUBLIC battle\taptap.wav)(ONENDTURN)" />
```

Both the TEXT and SOUND commands have a PUBLIC target, which can be any public output device depending on the current UI orchestration. The difference between both commands is simply whether a sound file is to be played or a text to be printed and/ or read to the players. Ending a player's active turn translates to:

```
<ONENDTURN action="(CANVAS/HIDESCROLL TURN)(SETLIGHT
0)(ENDTURN)" />
```

which means that the respective canvas on the private interaction device is hidden, so that the more sophisticated commands such as equipping a character, drinking a potion, casting a spell, etc. simply become unavailable to the player and do not require any special handling from the game rules. For instance, un-arming a weapon via

```
<UNARMWEAPON action="(UPDATE TURN weapon)(UPDATE WEAPONID
used)(DO (WEAPONID my_unuse))" arg0="WEAPONID" />
```

is valid for any player at any time, although only the currently active player is actually able to trigger that command due to the modification to the private user interface.

The game also allows for more complex rules such as flanking effects that are evaluated during combat. Flanking means that if two attackers from the same team both stand next to the potential target, they receive a bonus for jointly attacking. As can be seen from the following snippet, this is checked by evaluating if both figures are within a square around the target figure and then updating their status accordingly.

```
   <FLANK arg0="TRG" action="(IF (EQ (TRG team) 1)
(INSQUARE (TRG xLoc) (TRG yLoc) FLANK1)
(INSQUARE (TRG xLoc) (TRG yLoc) FLANK0))" />
     <FLANK1 arg0="X" arg1="Y" action="(UPDATEB+ X Y flankers1 1)" />
     <FLANK0 arg0="X" arg1="Y" action="(UPDATEB+ X Y flankers0 1)" />
```

INSQUARE simply evaluates all eight fields around the figure as can be seen from the next snippet.

```
     <INSQUARE arg0="X" arg1="Y" arg2="STR" action="(STR   (+ X
1) (+ Y 1)) (STR   (+ X 1) (- Y 1))(STR   (- X 1) (+ Y 1))(STR
(- X 1) (- Y 1))(STR   (+ X 1) (+ Y 0))(STR   (- X 1) (+ Y
0))(STR   (+ X 0) (+ Y 1))(STR   (+ X 0) (- Y 1))" />
```

The last two snippets also demonstrate implementation limitations of these constructs in GDL as for instance the global variables flankers0 and flankers1 allow for only two flanking participants. Implementing three flankers would result in more code to be written and allowing for different flankers per team is not possible at all (due to the turn-based interaction style, the latter is not a problem, as only one player is active at a time). Likewise, the implementation of INSQUARE is ineffective, especially considering what it would take to increase the radius from one to two fields. However, the point here is that both implementations should not matter to the average "end user programmer" as tweaking and adapting game rules can be expected to take place at a higher level of abstraction, That means, although it is technically possible to change what a flanking condition means or how being adjacent to another figure is defined, the average user should make use of these constructs instead of altering them. This is somehow similar to the capability of operator overloading in languages such as C++, where the average programmer and user of a class library is normally not concerned with actively utilizing this language feature, but benefit from the clarity provided by someone else having used that feature to facilitate writing (end user) code.

Outlook

In this section, the Caves & Creatures prototype was discussed on a platform and implementation level without providing insights on gameplay issues and how the game was perceived by actual players. Technically, the game is rather sophisticated and integrates all available UI components of the STARS platform as well as the GDL and UIDL domain specific languages. It also features quite complex game mechanics based on a Dungeons & Dragons –like miniatures roleplaying game.

What is more important about Caves & Creatures, however, is the opportunity to play the game with different degrees of "virtuality", as the game rules also allow for playing it without any kind of IT support (which is what pen&paper roleplaying gamers have been doing since the 1970s) or with a gradual transition from traditional physical to virtual elements. This interplay of domains is subject to the extensive summative evaluation that is discussed in the next and final chapter.

6.5. Conclusions

This chapter presented four proof-of-concept prototypes of hybrid games that are based on the STARS platform and utilize different aspects of the platform. The main purpose of this chapter was to illustrate that the platform has indeed been used for the development of hybrid games and thus contributes to demonstrating the internal validity of the platform.

Naturally, the advancement of the platform went on in parallel to the development of the presented prototypes. As these were discussed in the chronological order of their realization, it not only becomes clear by going through this chapter that the complexity of the demonstrators increased with the number of features available in the platform, but also how requirements from the demonstrators led to the advancement of certain features in the platform, or were integrated into the platform, respectively. For instance, for the SteinSchlag prototype that was realized only after finishing the first iteration of the PEGASUS subsystem, the main technical issues were related to actually creating components that PEGASUS could be used with, so that the game itself was not much more than a magic wand server component and two game board renderers that directly made it into the platform's component library. For the second game, Candyland, the components available were still very few, so that game board and dice cup components were created and consequently added to the platform. Additionally, the hard-coded narration and storytelling elements were found to be so cumbersome to work with that the need for scripting functionality became apparent. This was later realized with the GDL and UIDL domain specific languages that became part of the platform.

The Amulet and Caves & Creatures games marked a qualitative leap from the previous two prototypes as they were developed when much of the platform's foundation was already available, so that their primary purpose was not on building and advancing the platform itself, but on using the platform to create games that realize the conceptual hybrid games model. While both games still contributed to the platform significantly, as for instance each prototype development went together with the creation of one domain specific language, the focus and motivation stemmed however from game design issues. Technically, Amulet actually provided the most comprehensive additions to the platform, because not only the ambient light adapters and the UIDL were created, but the entire JAVA port of PEGASUS was developed for Amulet, so that arbitrary mobile devices using MIDlets could be integrated with the platform. Caves & Creatures, although the most sophisticated demonstrator so far realized, contributed less to the platform with only the GDL (that finally allowed for game rules to be completely dynamic) providing a significant improvement over previous versions of STARS. Otherwise, Caves & Creatures mainly improved on the quality of the rendering and artwork in order to provide some comparison to commercial video games. It is also the single prototype that brings together most of the features conceived for previous prototypes, so that it also demonstrates the proof-of-concept that STARS consists of re-usable components that *are* actually re-used.

While the internal validity of the platform has been shown with the prototypes presented in this chapter, the external validity will be demonstrated using two of the prototypes in the next and final chapter. In this respect, the next chapter will close the loop from the formative evaluation that motivated why it is worthwhile to start developing the STARS platform and hybrid games at all, over the realization of the platform and its software and hardware components, the proof-of-concept prototypes presented here, to finally using parts of these prototypes to conduct a final summative evaluation.

7. Summative Evaluation

As pointed out in the first chapter, this dissertation is structured around the central thesis that it is essential to provide hybrid gaming applications with the capability of dynamically integrating and flexibly administrating different user interface devices, because of the potential heterogeneity of end user interaction device setups. In order to evaluate and discuss this thesis, three different methods are applied that form a hierarchy with respect to their explicative power.

The first method deals with the *technical foundation*. As a precondition to actually having potential end users for hybrid games that in turn have heterogeneous device setups, it must be ensured that there is a hybrid games platform that is capable of providing respective applications. While the necessary hardware and software components have been discussed in chapter 4 and 5, the actual proof that this technical foundation is capable of providing games with different user interface devices was provided in the previous chapter. That means, by showing that several games were actually created and tested with the platform, the internal validity of the technical foundation was shown.

The next evaluative step relates to an *understanding* and appreciation of the target domain by the end users. If the technical foundation is available (as shown in the last chapter), the next condition for evaluating the thesis is that the concept of hybrid games is understood and appreciated by the end users, so that the external validity is ensured. This means that if hybrid games had no external relevance, it simply would not matter if there were differences in end user setups or interaction preferences. By letting end users interact with a hybrid game and utilizing a questionnaire in order to find out about their understanding and appreciation of several game aspects and concepts, it can be shown if the domain is relevant or not. The findings from testing the Amulet demonstrator with a questionnaire at two different public occasions are consequently reported in the next section.

Finally, a controlled experimental evaluation utilizing a within-subjects design is provided for the Caves & Creatures prototype regarding *alternative interaction device setups*. Here, the single same game was played by the same test users with very different setups of interaction devices. In particular, three different experimental conditions, namely playing the game without any virtual components as a traditional tabletop game vs. using the same game with only traditional graphical user interfaces in a way computer games are commonly played vs. a typical hybrid games setup that utilizes a set of the novel interaction devices provided by the platform. The results clearly show that the same game profits both by the hybrid games configuration and the capability of exchanging device setups which indicates that it is advantageous for a computer games platform to be capable of dynamically adding and integrating dedicated user interface devices.

7.1. Search for the Amulet

As "Search for the Amulet" was the first hybrid gaming prototype built with the STARS platform that actually related to the hybrid games conceptual model, it was essential to present the demonstrator to potential end users in order to receive meaningful feedback about the application itself and also to deduct indications whether the concept of hybrid games as such was worth pursuing further. As the demonstrator specifically implemented and addressed several aspects of the hybrid games model, the evaluation strategy included as a first step making sure that these aspects were addressed correctly and perceived by the end users as

7. Summative Evaluation

such. As a second step, provided that the demonstrator implemented the hybrid games model appropriately, the appreciation and interest among the end users was evaluated in order to decide on abandoning or modifying the concept or developing it further.

As discussed in the previous chapter, there were four design goals of the game that related to an implementation of the hybrid games model:

- Supporting the Social Domain (The interaction should first and foremost take place directly between the human players and not be moderated by computer displays and other devices alone.)

- Representation and Control (The game should implement tangible user interfaces and keep the interaction with standard graphical interfaces at a minimal level.)

- Multimodal Stimulation (The game should utilize multiple modalities for input and output to allow for a peripheral reception of game information in contrast to active interaction with a graphical user interface.)

- Effective Use of the Virtual Domain (A virtual game instance should be able to communicate with individual players and influence the flow of the game effectively by conveying private and public game information to the players.)

If these goals were adequately realized, no other deficiencies in technology or game design were identified by the end users, and they appreciated the game, then the evaluation would be considered successful and, consequently, the development of further hybrid games demonstrators would be justified.

Method

For the evaluation, "Search for the Amulet" was presented to the public on two occasions after the development of the first prototypical version. Since the game was initially planned for open house and exhibition situations, an average game session lasts about 30 minutes. This length allows for comfortable observations during a session and still leaves sufficient time to hand out respective questionnaires that were filled out by the players after the game sessions. Using a questionnaire allowed for a quantitative analysis of the respective items. The questionnaire is presented in the forthcoming section on the procedure.

Figure 60. Search for the Amulet version 1 (left) and 2 (right)

151

7. Summative Evaluation

The game was first publicly presented at an Open House Day at Fraunhofer IPSI (see Figure 60 left). A revised version with a slightly different and improved hardware setup was later presented for several days at the Comp21 symposium during the 150 years anniversary of the ETH Zürich (http://www.comp21.ethz.ch/). This second Amulet setup is shown in Figure 60 on the right.

Subjects

On both occasions, players were recruited from visitors to the respective events. The first sample consisted of 23 subjects randomly recruited from the open house day visitors at IPSI, 19 of them were male, four were female. The average age was 18 years. These subjects came from a larger sample of 28 players with 5 of these not returning the questionnaires at all or with too many missing items.

The second sample consisted of 21 subjects randomly recruited from the Comp21 event, 20 of them were male, one was female. The average age was 27 years. Here, the original sample was 24 players with three players not returning or filling out the questionnaires.

Apparatus

On both occasions, the deployment largely represented the description from the previous chapter. The most important difference related to the first version using ordinary, non touch sensitive private displays and button bars assembled beneath the private displays in order to trigger interactions. The second, improved version utilized smaller touch sensitive displays that allowed for a direct interaction with the controls displayed on the screens and thus eliminated the need for the additional physical button bars. In addition to that, the second version also included a few modifications to the game events, mostly increasing the number of items so that the trading game element would play a more significant role.

Procedure

As both parts of the evaluation took place in open exhibition style situations, the procedure came down to the investigator standing next to the demonstrator and inviting potential players that walked by to join in a short game session and to fill out the questionnaire after the game ended. The open house event had potential subjects mostly appear in groups of several visitors which made the recruitment process straightforward. At the comp21 event, however, most potential subjects arrived alone which aggravated the task of finding a second player, before the first would wander off to the next exhibit. This resulted in recruiting less subjects, although both the number of available subjects was bigger due to the bigger size of the event and the recruitment time was also longer with two full days compared to half a day at the open house event.

After the recruitment phase the game would start with a brief introduction of the core game mechanics. As the game rules and events were rather complex in relation to an exhibition situation, the investigator would continue explaining the interaction and game rules during the first turns that the players took in order to make sure that the goals were understood. This tutorial phase usually lasted no longer than five minutes, so that the game would go on for about 20-25 minutes on average, before one of the players was victorious. In about 20% of the cases, subjects asked for playing a second game which we did not encourage, but not prohibit either, because the gain of having a player come to a better informed assessment of the game through playing twice presumably does not outweigh the benefit of having two different players participate in the game during the same amount of time.

7. Summative Evaluation

When the game was over, each participant was asked to fill out the questionnaire that was created specifically for the Amulet game in order to obtain feedback not only in terms of general concepts such as attractively or immersion (for which a standard questionnaire based on a validated construction could have been used), but also to access means of improving concrete features and allow for an inference back to the hybrid games model.

The questionnaire itself was constructed as an operationalization of the hybrid gaming design goals and additionally contained concrete items related to specific issues of the technical realization.

Related to the social domain design goal, two items were included:
• Did you rather communicate directly with the other players or rather through the displays?
• How did you like the trading game element?
(The second item indirectly assesses the design goal, as the trading game element was the central game element that required face-to-face negotiation).

Representation and control was covered with these three items:
• Did you experience the game more like a board game or more like a video game?
• Where did you perceive the focus of the game (display/ game board)?
• How did you find the controls of the game compared to a comparable console or video game?

Multimodal stimulation was covered with one item:
• How did you perceive the fan and the lamp?

The effective use of the virtual domain translated to:
• How effective did you find the events (items, characters to meet)?
• How did you find the pacing of the game?
(The second item indirectly assesses the design goal, as the pacing was largely determined by the virtual domain through deliberately triggering respective game events to adjust the game length).

One item also related to the realization of the private displays.

The items were closed rating items that were based on bipolar scales, in which the participants should grade their responses between two extremes, as we were mainly interested in tendencies such as "was the focus more on the game board or more on the displays?". More exact ratings of details did not seem to be appropriate due to the prototypical state of the game and the short response times required by the exhibition type situations. The questionnaire also included open questions about what they liked and disliked and why.

Results

Chi^2 tests were used to determine, if there was a significant number of participants rating for one extreme rather than for the other. Neutral answers (marks exactly in the middle of the scale) were not included in the analysis. In Table 19 the statements illustrate the scales' respective endpoints. The frequencies measures given in the table include all participants who rated on this side of the scale, disregarding the magnitude of their responses in order to eliminate the effects of individual response biases of the participants.

Table 19: Evaluation of the first two design versions with a bipolar scales questionnaire

Item	Responses	Frequencies version 1 (IPSI)	Frequencies version 2 (ETH)
1. Did you experience the game more like a board game or more like a video game?	Board game	13	10
	Video game	3	5
	χ^2	6,25*	0,6
2. Where did you perceive the focus of the game?	Display	10	7
	Game board	4	6
	χ^2	13**	5,4*
3. How did you find the controls of the game compared to a comparable console or video game?	Very easy	16	15
	Very complicated	1	1
	χ^2	13,23**	12,25**
4. How was the handling of the private displays?	Very intuitive	13	17
	Very confusing	3	0
	χ^2	6,25*	17,0**
5. Did you rather communicate directly with the other players or rather through the displays?	Direct, verbal	8	12
	Through displays	7	5
	χ^2	0,6	1,0
6. How did you like the trading game element?	Very interesting	10	14
	Boring	4	2
	χ^2	4,57*	9,0**
7. How effective did you find the events (items, characters to meet)?	Very effective	12	14
	ineffective	4	2
	χ^2	4,0*	9,0**
8. How did you perceive the fan and the lamp?	Very helpful	14	12
	Superfluous or distracting	1	0
	χ^2	5,57*	13,24**
9. How did you find the pacing of the game?	Lengthy	4	1
	Entertaining	10	16
	χ^2	2,57	8,41**

---

* χ^2 test significant on a 5% level

** χ^2 test significant on a 10% level

Discussion

After evaluating the first version of the game, the results for the social domain design goal turned out to be unexpectedly low, as the responses for items #5 and #6 both indicated that a significant amount of subjects did not perceive the communication as focused on face-to-face interaction as we had desired. This low score also corresponded to our observations during the game sessions in which players spent much time with collecting and searching for items instead of trading them. The ratio of steps taken on the game board to the items found was obviously too low, so that most of the time in the early stages of the game, players would wander around looking for items without any necessity and little motivation to engage with the other player in order to negotiate advantageous deals with him. As item #5 had lower scores than #6 we concluded that the social game aspects were still perceived as positive, but due to not stimulating them adequately through the game design, they simply occurred with too little frequency to realize the social domain design goal.

As a result, we then worked towards changing the perceived focus and the lack of communication for the second design version. Consequently, we added more game events, especially more items to be found and picked up, to foster trading and thereby the use of direct communication between the players.

For representation and control we found a remarkably stable pattern of subjects indicating that the interaction style was clearly more similar to those of a board game in contrast to a computer game, but at the same time they found they were interacting more with the screen than with the game board. We interpret this as an indication that the physical aspects of traditional board games are less important than the face-to-face setting. While item #3 indicated that the controls as such were largely intuitive and easy to understand, the results for item #4 also indicated that the handling of the private displays was less effective, so that obviously the high score for item #3 could be attributed to the tangible game board and not to the private displays. As there was an additional layer of indirection with translating information shown on the displays to the button bars mounted below the displays, the mental effort of choosing and finding the adequate button could have been reduced by implementing a direct interaction scheme.

For the second version, we then replaced the large private displays and the physical buttons by the touch sensitive displays in order to eliminate interaction issues.

The multimodal stimulation design goal was only covered with the single item #8 and subjects generally seemed to appreciate it and understand its function. The weather game element was shown on the public screen and could be heard through the public speakers as well as being conveyed in an ambient way with the wind through the fan and the sunlight via the lamp shining on the game board. It could clearly be perceived with the very most subjects that initially, when the game started, they would frequently check the public display for the weather information, but then quickly adapted to relying on the ambient information presented on the additional channels. As the weather is a central game element affecting the available moves for the players, we can conclude that the reason for the shift away from the public display was not due to an insignificance of the information, but that the multimodal ambient display of information was sufficient and preferred by the subjects (which also goes in line with the rating of item #8).

As the multimodal stimulation design goal was reached already in the first version of the game, no modifications were created in the second version.

7. Summative Evaluation

The final design goal of an effective use of the virtual domain was addressed with items #7 and #9. Both were not rated as highly as initially expected and especially the pacing was not perceived as entertaining as intended. Clearly, there is a correlation with the items of the social domain design goal, as the pacing was depending on the events generation and effectiveness which in turn has an effect on the social domain design goal, because most events provide means of initiating the trade game element which takes place in the social domain.

The consequences for the second version thus came down to the design changes already described, namely adding more game events and more items in order to foster trading and direct communication between the players and likewise change the pace and effectiveness of the virtual domain.

After the second version was implemented and tested, the effects of the changes to the first prototype could be assessed. Comparing both evaluations' results indeed showed that the changes to the display interaction were rated significantly better than in the first version and that the improved events in the game had a noticeable effect on both the social domain design goal and the effectiveness of the virtual domain.

The questionnaires finally also included open questions, namely what the participants liked best and why, and what they did not like at all and why. As these were open questions, no statistical analysis was possible. In the first evaluation, many participants praised the combination of a board game and a computer game. Some mentioned the direct communication as a positive element. The negative remarks often mentioned a perceived bad balance of the game itself; some missed more stimuli for communication and some remarks concerned the massive hardware, including the unintuitive buttons. After the changes, the participants still liked the general idea of combining a game board with displays, sound and physical devices. They also mentioned the communication and interaction as very positive. On the negative side, they now mainly mentioned that winning the game largely depends on chance rather than ability. Some participants would prefer a more complex game with a larger and more flexible board. Nobody mentioned problems with the setup, the controls or the interaction any more. In the second evaluation we also specifically asked the participants to comment on the effects of the lamp and the fan, such as if they could explain their relations to the game. All players realized the devices, and most of them understood their function while playing. All of them liked the idea, but some missed different devices for each weather appearing in the game (we did not have a device for rain, and the fan was active for wind as well as for thunderstorm).

In general, the open questions therefore largely resembled the closed item ratings and for the two evaluations it can be stated that the game initially had some smaller flaws that affected mostly the social domain and effective use of the virtual domain design goals. The second version improved on the respective issues and finally all design goals were fulfilled, so that the overall goal of the user study, namely to investigate if the domain of hybrid games would be understood and appreciated by the end users, could also be fulfilled. It can therefore be concluded that these initial results indicate that hybrid gaming has an external relevance. Although the Chi² tests had statistical significance for some items such as the trading game element and the multimodal stimulation, the results should still be seen as indications, mostly because of the prototypical state of the demonstrator and the uncontrolled experimental conditions. For instance, the two samples of subjects were not equal, as the first sample consisted of younger subjects than the second in which presumably a higher share of academics was included. Therefore, the changes in the item responses between the two demonstrator versions could potentially be confounded, as the effects of the sample and the prototype were not controlled and varied jointly. This, however, should not be seen as a problem, because indications as results are sufficient for the respective research question. The hybrid games model was clearly supported by the study's results and a controlled experimental setting was then applied to the final evaluation discussed in the next section.

7.2. Caves & Creatures

The aim of the Caves & Creatures user study was to evaluate the effects of different interaction device setups on the perceived hedonic and pragmatic attributes of a single gaming application. As the thesis of the dissertation claims that it is essential to provide hybrid gaming applications with the capability of adapting to different user interface devices (due to the potential heterogeneity of end user interaction device setups), the study should show that the differences in interaction device setups actually matter and that it is possible with the STARS platform to provide an identical game with exactly the same game rules and mechanics to the players, but with completely different user interfaces. .

In addition to that primary goal of the evaluation, a secondary goal was also to prove that the concept of hybrid games and its conceptual model is useful and that the application domain of hybrid games is attractive for end users. The formative evaluation presented in chapter 3 already indicated that hybrid games could potentially be relevant for respective end users, but as that study revolved around fictitious scenarios and mock-ups, a more valuable approach is of course to provide a gaming application and compare different modes of realization. Taking the hybrid games model as a reference frame, the different realizations would then come down to different degrees of "virtuality", i.e. ranging from a purely physical setup to a purely virtual one with a prototypical hybrid game integrating from both domains.

The Caves & Creatures evaluation is also the only study presented here that follows an experimental setup in order to assess the isolated effects of explanatory or independent factors on the response or dependent variables. As this final summative evaluation does not serve the aims of justifying the beginning or continuation of development efforts, but to come to a detailed explanation for different factors, it is consequently not sufficient any more to discuss "tendencies" as results, but to provide a carefully crafted analysis that is free of potential confoundations and related issues. While parts of the variance between the two sessions of the Amulet evaluation could theoretically be attributed to the different samples, the different locations, different material, or other uncontrolled factors, the summative evaluation of Caves & Creatures should provide the same level of validity, reliability, and objectivity that standard controlled experimental settings usually provide.

The evaluation of a complex gaming application is naturally difficult to control, as many factors can vary between game sessions and therefore certain artifacts are likely to occur. For instance, different subjects might considerably vary in their own preferences and previous experiences with games, so that characteristics of a person might have a relatively high impact compared to characteristics of the game setup. In order to compensate for these effects, one could either include a very large amount of subjects in the study to mitigate any artifacts, or attempt to control and minimize subject factors by both going for a homogenous sample and use a within-subjects design, so that each subject is repeatedly confronted with a gaming situation. Mostly for economic reasons, the latter approach is taken for this study.

7. Summative Evaluation

Method

Pilot Study

According to Hix & Hartson (1993) it is generally advisable to perform a pilot study or dry run for experimental studies that have either not taken place before or that contain critical elements such as a complicated apparatus or procedure. Such a pilot study is especially useful for estimating the temporal dimensions, for finding flaws in the instructions, procedure or apparatus, and in general for ensuring a smooth execution of the real study.

Figure 61. Caves & Creatures pilot study

Consequently, a pilot study (see Figure 61) with two groups of participants was conducted a week before the actual user study was conducted on two days in order to ensure a smooth flow of the procedure and to evaluate the time needed for a complete execution of the study. Within the pilot study two times three subjects went through three experimental conditions (as described in the apparatus section) and played a game of Caves & Creatures with three different device setups. While initially the time for a complete cycle for a single group was estimated to be max. 2 hours, the pilot study indicated that this was an underestimation, as both the participants commented freely on the study which took some time, and the length of each game session showed some variance as the usage of potions and spells for healing could delay the defeat of characters significantly.

Furthermore, as the subjects were not experts in the domain of miniatures roleplaying games, there was also some time needed for giving detailed instructions on the game goals and mechanics, so that the overall slot size for a group was then finalized to be three hours. No technical issues came up during the dry run, so that no modifications to the hardware/ software became necessary.

Subjects

For the actual user study, there were 18 subjects recruited that participated in the study. All of them came from either the Fraunhofer IPSI research institute in Darmstadt, the technical University of Darmstadt, or were other appropriate contacts of colleagues and acquaintances. During the participants' selection process an emphasis was put on the requirement that participants had appropriate computer skills and had at least some knowledge about tabletop, video or board games. As discussed before, the reason for this little diverse sample was that due to the rather high effort of conducting the study, the expected effect strength should be kept high by a homogenous sample with the drawback of a potentially limited generalization.

7. Summative Evaluation

This limitation was taken into account because of the non-casual nature of the Caves & Creatures game application. 15 participants were male and 3 female. The average age was 27.5 years. The youngest participant was 16 years old, the oldest 39 years.

Three subjects each were assigned to one game group, so that overall six groups of players were formed. One group had to be disregarded in the analysis of the study due to a delay in the procedure that rendered a continuation of the study impossible, because one participant had to leave for another appointment.

Apparatus

The study took place with three configurations of the Caves & Creatures demonstrator deployed in the AMBIENTE laboratory at the FhG IPSI institute. The three different configurations related to the integration of user interface components with respect on how central game elements were realized. This is shown in Table 20.

Table 20: Three experimental setups

Game Element	Configuration I	Configuration II	Configuration III
Moving and selecting playing pieces	Sentient game board	Sentient game board without functionality	GUI game board
Readying equipment, weapons, & armor	iBracelet, RFID augmented playing cards	RFID augmented playing cards without functionality	GUI application
Generating variability	Smart Dice Cup	Conventional dice cup	Random number generator
Casting spells	Magic Wand	Conventional dice cup	Random number generator
Atmospheric display	Background sound & music, room illumination, Roomware ambient displays	Not available	Background sound & music
Administration of game data and rules	GDL definitions	Pen & paper	GDL definitions

As the table shows, the three configurations represent typical setups for a hybrid gaming application (configuration I), for a traditional pen & paper tabletop roleplaying game (configuration II) and for a traditional video game (configuration III). For configuration II the initial random distribution of items on the game board was not performed by a human game master, but was fixed for all subject groups, as each group played the game only once in each configuration, so that a random distribution was not necessary.

Procedure

The study took place on two consecutive days on which nine subjects each were invited to participate inside the FhG IPSI institute. Each group of three subjects was scheduled for a three hours period. Within that timeframe, the procedure started with a short assessment of basic personal data and gaming preferences.

7. Summative Evaluation

This initial assessment was included in order to be able to perform a median split among the participants regarding their gaming habits. As two of the three game configurations resembled a game type or technique they would probably be used to and prefer over other types, it was crucial to control this factor, as otherwise the results of the attractiveness ratings of the game conditions might have included confoundations with the participants' dispositions. Consequently, the subjects were to rate their own gaming habits on two likert scaled items for each video games and board games with the two ratings then being subtracted from each other. This "gaming habit" index was then used to discriminate the subjects between video gamers and board gamers for the analysis of variance (ANOVA) of the attractiveness ratings for the experimental conditions. The advantage of this procedure is that the actual magnitude of gaming preferences is eliminated in favor of the discrimination between the game types.

After the initial assessment, an introduction to the game and the game rules followed along with a short tutorial covering the main game elements as well as the respective user interface components. Each game element (such as casting a spell) was demonstrated consecutively with the different interaction devices used for each configuration, so that initial comparisons between the different configurations could be drawn implicitly already at this introductory stage. After the introduction, the players had the opportunity to ask questions and to practice the handling of any interaction device for a few minutes. After that phase of getting accustomed with the apparatus, the actual game sessions took place. Each group was exposed to all three experimental conditions. The order of the conditions was fully randomized in order to cope with ordering effects.

After each game session, the subjects were presented a subset of the proven and commonly used AttrakDiff questionnaire (Hassenzahl 2004) that measures hedonic and pragmatic qualities of interactive products. The measures taken with the questionnaire ("pragmatic quality", "hedonic quality-stimulation", and "attractiveness") were the main response valuables of the study. While the subjects filled out the questionnaires, the configuration of the next experimental condition was activated. As configuration I and III were running in parallel anyway (e.g. virtual and tangible game board were both active, but not exposed to the players at the same time) this came down to merely exchanging interaction devices.

There was no pause between the three game sessions except for the questionnaires, but afterwards a short break was scheduled as a soft transition to the concluding open interview phase in which the players could make any remarks or give any feedback in an open format.

Variables and Measurements

The explanatory or independent factors followed a 2x3 design with the gaming habit (video games, board games) and the experimental condition (condition I, II, III) allowing for a mixed-design ANOVA in which the gaming habit was the between-subjects factor and the experimental condition was the within-subject factor.

The response or dependent variables were taken with the questionnaires after each game session and included the following factors (from Hassenzahl 2004):

Pragmatic Quality (PQ):
The Pragmatic Quality describes a product's usability and indicates how successfully users are in achieving their goals using the product.

7. Summative Evaluation

Hedonic Quality – Stimulation (HQ-S)
This dimension indicates to what extent the product can support human needs for development and moving forward in terms of novel, interesting, and stimulating functions, contents, and interaction- and presentation styles.

Attractiveness (ATT)
Attractiveness describes a global value of the interactive product based on the overall quality perception of the user.

The response variables thus measured whether a condition was in general attractive to the user, and more specifically how the pragmatic and hedonic qualities were perceived in relation to the gaming habit of the users.

Results

The responses on the AttrakDiff scales for the three experimental conditions are shown in the following Table 21.

Table 21: Means and standard deviations for the three scales

Scale	EC I: M	EC I: s	EC II: M	EC II: s	EC III: M	EC III: s
PQ	2.21	0.51	-0.31	0.91	2.1	0.66
HQ-S	2.02	0.46	1.92	1.12	1.61	0.54
ATT	2.16	0.62	2.01	0.81	1.8	0.91

For all three scales ANOVAs were calculated in order to access the significance of the different scores.

Pragmatic Quality Explained By Experimental Condition and Gaming Habit

A mixed-design ANOVA with the gaming habit (GH) as the between-subjects factor and the experimental condition (EC) as the within-subject factor did not show a significant main impact of the between-subjects factor GH, although on a descriptive level, there was a slight tendency to a higher response value of PQ for condition III among subjects with a video GH.

The response values of the within-subject factor EC however varied significantly ($F = 4.815$, $df = 2$, $p < 0.5$). The pair wise t-tests for the different PQ values (EC condition I: $M = 2.21$, $s = 0.51$; condition II: $M = -0.31$, $s = 0.91$; condition III: $M = 2.1$, $s = 0.66$) were highly significant for condition I&II ($t = 9.35$, $p < 0.01$), not significant for condition I&III ($t = 0.51$, $p > 0.05$), and highly significant for condition II&III ($t = 9.35$, $p < 0.01$).

Hedonic Quality Explained By Experimental Condition and Gaming Habit

A mixed-design ANOVA with the gaming habit (GH) as the between-subjects factor and the experimental condition (EC) as the within-subject factor did not show a significant main impact of the between-subjects factor GH and no interaction effect between GH and EC.

The response values of the within-subject factor EC varied significantly ($F = 4.918$, $df = 2$, $p < 0.5$). The corresponding pair wise t-tests for the different HQ-S values (EC condition I: $M = 2.02$, $s = 0.46$; condition II: $M = 1.92$, $s = 1.12$; condition III: $M = 1.61$, $s = 0.54$) were significant for condition I&III ($t = 2.24$, $p < 0.05$), but not significant for condition I&II ($t = 0.97$, $p > 0.05$) and not for condition II&III ($t = 0.97$, $p > 0.05$).

7. Summative Evaluation

Attractiveness Explained By Experimental Condition and Gaming Habit

A mixed-design ANOVA with the gaming habit (GH) as the between-subjects factor and the experimental condition (EC) as the within-subject factor did not show a significant main impact of the between-subjects factor GH, as well as no significant within-subject factor EC, and also no significant interaction effects of EC and GH (Main effect GH: $F < 1$; Main effect EC: $F=1.69$, $p > 0.05$; Interaction effect EC * GH: $F=3.27$, $p > 0.05$).

Correspondingly, the different ATT scores (EC condition I: $M = 2.16$, $s = 0.62$; condition II: $M = 2.01$, $s = 0.81$; condition III: $M = 1.8$, $s = 0.91$) did not show significant differences between the three conditions.

Open Interviews

After all game sessions were over, an open interview and debriefing took place. The feedback gathered there included many questions regarding technical realizations that was presumably due to the nature of the subject sample consisting of many subjects with a technical background who were interested in the implementation of the system.

A comment that was frequently made related to the entire experiment which was positively perceived in general, independent of the concrete conditions and setups. After querying about the differences and advantages/ disadvantages of the conditions, many subjects referred to the manual and partly tedious tasks relevant in condition II, although not all subjects found them to be a disadvantage. While players with a video gaming preference generally regarded the impact more negative (several times the condition was labeled as "old fashioned") some (but not all) subjects with a board gaming preference regarded the manual tasks as adding to the overall experience. Apart from that, some subjects also noted that the game as such was similar between the conditions, so their verdict was not really strong and they liked the game independently of the condition. A few players also stated that condition III felt much like a computer game which they would probably prefer when they were alone, but not when playing together with friends. In such a situation, the novel controllers to the hybrid gaming setup would often be favored, especially the dice cup was liked by many participants. When it came to the discussion of the hybrid games condition, several subjects also asked when the sytem would be available for purchase and indicated that they would in principle appreciate a commercial realization.

Discussion

The most significant and plausible result relates to the main effect of the experimental condition on the perceived pragmatic quality. While there were no significant differences between the hybrid and video games conditions (I + III), both conditions were rated highly significantly better than condition II, which also received the only negative rating on the (-3..+3) scale of the AttrakDiff PQ scale. Although there was no significant interaction effect with GH, the increased variance within condition II compared to I + III still indicates that GH at least explains more variance here than in the other conditions. This means that the lower PQ value for condition II is not as uniformly found between subjects than the high scores in the other conditions (which explain the high overall significance of the t-tests). Taking the feedback from the open interview after the game sessions into account, it becomes obvious that the increased manual tasks in condition II such as manually looking up events and administering hit points explains the low perceived pragmatic value. While no item analysis was performed in the evaluation, it still goes in line with this interpretation that the most negatively rated items of the PQ scale were the "impractical" (vs. practical), "cumbersome" (vs. straightforward) and "unruly" (vs. manageable) items. It was therefore demonstrated

7. Summative Evaluation

clearly that condition II is of lower pragmatic value than the other conditions which, on the other side, seem to be of rather equal pragmatic value with no significant differences being found.

This directly leads to the question whether this low pragmatic value of condition II correlates with a lower hedonic value as well. Conceptually, both the hedonic and pragmatic dimensions are independent, and this also shows in the scores for the HQ-S scale. Here, condition I was rated higher than II which again was higher than III, but only the differences between I and III were significant, and even they were significant only on the 0.05 level. Although it could be hypothesized that the differences in the HQ-S values should be explained by the differences in GH (someone who has a habit and general preference for one type of game should enjoy it more than other types), there was no main effect of the GH factor on the HQ-S.

The findings from the open interview contradict the statistical result that GH has no effect on the perceived hedonic value, as several players uttered enjoyment statements corresponding with their own general preferences when it came to the difference between condition II and III. Interestingly, condition I seemed to bridge the gap between the other conditions as the interview results showed a consistent positive pattern independent of the GH factor which implies that the GH-related general dispositions against certain game types ("old fashioned traditional media", "feels like playing a computer game") did generally not apply to the hybrid gaming setup, although there was no consistent positive effect of the hybrid gaming setup in so far, as the GH disposition did not generally account for positive statements regarding the similarities to the respective GH disposition. The HQ-S scores nonetheless mark the most favorable result for the hybrid games condition so far, as a clear ranking of conditions can be seen in the data, although not all differences are significant, the tendencies are still obvious.

In contrast to the PQ items, it must be noted for the HQ-S items that these might be somewhat misleading, as item pairs such as "dull / captivating" or "undemanding / challenging" relate more to the game mechanics than to certain instances of ECs. However, as the variances of the HQ-S scores are not smaller than the variances of the PQ scores (which they should be, if the PQ items related only to the game mechanics which are identical for all ECs), the potential confounding effects should be negligible. What is probably more of an issue here is that two items, namely "conservative / innovative" and "ordinary / novel" do not only have a subjective interpretation, but also describe the fact that a hybrid games setup is not ordinary and thus have an objective notion to it beyond the hedonic quality. This might have led to a certain overestimation of condition I in the HQ-S scores, but it is still consistent with the open interview results and the (statistically non significant) negative dispositions against conditions II and III depending on the GH factor.

The overall attractiveness ratings followed the ranking from the HQ-S scores with condition I scoring higher than 2 and 3. Unfortunately, as all conditions had rather high scores, there was no significance between the different scores at all, so that all conditions must be seen as equally attractive. Also on a descriptive level, at least condition I and II are so close together (2.16 and 2.01) and have rather high variances that the hybrid games setup receiving the highest score again does not really mean a lot. What can be clearly stated is that the obvious and significantly identified pragmatic shortcomings of condition II do not correlate at all with the perceived attractiveness. As attractiveness is defined as a global measure of quality that contains aspects of hedonic and pragmatic qualities, it is obviously the case for gaming applications that hedonic aspects are simply more important than pragmatic ones. In addition, the selection of items in the attractiveness scale are [in accordance with the global concept of attractiveness as being explicative for the variance of both hedonic and pragmatic qualities, while HQ-S and PQ are conceptually highly independent of each other] more broadly defined and global with pairs such as "bad / good" or "repelling / appealing" potentially including broader aspects of the experimental condition including aspects of the game mechanics that are invariant between conditions. This goes in line with frequent feedback from the open interviews where subjects stated that they liked the entire experiment which naturally aggravates the discriminative power between experimental conditions. The consistently high attractiveness scores can therefore also be interpreted on a meta level as an indication that it is valuable to allow for all the different configurations, as they are obviously all attractive to the end users.

The bottom line of the test results is that the different configurations are not equal in terms of their pragmatic value (with PQ being significantly lower in condition II) and that also the hedonic qualities differ, although not as significantly as PQ, which certainly relates to the invariant game mechanics explaining some of the variance in HQ-S, but not in PQ. When it comes to addressing the question which setup is the most favorable one, the hybrid games condition consistently marks the highest scores, although the differences to the other conditions are not always significant. Its main benefit is clearly the lack of major drawbacks such as the pragmatic problems of condition II and the least perceived enjoyment and isolating aspects of condition III. In that respect, it is unfortunate that the GH factor contributed so little to the statistical analysis, although it became clear in the open interview that there are indeed different types of gaming preferences that have an impact on the rating of certain HQ-S and PQ aspects. In retrospect, more subjects should have been included in the study, as more significant results can generally be realized with a growing subjects count. For the GH factor, this could have been especially valuable.

As the ranking of the hybrid gaming condition is mostly relevant for the validation of the hybrid games model and the justification of the application domain as such, the other major issue relates to the thesis of this dissertation, namely if it is essential to provide hybrid gaming applications with the capability of adapting to different user interface devices, the consistent high scores of ATT together with the open feedback regarding the situations in which certain setups would be preferable (e.g. when being alone a video game type of configuration is more appropriate than in other situations) seem to suggest that it is indeed favorable, if a hybrid gaming platform supports this adaptation functionality. While the initial thesis provided the rationale that the potential heterogeneity of end user interaction device setups requires this adaptation functionality (which could not really have been proven in the experiment, but only backed up with claims of sales data for comparable video games systems such as the Nintendo Wii for which a multitude of controllers and peripherals exist), the finding that the very different configurations do have their benefits and drawbacks and the indication that there are situations in which they are more or less appropriate supports the thesis of this dissertation even more.

7.3. Conclusions

The summative evaluation closes the cycle presented in this dissertation. Starting from a discussion of the current state of the art in smart environment infrastructures, the foundations of user interaction in pervasive computing environments, and the motivation for a novel development and runtime platform this dissertation has discussed the theory and concept and of hybrid games. This discussion has included the specific perceptive qualities of hybrid

7. Summative Evaluation

games and the emerging conceptual approaches. By conducting a formative evaluation about the acceptance and requirements of the target audience early on the dissertation's concept and theoretical model could be verfied, before investing further in this emerging field. Due to the complexity of introducing virtual, social, and physical domains that open up a large design space for user interfaces which motivates the central thesis of this dissertation, namely that hybrid games benefit from a flexible and dynamically changing integration of user interfaces which a development and runtime platform should consequently target at.

Two chapters dealing with the hardware and software components that form the basis for user interaction in hybrid games then followed as a central contribution of the dissertation. First, appropriate hardware interfaces and smart artifacts developed as building blocks for hybrid games were discussed. Several tangible interaction devices were specifically designed and implemented to provide the affordances of well known user interfaces from the domain of traditional gaming such as game boards, dice, or magic wands. In addition, the combination of tangible and graphical user interface components with Roomware technologies was presented. In order to flexibly integrate and re-combine the respective user interface devices with gaming applications a complementary software platform that provides a distributed communication and coordination infrastructure was presented in the next chapter. By providing a decoupled communication scheme and consistency management between components it addresses the anticipated heterogeneity in future smart home environments, completety separating game rules and mechanics from the configuration of user interfaces. A dedicated definition language for game rules that allows for a high level specification of games and the alteration of game rules during runtime was presented as well as a description language for gaming user interfaces and several components such as game board renderers that facilitate the development of hybrid games.

The development of concrete proof-of-concept prototypes that utilize the software and hardware platform was then discussed in order to prove that the platform is actually able to support the development process of hybrid games. Four such prototypes of different complexity were presented, each integrating a certain selection of the platform's functionality. Two of these prototypes were then finally used in the summative evaluation that shows the appreciation of the hybrid games domain as such as well as providing an indication for the validity of the central thesis of this dissertation.

In parallel to the development of the STARS platform some of the concepts and approaches presented in this dissertation such as the utilization of novel game controllers have also been applied to the commercial world with e.g. the Nintendo Wii being extremely successful despite the inferior graphics capabilities compared to other next gen home entertainment systems. Likewise, in the domain of traditional tabletop games some elements of hybrid games, such as the voice output and processing unit within Ravensburger's King Arthur demonstrate the external vailidity of the hybrid games concept. Naturally, as commercial realizations are prone to many more constraints and market considerations than research prototypes, not every aspect that might be interesting and sensible to pursue in a research context will find its way to the commercial market. Despite that, the trend in the mainstream market towards an integration of the formerly different game classes goes in line with the work presented in this dissertation.

Another current trend that is however not covered within this work, but seems to play a huge role in future gaming scenarios as well, is that of mobile phone integration including location information and location based services. With the upcoming generation of very attractive

7. Summative Evaluation

touch controlled phones that offer well-crafted service and application marketplaces as well as providing cameras finally capable of reading barcodes reliably, the notion of ubiquitous gaming and interaction with arbitrary real-world objects with meaningful location information will certainly catch on. It can be seen as a limitation of the work presented in this dissertation that the focus is mostly on static locations and home environments, but then again this can also be seen as a specialization and certain features of the platform such as the Roomware integration only make sense in this context.

Nonetheless, the next steps and future research agenda for the STARS platform and its successors include the stronger integration of next-gen mobile devices as central platform elements and not just peripherals for displaying private information as they are currently used. This includes both the utilization of novel services accessible on mobile phones involving barcode scanning and location information, but also iussues of synchronicity and mobility of devices for which the current architecture is not optimized. Hybrid games will continue to evolve with toolkits and platforms such as STARS allowing for quickly prototyping and realizing novel interaction and gaming concepts aligned with future technological developments.

8. References

Abowd, G., Atkeson, C., Bobick, A. F., Essa, I. A., MacIntyre, B., Mynatt, E., Starner, T. E. (2000). Living laboratories: the future computing environments group at the Georgia Institute of Technology. In CHI '00 Extended Abstracts on Human Factors in Computing Systems (The Hague, The Netherlands, April 01 - 06, 2000). CHI '00. ACM Press, New York, NY, 215-216.

Abowd G, Mynatt E, Rodden T. (2002). The Human Experience. IEEE Pervasive Computing journal, 1(1): 48-57.

Abowd, G., Mynatt, E. (2005). Designing for the Human Experience in Smart Environmkents. In: Cook, D.J., Das, S. Smart Environments: Technologies, Protocols, and Applications. Wiley-IEEE, 2005, 153-174.

Akyildiz, I. F., Su, W., Sankarasubramaniam, Y., Cayirci, E. (2002). Wireless sensor networks: A survey. Computer Networks, vol. 38, 393-422.

Altherr, M., Erzberger, M., Maffeis, S. (1999). iBus - a Software Bus Middleware for the Java Platform. In International Workshop on Reliable Middleware Systems of the 13th IEEE Symposium On Reliable Distributed Systems, 43-53.

Bahl, P., Padmanabhan, V.N. (2000). RADAR: An In-Building RF based User Location and Tracking System", Proceedings of IEEE INFOCOM 2000, Tel-Aviv, Israel, March 2000, 775-784.

Bandura, A. (1989). Social cognitive theory. In R. Vasta (Ed.), Annals of child development. Vol. 6: Theories of child development: Revised formulations and current issues. Greenwich, CT: JAI Press.

Balazinska, Magdalena & Balakrishnan, Hari (2001). Twine: A Scalable Peer-to-Peer Architecture for Intentional Resource Discovery (retrieved from http://sow.csail.mit.edu/2001/proceedings/balazinska.pdf).

Ballagas, R., Ringel, M., Stone, M., and Borchers, J. (2003). iStuff: a physical user interface toolkit for ubiquitous computing environments. In Proceedings of the SIGCHI Conference on Human Factors in Computing Systems (Ft. Lauderdale, Florida, USA, April 05 - 10, 2003). CHI '03. ACM Press, New York, NY, 537-544.

Barkhi, R., Jakob, V.S., & Pirkul, H. (1999). An Experimental Analysis of Face to Face versus Computer Mediated Communication Channels. Group Decision and Negotiation, 8, 325-347.

Beigl, M., Gellersen, H. (2003). Smart-Its: An Embedded Platform for Smart Objects. In Proc. Smart Objects Conference (SOC 2003), Grenoble, France.

Benford, S., Magerkurth, C., Ljungstrand, P. (2005). Bridging the physical and digital in pervasive gaming. Communications of the ACM 48, 3 (Mar. 2005), 54-57.

Bernsen, N.O (1997). Defining a Taxonomy of Output Modalities from an HCI Perspective. Computer Standards and Interfaces, Special Double Issue, 18, 6-7, 1997, 537-553.

Block, F., Schmidt, A., Villar, N., Gellersen, H.-W. (2004). Towards a Playful User Interface for Home Entertainment Systems. In: Proceedings of the European Symposium on Ambient Intelligence 2004; ISBN: 3-540-23721-6. Springer, 207-217.

Bodnar, A., Corbett, R., Nekrasovski, D. (2004). AROMA: ambient awareness through olfaction in a messaging application. In Proceedings of the 6th international Conference on Multimodal interfaces (State College, PA, USA, October 13 - 15, 2004). ICMI '04. ACM Press, New York, NY, 183-190.

Bohn, J.: The Smart Jigsaw Puzzle Assistant: Using RFID Technology for Building Augmented Real-World Games, Workshop on Gaming Applications in Pervasive Computing Environments at Pervasive 2004, Vienna, Austria. http://www.pergames.de.

Bolt, R. A. (1980). "Put-that-there": Voice and gesture at the graphics interface. In Proceedings of the 7th Annual Conference on Computer Graphics and interactive Techniques (Seattle, Washington, United States, July 14 - 18, 1980). SIGGRAPH '80. ACM Press, New York, NY, 262-270.

Brumitt, B., Meyers, B., Krumm, J., Kern, A., Shafer, S. (2000). EasyLiving: Technologies for Intelligent Environments. Proceedings of the International Conference on Handheld and Ubiquitous Computing 2000, Springer-Verlag, 12-29.

Bruner, J. S. (1972). The nature and uses of immaturity. American Psychologist, 27, 687-708.

Beigl, M., Gellersen, H.W (2003). Smart-its: An embedded platform for smart objects. In: Proceedings of Smart Objects Conference (SOC 2003), Grenoble, France.

Cao, X., Balakrishnan, R. (2003). VisionWand: interaction techniques for large displays using a passive wand tracked in 3D. In Proceedings of the 16th Annual ACM Symposium on User interface Software and Technology (Vancouver, Canada, November 02 - 05, 2003). UIST '03. ACM Press, New York, NY, 173-182.

Chalmers, M., Barkhuus, L., Bell, M., Brown, B., Hall, M., Sherwood, S., Tennent, P. (2003). Gaming on the Edge: Using Seams in Pervasive Games. Position Paper at PerGames 2005 Workshop, www.pergames.de.

Chen, Y., Clark, D.W., Cook, P. Damianakis, G., Essel, A., Finkelstein, T. (2000). Early Experiences and challenges in building and using a scalable display wall system. IEEE Computer Graphics and Applications, 20(4), 671-680.

Cheok, A., Yang, X., Ying, Z., Billinghurst, M., Kato, H. (2002). Touch-Space: Mixed Reality Game Space Based on Ubiquitous, Tangible, and Social Computing. Personal Ubiquitous Comput. 6, 5-6 (Jan. 2002), 430-442.

Ciger, J., Gutierrez, M., Vexo, F., Thalmann, D. (2003). The magic wand. In Proceedings of the 19th Spring Conference on Computer Graphics (Budmerice, Slovakia, April 24 - 26, 2003). L. Szirmay-Kalos, Ed. SCCG '03. ACM Press, New York, NY, 119-124.

Coen, M., Phillips, B., Warshawsky, N., Weisman, L., Peters, S., Finin, P. (1999). Meeting the Computational Needs of Intelligent Environments: The Metaglue System. In Proceedings of 1st International Workshop on Managing Interactions in Smart Environments (MANSE'99), Dublin, Ireland, 201—212.

Cohen, P.R., McGee, D. (2004), Tangible Multimodal Interfaces for Safety-Critical Applications. In: Communications of the ACM, January 2004, vol. 47, No. 1, 41-46.

Connolly, J. A., & Doyle, A. (1984). Relation of social fantasy play to social competence in preschoolers. Developmental Psychology, 20, 797-806.

Coroama, V., Kapic, T., Röthenbacher, F. (2004). Improving the Reality Perception of Visually Impaired through Pervasive Computing. In: Ferscha, A., Hoertner, H., Kotsis, G. (eds.): Advances in Pervasive Computing, Austrian Computer Society (OCG), Vienna, Austria, 369-376.

Costikyan, G. (2007): I Have No Words & I Must Design, (http://www.costik.com/nowords.html)

Crabtree, A., Benford, S., Rodden, T., Greenhalgh, C., Flintham, M., Anastasi, R., Drozd, A., Adams, M., Row-Farr, J., Tandavanitj, N., Steed, A. (2004). Orchestrating a mixed reality game 'on the ground'. In Proceedings of the SIGCHI Conference on Human Factors in Computing Systems (Vienna, Austria, April 24 - 29, 2004). CHI '04. ACM Press, New York, NY, 391-398.

Cugola, G., Di Nitto, E., Fuggetta, A. (2001). The JEDI event-based infrastructure and its application to the development of the OPSS WFMS. IEEE Transactions on Software Engineering, 27(9).

Das, S. K., Cook, D. J., Bhattacharya, A., Heierman, E. O., Lin, T.Y. (2002). The Role of Prediction Algorithms in the MavHome Smart Home Architecture. IEEE Wireless Communications Special Issue on Smart Homes, vol. 9, 6, 77-84.

de Ruyter, B., Aarts, E. (2004). Ambient intelligence: visualizing the future. In Proceedings of the Working Conference on Advanced Visual interfaces (Gallipoli, Italy, May 25 - 28, 2004). AVI '04. ACM Press, New York, NY, 203-208.

Denoue, L., Nelson, L., Churchill, E. (2003). AttrActive windows: dynamic windows for digital bulletin boards. In CHI '03 Extended Abstracts on Human Factors in Computing Systems (Ft. Lauderdale, Florida, USA, April 05 - 10, 2003). CHI '03. ACM Press, New York, NY, 746-747.

Dietz, P., Leigh, D. (2001). DiamondTouch: a multi-user touch technology. In Proceedings of the 14th Annual ACM Symposium on User interface Software and Technology (Orlando, Florida, November 11 - 14, 2001). UIST '01. ACM Press, New York, NY, 219-226.

Dix, Alan (2003). Human-Computer Interaction. Prentice Hall, Englewood Cliffs, 2003. ISBN 0130461091.

Dustdar, S., Gall, H., Hauswirth, M. (2003). Software-Architekturen für Verteilte Systeme: Prinzipien, Bausteine und Standardarchitekturen für moderne Software. Berlin: Springer Verlag.

Eugster, P. T., Felber, P. A., Guerraoui, R., Kermarrec, A. (2003). The many faces of publish/subscribe. ACM Computing Surveys. 35, 2 (Jun. 2003), 114-131.

Erikson, E. H. (1950). Childhood and Society. New York: Norton.

Falk, J., Ljungstrand, P., Björk, S., Hansson, R. (2001). Pirates: proximity-triggered interaction in a multi-player game. In CHI '01 Extended Abstracts on Human Factors in Computing Systems (Seattle, Washington, March 31 - April 05, 2001). CHI '01. ACM Press, New York, NY, 119-120.

Fishkin, K.P., Moran, T.P., Harrison, B.L. (1998). Embodied user interfaces: Towards invisible user interfaces. In Proceedings of EHCI'98 (Heraklion, Greece, Sept. 1998), 1-18.

Fitzmaurice, G.W. (1996). Graspable User Interfaces, Ph.D. thesis, University of Toronto.

Flieder, K., Mödritscher, F. (2006). Foundations of a pattern language based on Gestalt principles. In CHI '06 Extended Abstracts on Human Factors in Computing Systems (Montréal, Québec, Canada, April 22 - 27, 2006). CHI '06. ACM, New York, NY, 773-778.

Foley, J., Wallace, V. Chan, P. (1984). The Human Factors of Computer Graphics Interaction Techniques. IEEE Computer Graphics and Applications, 4(11), November 1984, 13–48.

Frapolli, F., Hirsbrunner, B., Lalanne, D. (2007). Dynamic Rules: Towards interactive games intelligence. Tangible Play: Research and Design for Tangible and Tabletop Games. Workshop at the 2007 Intelligent User Interfaces Conference, IUI 2007, January 2007, Hawaii, USA, 29-32.

Garlan, D. (2000). Software Architecture: a Roadmap. In: Proceedings of the 22st International
Conference on Software Engineering (ICSE'00), ACM Press, New York, NY, 93–101.

Gelernter, D. (1985). Generative communication in Linda. ACM Trans. Program. Lang. Syst. 7, 1 (Jan. 1985), 80-112.

Gelernter, D., Carriero, N. (1992). Coordination languages and their significance. Communications of the ACM 35, 2 (Feb. 1992), 96.

Gellersen, H.W., Beigl, M., Krull, H. (1999). The MediaCup: Awareness Technology embedded in an Everyday Object. In: Gellersen, H.W. (ed.): Handheld & Ubiqutious Computing, Lecture notes in computer science; Vol 1707, Springer, 308-310.

Gerber, A. (2005). IuK-News: Technologien statt Tabus – Forschen für die Spieleindustrie.

Greenberg, S., Boyle, M. (2002). Customizable physical interfaces for interacting with conventional applications. In Proceedings of the 15th Annual ACM Symposium on User interface Software and Technology (Paris, France, October 27 - 30, 2002). UIST '02. ACM Press, New York, NY, 31-40.

Greenberg, S., Boyle, M., LaBerge, J. (1998). PDAs and Shared Public Displays: Making Personal Information Public, and Public Information Personal. In: Personal Technologies, Vol. 3, 1. Elsevier.

Greenberg, S., Fitchett, C. (2001). Phidgets: easy development of physical interfaces through physical widgets. In Proceedings of the 14th Annual ACM Symposium on User interface Software and Technology (Orlando, Florida, November 11 - 14, 2001). UIST '01. ACM Press, New York, NY, 209-218.

Grieg, S., Muzyka, R., Ohlen, J., Oster, T. Zeschuk, G. (2002). Postmortem: BioWare's Neverwinter Nights. http://www.gamasutra.com/features/20021204/greig_03.htm

Gibson, J. J. (1979). The Ecological Approach to Visual Perception. Boston: Houghton Mifflin.

Harihar, K., Kurkovsky, S. (2005). Using Jini to enable pervasive computing environments. In Proceedings of the 43rd Annual Southeast Regional Conference - Volume 1 (Kennesaw, Georgia, March 18 - 20, 2005). ACM-SE 43. ACM, New York, NY, 188-193.

Hartmann, B., Klemmer, S. R., Bernstein, M., Abdulla, L., Burr, B., Robinson-Mosher, A., Gee, J. (2006). Reflective physical prototyping through integrated design, test, and analysis. In Proceedings of the 19th Annual ACM Symposium on User interface Software and Technology (Montreux, Switzerland, October 15 - 18, 2006). UIST '06. ACM, New York, NY, 299-308.

Hassenzahl, M. (2004). The interplay of beauty, goodness, and usability in interactive products. Hum.-Comput. Interact. 19, 4 (Dec. 2004), 319-349.

Hightower, J., Borriello, G. (2001). Location Systems for Ubiquitous Computing, IEEE Computer, Vol. 34(8), 57-66.

Hindus, D., Mainwaring, S.D., Hagstrom, A.E., Leduc, N., Bayley, 0. (2001). Casablanca: Designing social communications devices for the home. In: Proceedings of CHI 2001, 325-332.

Hinske, S., Lampe, M., Magerkurth, C., Röcker, C. (2007). Classifying Pervasive Games: On Pervasive Computing and Mixed Reality. In: Magerkurth, C., Röcker, C. (eds). Concepts and Technologies for Pervasive Games: A Reader for Pervasive Gaming Research. Shaker Verlag, 2007.

Hix, D., Hartson, H.R. (1993). Developing User Interfaces: Ensuring through product and process. New York: John Wiley.

Holland, J. H. (1998). Emergence. From Chaos to Order. Oxford: Oxford University Press.

Huang, Y., Garcia-Molina, H. (2001). Publish/Subscribe in a mobile enviroment. In Proceedings of the 2nd ACM international Workshop on Data Engineering For Wireless and Mobile Access (Santa Barbara, California, United States). S. Banerjee, Ed. MobiDe '01. ACM Press, New York, NY, 27-34.

Ishii, H., Ullmer, B. (1997). Tangible bits: towards seamless interfaces between people, bits and atoms. In Proceedings of the SIGCHI Conference on Human Factors in Computing Systems (Atlanta, Georgia, United States, March 22 - 27, 1997). S. Pemberton, Ed. CHI '97. ACM Press, New York, NY, 234-241.

Johanson, B. Fox, A. (2002). The Event Heap: A Coordination Infrastructure for Interactive Workspaces. In Proceedings of the Fourth IEEE Workshop on Mobile Computing Systems and Applications (June 20 - 21, 2002). WMCSA. IEEE Computer Society, Washington, DC, 83-93.

Johanson, B., Fox, A., Winograd, T. (2002). The Interactive Workspaces Project: Experiences with Ubiquitous Computing Rooms. IEEE Pervasive Computing Magazine, Vol. 1, Issue 2, (2002) 71-78.

Juul, J. (2003). The Game, the Player, the World: Looking for a Heart of Gameness, in Marinka Copier & Joost Raessens (Eds.): Level Up: Digital Games Research Conference Proceedings. Utrecht: Universiteit Utrecht, 2003, 30-45.

Hinckley, K., Pierce, J., Sinclair, M., Horvitz, E. (2000). Sensing techniques for mobile interaction. In: Proceedings of UIST 2000, 91-100.

Kahan, J., Koivunen, M. (2001). Annotea: an open RDF infrastructure for shared Web annotations. In Proceedings of the 10th international Conference on World Wide Web (Hong Kong, Hong Kong, May 01 - 05, 2001). WWW '01. ACM Press, New York, NY, 623-632.

Kahn, J. M., Katz, R. H., Pister, K. S. (1999). Next century challenges: mobile networking for "Smart Dust". In Proceedings of the 5th Annual ACM/IEEE international Conference on Mobile Computing and Networking (Seattle, Washington, United States, August 15 - 19, 1999). MobiCom '99. ACM Press, New York, NY, 271-278

Kampmann Walther, B. (2005): Atomic Actions. International Workshop on Pervasive Gaming Applications, PerGames 2005

Kanjo, E., Astheimer, P (2002): Interactive environment by narrative playmate toys; ACM SigGroup Bulletin, Volume 23 , Issue 2 (August 2002), 6-7.

Kijanka, B. (2002): Postmortem: Gas Powered Games' Dungeon Siege http://www.gamasutra.com/features/20021218/kijanka_01.htm

Klabbers, J. H. G. (2003): The gaming landscape: A taxonomy for classifying games and simulations, presented at LEVEL UP: Digital Games Research Conference (2003)

Klemmer, S. R., Li, J., Lin, J., Landay, J. A. (2004): Papier-Mache: toolkit support for tangible input. In Proceedings of the SIGCHI Conference on Human Factors in Computing Systems (Vienna, Austria, April 24 - 29, 2004). CHI '04. ACM Press, New York, NY, 399-406.

Kaptelinin, V., Czerwinski, M. (2007): The Desktop Metaphor and New Uses of Technology. In Kaptelinin, V., Czerwinski, M. (Eds.): Beyond the Desktop Metaphor: Designing Integrated Digital Work Environments. MIT Press, 1-11.

Konkel, M., Leung, V., Ullmer, B., Hu, C. (2004). Tagaboo: a collaborative children's game based upon wearable RFID technology. Personal Ubiquitous Comput. 8, 5 (Sep. 2004), 382-384.

Krohn, A., Zimmer, T., Beigl, M. (2004). Enhancing Tabletop Games with Relative Positioning Technology. Advances in Pervasive Computing, Oesterreichische Computer Gesellschaft, Wien 2004.

Lampe, M., Strassner, M., Fleisch, E. (2004). A Ubiquitous Computing environment for aircraft maintenance. In Proceedings of the 2004 ACM Symposium on Applied Computing (Nicosia, Cyprus, March 14 - 17, 2004). SAC '04. ACM Press, New York, NY, 1586-1592.

Lee, J. C., Avrahami, D., Hudson, S. E., Forlizzi, J., Dietz, P. H., Leigh, D. (2004). The calder toolkit: wired and wireless components for rapidly prototyping interactive devices. In Proceedings of the 2004 Conference on Designing interactive Systems (Cambridge, MA, USA, August 01 - 04, 2004). DIS '04. ACM Press, New York, NY, 167-175.

Lindley, C. A. (2003): Game Taxonomies: A High Level Framework for Game Analysis and Design. http://www.gamasutra.com/features/20031003/lindley_02.shtml

Magerkurth, C., Cheok, A. D., Mandryk, R. L., Nilsen, T. (2005). Pervasive games: bringing computer entertainment back to the real world. ACM Computers in Entertainment. 3, 3 (July 2005), 4-23.

Magerkurth, C., Engelke, T., Grollman, D. (2006). A component based architecture for distributed, pervasive gaming applications. In Proceedings of the 2006 ACM SIGCHI international Conference on Advances in Computer Entertainment Technology (Hollywood, California, June 14 - 16, 2006). ACE '06, vol. 266. ACM, New York, NY, 15.

Magerkurth, C., Engelke, T., Memisoglu, M. (2004 a). Augmenting the virtual domain with physical and social elements: towards a paradigm shift in computer entertainment technology. In Proceedings of the 2004 ACM SIGCHI international Conference on Advances in Computer Entertainment Technology (Singapore, June 03 - 05, 2005). ACE '04, vol. 74. ACM, New York, NY, 163-172.

Magerkurth, C., Memisoglu, M., Engelke, T., Streitz, N.A. (2004 b). Towards the next generation of tabletop gaming experiences. In: Graphics Interface 2004 (GI'04), London (Ontario), Canada, AK Peters, May 17-19, 73-80.

Magerkurth, C., Memisoglu, M., Hinrich, W. (2005). Entwurf und Umsetzung Hybrider Spielanwendungen. In: Proceedings of Mensch & Computer 2005 (M&C 2005), Linz, Österreich, Oldenbourg-Verlag, München, September 4-7, 211-220.

Magerkurth, C., Röcker, C. (2006). User Interfaces for Pervasive Games: Experiences of a Formative Multi-Method Evaluation and its Implications for System Development. In: Proceedings of the Ninth ERCIM Workshop on User Interfaces For All (UI4All'06), Königswinter (Bonn), Germany, September 27 - 28, 2006.

Magerkurth, C., Stenzel, R. (2003). A pervasive keyboard - separating input from display. Proceedings of the First IEEE International Conference on Pervasive Computing and Communications (PerCom 2003), 388- 395.

Magerkurth, C., Stenzel, R. (2003). Computerunterstütztes Kooperatives Spielen – Die Zukunft des Spieltisches. In: Proceedings of Mensch & Computer 2003 (MC '03), Stuttgart, Teubner, 123-133.

Magerkurth, C., Stenzel, R. (2004). Spielanwendungen im Kontext realweltlicher Parameter. In: Tagungsband der 34. Jahrestagung der Gesellschaft für Informatik, Ulm, Germany.

Magerkurth, C., Stenzel, R., Prante, T. (2003). STARS - A Ubiquitous Computing Platform for Computer Augmented Tabletop Games. In: Video Track and Adjunct Proceedings of the Fifth International Conference on Ubiquitous Computing (UBICOMP'03), Seattle, Washington, USA.

Magerkurth, C., Prante, T. (2001). Towards a unifying Approach to Mobile Computing. In: SIGGROUP Bulletin, April, 2001. Vol.22, No.1, 16-18.

Mandryk, R. L., Maranan, D. S. (2002). False prophets: exploring hybrid board/video games. In CHI '02 Extended Abstracts on Human Factors in Computing Systems (Minneapolis, Minnesota, USA, April 20 - 25, 2002). CHI '02. ACM Press, New York, NY, 640-641.

Mandryk, R., Stanley, K.G. (2004). Gemini: Accumulating Context for Play Applications, Proceedings of UbiComp 2004.

Marquardt, N. and Greenberg, S. (2007). Distributed physical interfaces with shared phidgets. In Proceedings of the 1st international Conference on Tangible and Embedded interaction (Baton Rouge, Louisiana, February 15 - 17, 2007). TEI '07. ACM, New York, NY, 13-20.

Matsumoto, M., Nishimura, T. (1998). Mersenne twister: a 623-dimensionally equidistributed uniform pseudo-random number generator. ACM Trans. Model. Comput. Simul. 8, 1, 3-30.

Mauney, D., Masterton, C.:(2008). Small-Screen Interface. In: Kortum, P. (Hrsg.): HCI Beyond the GUI. Design for Haptic, Speech, Olfactory and Other Nontraditional Interfaces, Elsevier/Morgan Kaufmann, Amsterdam, 307-357.

Mavrommati, I., Kameas, A. (2003). The evolution of objects into hyper-objects: will it be mostly harmless? Personal and Ubiquitous Computing. 7, 3-4 (Jul. 2003), 176-181.

Milgram, P., Kishino, A.F. (1994). Taxonomy of Mixed Reality Visual Displays IEICE Transactions on Information and Systems, E77-D(12), pp. 1321-1329.

Millien, E., Roux, C. (2003). User's input to the design of a 'communicating pen': a participatory approach. In: Proceedings of Smart Objects Conference (SOC'03)

Minar, N., Gray, M., Roup, O., Krikorian, R., Maes, P. (1999). Hive: Distributed Agents for Networking Things. First International Symposium on Agent Systems and Applications (ASA'99).

Minkley, J. (2003). Eyetoy shifts a million. Online article at Computer and Video Games Market. http://www.computerandvideogames.com/news/news_story.php(que)id=97876

Mitchell, K., McCaffery, D., Metaxas, G., Finney, J., Schmid, S., Scott, A. (2003). Six in the city: introducing Real Tournament - a mobile IPv6 based context-aware multiplayer game. In Proceedings of the 2nd Workshop on Network and System Support For Games (Redwood City, California, May 22 - 23, 2003). NETGAMES '03. ACM Press, New York, NY, 91-100.

Morris, M. R., Ryall, K., Shen, C., Forlines, C., Vernier, F. (2004). Beyond "social protocols": multi-user coordination policies for co-located groupware. In Proceedings of the 2004 ACM Conference on Computer Supported Cooperative Work (Chicago, Illinois, USA, November 06 - 10, 2004). CSCW '04. ACM, New York, NY, 262-265.

Müller, F., Agamanolis, S., Picard, R. (2003). Exertion interfaces: sports over a distance for social bonding and fun. In Proceedings of the SIGCHI Conference on Human Factors in Computing Systems (Ft. Lauderdale, Florida, USA, April 05 - 10, 2003). CHI '03. ACM Press, New York, NY, 561-568

Müller-Tomfelde, C., Streitz, N.A., Steinmetz, R. (2003). Sounds@Work - Auditory Displays for Interaction in Cooperative and Hybrid Environments. In: C. Stephanidis, J. Jacko (Ed.): Human-Computer Interaction: Theory and Practice (Part II), Lawrence Erlbaum Publishers. Mahwah, 751-755.

Murphy, A. L., Picco, G. P., Roman, G. (2006). LIME: A coordination model and middleware supporting mobility of hosts and agents. ACM Trans. Softw. Eng. Methodol. 15, 3 (Jul. 2006), 279-328.

Myers, B. A. (2001). Using handhelds and PCs together. Communications of the ACM 44, 11 (Nov. 2001), 34-41.

Mynatt, E. D., Back, M., Want, R., Baer, M., Ellis, J. B. (1998). Designing audio aura. In Proceedings of the SIGCHI Conference on Human Factors in Computing Systems (Los Angeles, California, United States, April 18 - 23, 1998). ACM Press/Addison-Wesley Publishing Co., New York, NY, 566-573.

Naef, M., Staadt, O., Gross, M. (2002). Spatialized audio rendering for immersive virtual environments. In Proceedings of the ACM Symposium on Virtual Reality Software and Technology (Hong Kong, China, November 11 - 13, 2002). VRST '02. ACM Press, New York, NY, 65-72.

Lundgren, S., Björk, S. (2004). Game Mechanics: Describing Computer-Augmented Games in Terms of Interaction (retrieved from http://www.playresearch.com).

O'Connor, M.C. (2004). Intel Demos RFID-Enabled Projects. RFID Journal article online at http://www.rfidjournal.com/article/articleview/946/1/1/.

Ogden, S. (1999). Advancing game graphics: A war of escalation. SIGGRAPH Comput. Graph. 33, 4 (Nov. 1999), 5-8.

Olszewski, P. (1987). Individual differences in preschool children's production of verbal fantasy play. Merrill-Palmer Quarterly, 33, 69-86.

Patten, J, Ishii, H. (2000). A comparison of spatial organization strategies in graphical and tangible user interfaces. In Proceedings of DARE 2000 on Designing Augmented Reality Environments (Elsinore, Denmark). DARE '00. ACM Press, New York, NY, 41-50.

Patterson-McNeill, H. Binkerd, C. L. (2001). Resources for using lego mindstorms. In Proceedings of the Seventh Annual Consortium For Computing in Small Colleges (Branson, Missouri, United States). J. G. Meinke, Ed. Consortium for Computing Sciences in Colleges, 48-55.

Pearce, C. (1997). The Interactive Book. New York: Macmillan Technical Publishing, 422–423.

Piaget, J. (1965). The moral judgment of the child. New York: Free Press (Original work published in 1932).

Prante, T., Streitz, N.A., Tandler, P. (2004). Roomware: Computers Disappear and Interaction Evolves. In: IEEE Computer, December 2004, 47-54.

Preece, Jennifer (2002). Interaction Design. J. Wiley and Sons, New York, 2002.

Priyantha, N. B., Chakraborty, A., Balakrishnan, H. (2000). The Cricket location-support system. In Proceedings of the 6th Annual international Conference on Mobile Computing and Networking (Boston, Massachusetts, United States, August 06 - 11, 2000). MobiCom '00. ACM Press, New York, NY, 32-43.

Resnick, M., Martin, F. Sargent, R., Silverman, B. (1996). Programmable Bricks: Toys to Think With. IBM Systems Journal, vol. 35, no. 3-4, 443-452.

Robertson, J., Good, J. (2003): Ghostwriter: a narrative virtual environment for children; Interaction Design And Children, Proceeding of the 2003 conference on Interaction design and children; Preston, England; SESSION: Papers; 85 – 91.

Röcker, C., Janse, M. D., Portolan, N., and Streitz, N. (2005). User requirements for intelligent home environments: a scenario-driven approach and empirical cross-cultural study. In Proceedings of the 2005 Joint Conference on Smart Objects and Ambient intelligence: innovative Context-Aware Services: Usages and Technologies (Grenoble, France, October 12 - 14, 2005). sOc-EUSAI '05, vol. 121. ACM Press, New York, NY, 111-116.

Röcker, C., Magerkurth, C. (2006). User Interfaces for Pervasive Games: Experiences of a Formative Multi-Method Evaluation and its Implications for System Development. In: Proceedings of the Ninth ERCIM Workshop on User Interfaces For All (UI4All'06), Königswinter (Bonn), Germany, September 27 - 28, 2006.

Römer, K. Domnitcheva, S. (2002). Smart Playing Cards: A Ubiquitous Computing Game. Personal & Ubiquitous Computing. 6, 5-6 (Jan. 2002), 371-377.

Römer, K., Schoch, T., Mattern, F., Dübendorfer, T. (2004). Smart identification frameworks for ubiquitous computing applications. Wireless Networks 10, 6 (Nov. 2004), 689-700.

Russell, D. M., Streitz, N. A., Winograd, T. (2005). Building disappearing computers. Communications of the ACM 48, 3 (Mar. 2005), 42-48.

Salen, K., Zimmermann, E. (2003). Rules of Play: Game Design Fundamentals: MIT Press

Sanneblad, J., Holmquist, L. E. (2003). OpenTrek: A Platform for Developing Interactive Networked Games on Mobile Devices. In Proceedings of Mobile HCI (Udine, Italy, September 8-11, 2003), 224-240.

Sanneblad, J., Holmquist, L. E. (2004). The GapiDraw platform: high-performance cross-platform graphics on mobile devices. In Proceedings of the 3rd international Conference on Mobile and Ubiquitous Multimedia (College Park, Maryland, October 27 - 29, 2004). MUM '04, vol. 83. ACM Press, New York, NY, 47-53.

Scherer, K.; Grinewitschus, V.; Vom Bögel, G. (2004). Das vernetzte Haus. In: Tagungsband Innovationen für Menschen. Berlin: VDE-Verlag, 27-32.

Schmidt, A., Gellersen, H.W. (2001). Modell, Architektur und Plattform für Informationssysteme mit Kontextbezug. Informatik Forschung und Entwicklung. Band 16, Heft 4, 213-224.

Schuckmann, C., Schümmer, J., Seitz, P. (1999). Modeling collaboration using shared objects. In Proceedings of the international ACM SIGGROUP Conference on Supporting Group Work (Phoenix, Arizona, United States, November 14 - 17, 1999). GROUP '99. ACM Press, New York, NY, 189-198.

Searle, John (1995). The Construction of Social Reality. New York: The Free Press.

Shafer, S. A. N., Brumitt, B., and Cadiz, J. (2001). Interaction Issues in Context-Aware Intelligent
Environments, Human-Computer Interaction 16 (2–4), 363–378.

Shaer, O., Leland, N., Calvillo-Gamez, E. H., Jacob, R. J. (2004). The TAC paradigm: specifying tangible user interfaces. Personal and Ubiquitous Computing. 8, 5 (Sep. 2004), 359-369.

Shen, C., Lesh, N.B., Vernier, F., Forlines, C., Frost, J. (2002): Sharing and Building Digital Group Histories. Proceedings of CSCW'02, 324-333.

Shen, C., Vernier, F. D., Forlines, C., Ringel, M. (2004). DiamondSpin: an extensible toolkit for around-the-table interaction. In Proceedings of the SIGCHI Conference on Human Factors in Computing Systems (Vienna, Austria, April 24 - 29, 2004). CHI '04. ACM Press, New York, NY, 167-174.

Shirehjini, A. A. (2005). A generic UPnP architecture for ambient intelligence meeting rooms and a control point allowing for integrated 2D and 3D interaction. In Proceedings of the 2005 Joint Conference on Smart Objects and Ambient intelligence: innovative Context-Aware Services: Usages and Technologies (Grenoble, France, October 12 - 14, 2005). sOc-EUSAI '05, vol. 121. ACM, New York, NY, 207-212.

Shneiderman , B. (1998). Designing the User Interface. Addison Wesley Longman.

Shoemaker, G. B., Inkpen, K. M. (2001). Single display privacyware: augmenting public displays with private information. In Proceedings of the SIGCHI Conference on Human Factors in Computing Systems (Seattle, Washington, United States). CHI '01. ACM Press, New York, NY, 522-529.

Singer, J. L. (Ed.) (1973). The child's world of make-believe: Experimental studies of imaginative play. New York: Academic Press.

Smith, I., Consolvo, S., LaMarca, A. (2005). The Drop: pragmatic problems in the design of a compelling, pervasive game. ACM Transactions on Computers in Entertainment, 3, 3 (July 2005), 4-4.

Smith, J. R., Fishkin, K. P., Jiang, B., Mamishev, A., Philipose, M., Rea, A. D., Roy, S., Sundara-Rajan, K. (2005). RFID-based techniques for human-activity detection. Commun. ACM 48, 9 (Sep. 2005), 39-44.

Sommerville, I. (2006). Software Engineering. Addison-Wesley Longman, Amsterdam.

Sousa, J., Garlan, D. (2002). Aura: An Architectural Framework for User Mobility in Ubiquitous Computing Environments. In: Software Architecture: System Design, Development, and Maintenance
(Proceedings of the 3rd Working IEEE/IFIP Conference on Software Architecture), 29–43.

Stapleton, C., Hughes, C., Moshell, M., Micikevicius, P., Altman, M. (2002). Applying Mixed Reality to Entertainment. Computer 35, 12 (Dec. 2002), 122-124.

Starner, T., Leibe, B., Singletary, B., Pair, J. (2000). Mind-Warping: Towards creating a compelling collaborative augmented reality game. In Proceedings of the 5th international Conference on intelligent User interfaces (New Orleans, Louisiana, United States, January 2000). IUI '00. ACM Press, New York, NY, 256-259.

Steurer, P., Srivastava, M.B. (2003): System Design of Smart Table. Proceedings of IEEE PerCom'03, Dallas-Fort Worth, Texas, March 2003, 473-480.

Stewart, J. (2007). Trends in real-time rendering: an interview with bioware's Ben Earhart. Crossroads 14, 1.

Streitz, N.A. (2005). From Human-Computer Interaction to Human-Artefact Interaction Design for Smart Environments. In: Hemmje, M., Niederee, C., Risse,T. (Ed.): From Integrated Publication and Information Systems to Virtual Information and Knowledge Environments, Springer LNCS 3379, 232-240.

Streitz, N.A., Geißler, J., Holmer, T. (1997). Roomware for Cooperative Buildings: Integrated Design of Architectural Spaces and Information Spaces. In: Streitz, N.A., Konomi, S., Burkhardt, H. (Ed.): Proceedings of CoBuild '98, Darmstadt, Germany, LNCS Vol. 1370, Heidelberg, Germany, Springer, 4-21.

Streitz, N.A., Magerkurth, C., Prante, T., and Röcker, C. (2005 a). From information design to experience design: smart artefacts and the disappearing computer. ACM Interactions, 12, 4 (Jul. 2005), 21-25.

Streitz, N.A., Prante, T., Müller-Tomfelde, C., Tandler, P., Magerkurth, C. (2002). Roomware: The Second Generation. In: Video Proceedings and Extended Abstracts of the ACM Conference on Human Factors in Computing Systems (CHI'02), Minneapolis, MN, USA, ACM Press, April 20-25, 2002, 506-507.

Streitz, N.A., Röcker, C., Prante, T., van Alphen, D., Stenzel, R., Magerkurth, C. (2005 b). Designing Smart Artifacts for Smart Environments. In: IEEE Computer, March 2005, 41-49.

Streitz, N.A., Röcker, C., Prante, Th. (2003). Situated Interaction With Ambient Information: Facilitating Awareness and Communication in Ubiquitous Work Environments. Proc. HCI 2003, 133-137.

Streitz, N.A., Tandler, P., Müller-Tomfelde, C., Konomi, S. (2001). Roomware. Towards the Next Generation of Human-Computer Interaction based on an Integrated Design of Real and Virtual Worlds. In: J. A. Carroll (Ed.): Human-Computer Interaction in the New Millennium, Addison Wesley, 553-578.

Strommen, E. (1998) When the interface is a talking dinosaur: learning across media with ActiMates Barney, Proceedings of the SIGCHI conference on Human factors in computing systems; Los Angeles, California, United States; 288 – 295.

Sutton-Smith, B. (1971). A Syntax for Play and Games. In Child's Play, Brian Sutton-Smith and R.E. Herron , New York: John Wiley and Sons, 304.

Sutton-Smith, B. (1986). Toys as Culture. New York: Gardner Press, Incorporated.

Tandler, P. (2004). The BEACH Application Model and Software Framework for Synchronous Collaboration in Ubiquitous Computing Environments. In: J.J. Barton, R. Cerqueira and M. Fontoura (Ed.): The Journal of Systems & Software, Vol 69/3, 267-296.

Taguchi, G., Rajesh, J. (2000). New Trends in Multivariate Diagnosis. Sankhya: The Indian Journal of Statistics, Volume 62, Series B, Pt. 2,. 233-248.

Torrance, M. (1995). Advances in Human Computer Interaction: The Intelligent Room. In Working Notes of the CHI '95 Research Symposium, Denver, Colorado.

Tse, E., Greenberg, S. (2002). SDGToolkit: A Toolkit for Rapidly Prototyping Single Display Groupware", Poster in ACM CSCW 2002.

Ullmer, B., Ishii, H. (2000). Emerging frameworks for tangible user interfaces. IBM Systems Journal, 39(3):915–931.

Ullmer, B., Ishii, H., Glas, D. (1998). mediaBlocks: physical containers, transports, and controls for online media. In Proceedings of the 25th Annual Conference on Computer Graphics and interactive Techniques SIGGRAPH '98. ACM Press, New York, NY, 379-386.

Underkoffler, J., Ishii, H. (1999). Urp: a luminous-tangible workbench for urban planning and design. In Proceedings of the SIGCHI Conference on Human Factors in Computing Systems, CHI '99. ACM Press, New York, NY, 386-393.

van Vliet, H. (2008). Software Engineering, Principles and Practice. John Wiley & Sons, Chichester.

Vygoysky, L. S. (1967). Play and its role in the mental development of the child. Soviet Psychology, 12, 62 – 76.

Wagner, M. and Kellerer, W. (2004). Web services selection for distributed composition of multimedia content. In Proceedings of the 12th Annual ACM international Conference on Multimedia (New York, NY, USA, October 10 - 16, 2004). MULTIMEDIA '04. ACM, New York, NY, 104-107.

Walther, B. K. (2003): Playing and Gaming - Reflections and Classifications, Game Studies, vol. 3

Want, R., Hopper, A., Falcao, V., Gibbons, J. (1992). The active badge location system. ACM Transactions on Information Systems, 10 (1), 91-102.

Weiser, M. (1991). The Computer for the Twenty-First Century. Scientific American, September 1991, 86—93.

Wellner, P. (1993). Interacting with paper on the DigitalDesk. Communications of the ACM, 36, 7 (Jul. 1993), 87-96.

Zagal, J.P., Nussbaum, M., Rosas, R. (2000). A Model to Support the Design of Multiplayer Games. Presence: Teleoperators and Virtual Environments, 9, MIT Press

9. Appendix

Caves & Creatures Game Definition

Data Objects:

```
<!--characters-->
<gid50 dexterity="8"      intelligence="11"  max_hp="11"      name="Dan"
speed="8" strength="9" model='0'> </gid50>
<gid51 dexterity="9"      intelligence="5"   max_hp="14" name="Carsten"
speed="7" strength="7" model='1' > </gid51>
<gid52 dexterity="9"      intelligence="13" max_hp="8"       name="Timo"
speed="8" strength="8" model='2' ></gid52>
<gid53 dexterity="12"  intelligence="7"     max_hp="9"    name="Richard"
speed="6" strength="6" model='3' > </gid53>
<gid54 dexterity="13"  intelligence="9"     max_hp="10" name="Michael"
speed="9" strength="11" model='4' ></gid54>
<gid55 dexterity="8"      intelligence="13"  max_hp="14" name="Norbert"
speed="6" strength="11" model='0' ></gid55>
<gid56 dexterity="11"  intelligence="12"  max_hp="6"       name="Bjork"
speed="7" strength="7" model='1' ></gid56>
<gid57     dexterity='8'              intelligence='12'           max_hp='12'
name='Thorsten' speed='8' strength='12' model='2' />


<!--weapons-->
<gid100 damage="3" name="Unwieldy Axe" range="short" model='1'
                unuse="(UNARMWEAPON 100)"
                my_unuse="(UPDATE+ TURN dexterity 2)"
                use="(ARMWEAPON 100)"
                my_use="(UPDATE- TURN dexterity 2)"></gid100>
<gid101 damage="2" name="Broadsword" range="short" model='2'
                unuse="(UNARMWEAPON 101)"
                use="(ARMWEAPON 101)"></gid101>
<gid102 damage="1" name="Short Bow" range="long" model='4'
                unuse="(UNARMWEAPON 102)"
                use="(ARMWEAPON 102)"></gid102>
<gid103 damage="1" name="Short Sword" range="short" model='2'
                unuse="(UNARMWEAPON 103)"
                use="(ARMWEAPON 103)"></gid103>
<gid104 damage='2' name='Bola' range='long' model='4'
                use='(ARMWEAPON 104)'
                unuse='(UNARMWEAPON 104)'
                hit='(UNARMWEAPON 104)(TEXT PUBLIC [CAT (TARGET name) "
has the " (104 name)])'
                miss='(DO (104 hit))'/>
<gid105 name="Poisoned Bow" damage='1' range='long' model='4'
                use='(ARMWEAPON 105)'
                unuse='(UNARMWEAPON 105)'
                hit='(UPDATE TARGET poisoned 1)'/>
<gid106 name="TwoHander" damage='2' range='short' model='2'
                use='(ARMWEAPON 106)'
                my_use='(UPDATE+ TURN strength 2)'
                unuse='(UNARMWEAPON 106)'
```

```
                    my_unuse='(UPDATE- TURN strength 2)'/>
    <gid107 name="Hurican Spell" damage='2' range='long' model='2'
                    use='(ARMWEAPON 107)'
                    unuse='(UNARMWEAPON 107)'/>


    <gid108 name="MagicWand" damage='2' range='short' model='2'
                    use='(ARMWEAPON 108)'
                    my_use='(UPDATE+ TURN strength 2)'
                    unuse='(UNARMWEAPON 108)'
                    my_unuse='(UPDATE- TURN strength 2)'/>
<!--WandSpells-->
    <gid110 name="Gesture of Darkness" damage='3' range='long' model='10'
use='(SHOWIMG TURN)'unuse='(UNARMWEAPON 108)'/>


    <gid111 name="Gesture of Fire" damage='5' range='long' model='7'
                    use='(ARMWEAPON 108)(SHOWIMG TURN)'
                    unuse='(UNARMWEAPON 108)'/>


<!--Scrolls-->
    <gid130 name="Scroll of Paralysis" use="(CASTSCROLL 130)"
                    sound='battle\freeze.wav'
                    my_use="(UPDATE TARGET paralyzed 1)
                            (UPDATES+ TARGET do_turn (130 my_str))"
                    my_str='[IF (EQ 1 (TURN paralyzed))
                            {(TEXT  PUBLIC  [CAT  (TURN  name)  "  roll
                                against intelligence to unparalyze"])
                            (ROLL   0   20)[IF   (LE   (DICE   0)   (TURN
                                intelligence))
                            (UPDATE TURN paralyzed)(ENDTURN)]}
                    (UPDATES- TURN do_turn (130 my_str))]'></gid130>
    <gid131 name="Scroll of Fire"
                    sound="battle\fire.wav"
                    use="(CASTSCROLL 131)"
                    my_use="(RANDOM 0 6)
                            (DAMAGE (DICE 0) TARGET)"></gid131>
    <gid132 name="Scroll of Ice"
                     sound="battle\freez2.wav"
                    use="(CASTSCROLL 132)"
                    my_use="(RANDOM 0 5)
                            (DAMAGE (+ (DICE 0) 1) TARGET)"/>
    <gid133 name="Flame of weakness"
                    sound="battle\defscroll.wav"
                    use="(CASTSCROLL 133)"
                    my_use='[IF (GE (TARGET strength) 3)
                            {(UPDATE-  TARGET  strength  3)(DOIN  TARGET  3
                                "(UPDATE+ TURN strength 3)")}]'/>
    <gid134 name="Circle of smoothness"
                    use='(TEXT        PUBLIC        "Tap        a        square")
                        (TAPSQUARE)(UPDATE+ LOCATION speed 1)'/>


<!--Potions-->
    <gid150 name="Potion of Health" use="(DRINKPOTION 150)"
     my_use="(UPDATE+ TURN hp 10)(UPDATE TURN poisoned)"/>
```

182

```
<gid151 name="Potion of Strength" use="(DRINKPOTION 151)"
 my_use='(UPDATE+ TURN strength 5)
          (DOIN TURN 5 "(UPDATE- TURN strength 5)")'></gid151>
<gid152 name="Potion of Thorns" use='(DRINKPOTION 152)'
 my_use='(UPDATES+ TURN when_hit  (152 my_str))
          (DOIN TURN 5  "(UPDATES- TURN when_hit (152 my_str))")'
                my_str='(UPDATE- TURN hp 4)'/>
    <gid153   name="Potion   of   intelligence"   use='(DRINKPOTION    153)'
my_use='(UPDATE+  TURN  intelligence  3)(DOIN   TURN   3   "(UPDATE-   TURN
intelligence 3)")'/>
    <gid154 name="Potion of speed" use='(DRINKPOTION 154)' my_use='(UPDATE+
TURN speed 2)(DOIN TURN 2 "(UPDATE- TURN speed 2)")'/>

<!--Items-->
    <gid170 name='Amulet of Command (Speed)' use='(WEAR 170)'
                my_use='(UPDATES+ TURN command (170 my_str))'
                my_str='(UPDATE+    TURN    speed    1)(DOIN    TURN    1
                    "(UPDATE- TURN speed 1)")'
                my_unuse='(UPDATES- TURN command (170 my_str))' />

    <gid171 name='Cloak of nimbleness'  use='(WEAR 171)' my_use='(UPDATE+
TURN dexterity 1)' my_unuse='(UPDATE- TURN dexterity 1)'/>

    <gid172 name='Shield of Chaos' use='(WEAR 172)'
                my_use='(UPDATES+ TURN when_hit (172 my_str))'
                my_unuse='(UPDATES- TURN when_hit (172 my_str))'
                my_str='(TELEPORT                         TURN)'/>

    <gid173 name='Amulet of Command (Intelligence)' use='(WEAR 173)'
                my_use='(UPDATES+ TURN command (173 my_str))'
                my_str='(UPDATE+  TURN  intelligence  1)(DOIN   TURN   1
                    "(UPDATE- TURN intelligence 1)")'
                my_unuse='(UPDATES- TURN command (173 my_str))' />

<!--locations-->
    <gid200 name='Tile of Life' action='(TEXT TURN "Welcome to the Tile of
Life")
    (UPDATE TURN hp (TURN max_hp))
    (UPDATES- LOCATION step_on "(DO (200 action))")
    (HIDE "(DO (200 action))")'/>
```

Game Rules:

```
<GAME     end_music="battle\outro.wav"     start_music="battle\intro.wav"
title="The   Battle-Royal"   name="gameCode"   file="xml\battle_royal.xml"
persist="true" persfile="xml\battle_royal.xml" DebugLevel="1">

<INIT    action='(GAMEINFO    &quot;Initializing    game...&quot;)(SETLIGHT
0)(DISPLAYGAMEINFO     false)(HIDEITEM     100)(HIDEITEM     101)(HIDEITEM
102)(HIDEITEM   103)(HIDEITEM   104)(HIDEITEM   105)(HIDEITEM   106)(HIDEITEM
130)(HIDEITEM   131)(HIDEITEM   132)(HIDEITEM   133)(HIDEITEM   134)   (HIDEITEM
150)(HIDEITEM   151)(HIDEITEM   152)(HIDEITEM   153)(HIDEITEM   154)(HIDEITEM
```

```
170) (HIDEITEM   171) (HIDEITEM   172) (HIDEITEM   173) (HIDE   &quot; (DO   (200
action)) &quot;) (UPDATE -1 inited 1) (UPDATE -1 goalPts 5) (DISPLAYGAMEINFO
true) (TEXT PUBLIC (CAT (GETATT title) &quot; can begin!&quot;)) (SETLIGHT
255)' />

<CLEARFIELDS action=" (DOFOREVERYCHILDELEMENT gboard: ONCLEARELEMENT)"/>

<ONCLEARELEMENT   arg0="PATH"   action=' (GAMEINFO   PATH) (DELATT   (CAT   PATH
&quot;/step_on&quot;))' />
<CANVAS>
        <UPD_MODEL      arg0="GID"      action=' (CHANGEATT      (CAT      (CAT
&quot;Canvas:gid&quot; GID) &quot;/Layers/PlayerInfo/Image/img&quot;) (CAT
&quot;img/chars/&quot; (CAT (GID device) (CAT &quot;_Model_&quot; (CAT (GID
model) &quot;.png&quot;)))))' />
        <UPD_PLAYERNAME   arg0="GID"   action=' (CHANGEATT   (CAT   (CAT
&quot;Canvas:gid&quot; GID) &quot;/Layers/PlayerInfo/Name/text&quot;) (GID
name))' />
        <UPD_HP      arg0="GID"      action=' (CHANGEATT      (CAT      (CAT
&quot;Canvas:gid&quot;                                                     GID)
&quot;/Layers/PlayerInfo/Stats/HP/Value/text&quot;) (GID hp))' />
        <UPD_DX      arg0="GID"      action=' (CHANGEATT      (CAT      (CAT
&quot;Canvas:gid&quot;                                                     GID)
&quot;/Layers/PlayerInfo/Stats/DX/Value/text&quot;) (GID dexterity))' />
        <UPD_MP      arg0="GID"      action=' (CHANGEATT      (CAT      (CAT
&quot;Canvas:gid&quot;                                                     GID)
&quot;/Layers/PlayerInfo/Stats/MP/Value/text&quot;) (GID mv_pts))' />
        <UPD_INTEL      arg0="GID"      action=' (CHANGEATT      (CAT      (CAT
&quot;Canvas:gid&quot;                                                     GID)
&quot;/Layers/PlayerInfo/Stats/INTEL/Value/text&quot;) (GID intelligence))'
/>
        <UPD_USRMSG      arg0="GID"      action=' (CHANGEATT      (CAT      (CAT
&quot;Canvas:gid&quot;                                                     GID)
&quot;/Layers/UserMessage/MessageText/text&quot;)    (GETATT    (CAT    (CAT
&quot;audio:gid&quot; GID) &quot;/speak&quot;)))' />
        <UPD_SPEED      arg0="GID"      action=' (CHANGEATT      (CAT      (CAT
&quot;Canvas:gid&quot;                                                     GID)
&quot;/Layers/PlayerInfo/Stats/SPEED/Value/text&quot;) (GID speed))' />
        <UPD_STRENGTH      arg0="GID"      action=' (CHANGEATT      (CAT      (CAT
&quot;Canvas:gid&quot;                                                     GID)
&quot;/Layers/PlayerInfo/Stats/STRENGTH/Value/text&quot;) (GID strength))'
/>
        <SHOWSCROLL action=' (SETATT (CAT (CAT &quot;Canvas:gid&quot; TURN)
&quot;/Layers/activeScroll/Symbol/img&quot;)
&quot;img/gestureScrolls/geste11.png&quot;) (SETATT      (CAT      (CAT
&quot;Canvas:gid&quot;   TURN)   &quot;/Layers/activeScroll/visible&quot;)
&quot;true&quot;) ' />
        <HIDESCROLL action=' (SETATT (CAT (CAT &quot;Canvas:gid&quot; GID)
&quot;/Layers/activeScroll/visible&quot;) &quot;false&quot;)' arg0="GID" />
        <UPD_TURNNAME      arg0="GID"      action=' (CHANGEATT      (CAT      (CAT
&quot;Canvas:gid&quot;   GID)   &quot;/Layers/PlayerInfo/TurnName/text&quot;)
(TURN name))' />
</CANVAS>
```

```
<CANVUPDATE      action="(CANVAS/UPD_PLAYERNAME      GID)(CANVAS/UPD_HP
GID)(CANVAS/UPD_DX       GID)(CANVAS/UPD_MP       GID)(CANVAS/UPD_STRENGTH
GID)(CANVAS/UPD_INTEL     GID)(CANVAS/UPD_SPEED     GID)(CANVAS/UPD_USRMSG
GID)(CANVAS/UPD_MODEL GID)(CANVAS/UPD_TURNNAME GID)" arg0="GID" />

<CANVUPDATEFROMGID action="(CANVUPDATE GID)" arg0="GID" arg1="ATTR" />

<SETLIGHT arg0="VAL" action="(SETATT light:value VAL)" />

<PLAYSOUND arg0="FNAME" action='(SETATT audio:file (CAT &quot;battle/&quot;
FNAME &quot;.wav&quot;))(SETATT audio:play once)' />

<SETDICEBOXTEXT arg0="TXT" action="(SETATT dbox:text TXT)" />

<BUTTON_MSG action='(GAMEINFO [CAT (GID name) &quot; pressed MSG&quot;])'
arg0="GID" />

<BUTTON_STATS    action='(GAMEINFO    [CAT    (GID    name)    &quot;    pressed
STATS&quot;])' arg0="GID" />

<WAND_MOVED       action='(TEXT        PUBLIC        &quot;&quot;)(SETLIGHT
100)(CANVAS/SHOWSCROLL)' />

<WAND_GESTURE action='(SETLIGHT 255)(PLAYSOUND roar)(TEXT PUBLIC &quot;You
fired the Spell of Darkness!&quot;)(CANVAS/HIDESCROLL TURN)' />

<WAND>
<HEAR    action="(CHANGEATT    wand:wandSet/notifyWandMoved    true)(CHANGEATT
wand:wandSet/recognize false)" />

<WAITFORGESTURE        action="(CHANGEATT        wand:wandSet/notifyWandMoved
true)(CHANGEATT wand:wandSet/recognize true)" />

<DONTCARE    action="(SETATT    wand:wandSet/notifyWandMoved    false)(SETATT
wand:wandSet/recognize false)" />

</WAND>

<HIDE arg0="STR" action="(RANDOM 0 8 8)(UPDATEBS+   (- (DICE 0) 1) (- (DICE
1) 1) step_on STR)" />

<HIDEITEM    arg0="ITM"    action='(HIDE    [CAT    &quot;(FINDITEM    &quot;   ITM
&quot;)&quot;])' />

<TURN       action="(IF       [NEQ       (-1       inited)       1]       (INIT))
(UPDATE+ TURN turn_count 1)
(IF (EQ (TURN poisoned) 1)
    (DAMAGE 1 TURN))
    [IF (EQ (TURN death) 1)
            { (UPDATE TURN death 0)(UPDATE TURN hp (TURN max_hp))(ENDTURN)}
            {(SOUND PUBLIC (TURN theme_song))
(TEXT    TURN    (CAT    (TURN    name)    &apos;    take    your    turn&apos;))
(UPDATE            TURN            mv_pts            (TURN            speed))
(INTURNSQUARE COMMAND)
```

```
(DO (TURN do_turn))}]" order_attr="speed" ordering="ORDERBYG" />

<COMMAND arg0="X" arg1="Y" action="(DO (BOARD X Y piece command))" />

<TAP action='(TTARG)[IF (LEGALTARGET)(FIGHT)(TEXT PUBLIC &quot;Not a legal
target&quot;)]' />

<TTARG action="(SOUND PUBLIC battle\tap.wav)(TAPTARG)" />

<TAPTAP action="(SOUND PUBLIC battle\taptap.wav)(ONENDTURN)" />

<FIGHT            action='(SOUND       ·    PUBLIC          battle\fight.wav)
(TEXT PUBLIC [CAT (TURN name) &quot; roll for attack&quot;])(SETDICEBOXTEXT
[CAT &quot;Rolldice&quot; (TURN name)])                            (ROLL 0
20)                       (TEXT PUBLIC [CAT (TARGET name) &quot;
roll for defense&quot;])(SETDICEBOXTEXT [CAT &quot;Rolldice&quot; (TURN
name)])                                                    (ROLL 1 20)
(UPDATES TURN attacking TARGET)                            [IF (GE [+
(DICE 0) (TURN dexterity)    (* 2 (- (LOCATION [CAT &quot;flankers&quot;
(TURN team)]) 1))]                                     [+ (DICE 1)
(TARGET dexterity)])                                                {
(SOUND PUBLIC battle\hit.wav)                              (DO (TURN
weapon hit))                     [IF (SEQ (TURN weapon range)
short)                                 (DO (TARGET when_hit))]
(DAMAGE [+ 1 [/ (TURN strength) 4] (TURN weapon damage)] TARGET)
}                    {(TEXT TURN [CAT &quot;You missed to hit
&quot; (TARGET name)]])(TEXT TARGET [CAT &quot;You have not been hit by
&quot; (TURN name)])                          (SOUND PUBLIC
battle\fightmiss.wav)                          (DO (TURN weapon
miss))                                                         }]
(ONENDTURN)' />
(SOUND                    PUBLIC                  battle\death.wav)
(UPDATE TRG poisoned)                                (UPDATE TRG
death 1)                          (IF [NEQ (TRG team) (TURN
team)]                                  {(UPDATE+ TURN points) (-
1)                             (IF [EQ (TURN points) (-
1 goalPts)]                                   {(TEXT
PUBLIC [CAT (TURN name) &apos; has won&apos;])(ENDGAME)}}})
(IF (EQ (TRG team) 1) (UPDATE TRG team 0)(UPDATE TRG team 1))
}]" />

<MOVE action='(IF [AND (LEGALMOVE) (GE [+ (TURN mv_pts) (LOCATION speed)]
0)]{(UNFLANK    TURN)    (UPDATE+    TURN    mv_pts    (LOCATION    speed))
(UPDATE TURN xLoc (LOCATION xLoc))(UPDATE TURN yLoc (LOCATION yLoc))(FLANK
TURN)(SOUND PUBLIC &quot;battle\walk.wav&quot;)(DO (LOCATION step_on))}
{(SOUND TURN &quot;battle\nowalk.wav&quot;)(TEXT PUBLIC (CAT &quot;Oh oh!
Please go back to field &quot; (CAT (TURN yLoc) (CAT &quot; &quot;(TURN
xLoc))))))(TEXT TURN (CAT &quot;Not a legal turn, please go back to
position &quot; (CAT (TURN yLoc) (CAT &quot;/&quot;(TURN xLoc)))))))' />

<LEGALMOVE   bool="(AND   (LE   (LOCATION   xLoc)   [+   (TURN   xLoc)   1])
(LE     (LOCATION     yLoc)     [+      (TURN     yLoc)      1])
(GE     (LOCATION     xLoc)     [-      (TURN     xLoc)      1])
(GE (LOCATION yLoc) [- (TURN yLoc) 1]))" />
```

```
<LEGALTARGET bool="{OR [AND (SEQ (TURN weapon range) short) (LEGALMOVE)]
[AND (SEQ (TURN weapon range) long) (NOT (LEGALMOVE))]}" />

<FLANK       arg0="TRG"      action="(IF      (EQ      (TRG      team)      1)
(INSQUARE           (TRG           xLoc)           (TRG           yLoc)      FLANK1)
(INSQUARE (TRG xLoc) (TRG yLoc) FLANK0))" />          .

<FLANK1 arg0="X" arg1="Y" action="(UPDATEB+ X Y flankers1 1)" />

<FLANK0 arg0="X" arg1="Y" action="(UPDATEB+ X Y flankers0 1)" />

<UNFLANK       arg0="TRG"      action="(IF      (EQ      (TRG      team)      1)
(INSQUARE           (TRG           xLoc)           (TRG           yLoc)      UNFLANK1)
(INSQUARE   (TRG xLoc)   (TRG yLoc) UNFLANK0))" />
     <UNFLANK1 arg0="X" arg1="Y" action="(UPDATEB- X Y flankers1 1)" />
     <UNFLANK0 arg0="X" arg1="Y" action="(UPDATEB- X Y flankers0 1)" />
     <ARMWEAPON       arg0="WEAPONID"      action="[IF      [EQ     (WEAPONID      used)      1]
(TEXT           PUBLIC          &apos;Weapon          already          being          used&apos;)
{                                                                   (DO (TURN weapon
unuse))                                                            (UPDATE TURN
weapon                                                                    WEAPONID)
(UPDATE                   WEAPONID                    used                    1)
(SOUND   PUBLIC   battle\weaponarm.wav)           (DO  (WEAPONID   my_use))
}]" />

<UNARMWEAPON     action="(UPDATE    TURN    weapon)(UPDATE     WEAPONID    used)(DO
(WEAPONID my_unuse))" arg0="WEAPONID" />

<CASTSCROLL arg0="SCROLLID" action="(TTARG)(TEXT PUBLIC [CAT (TARGET name)
&apos;     roll      against      intelligence&apos;])(ROLL      0      20)
(UPDATES                  TURN                  casting                   TARGET)
[IF         (GE        (DICE        0)        (TARGET        intelligence))
{(SOUND PUBLIC (SCROLLID sound))(DO (SCROLLID my_use))}
(SOUND                    PUBLIC                    battle\scrollmiss.wav)]
(ENDTURN)" />

<NEWPIECE      action='(UPDATE     TARGET     xLoc    (LOCATION     xLoc))
(UPDATE             TARGET            yLoc           (LOCATION            yLoc))
(IF   (EQ   (-1   team)   0)   (UPDATE   -1   team   1)(UPDATE   -1   team   0))
(UPDATE             TARGET            team            (-1            team))
(UPDATE            TARGET            hp            (TARGET            max_hp))
(FLANK   TARGET)(TEXT   PUBLIC   (CAT   (TARGET   name)   &quot;   entered   the
game!&quot;))                                       ' />

<INTURNSQUARE arg0="STR" action="(INSQUARE (TURN xLoc) (TURN yLoc) STR)" />

<INSQUARE arg0="X" arg1="Y" arg2="STR" action="(STR   (+ X 1)   (+ Y 1))(STR
(+ X 1) (- Y 1))(STR   (- X 1)   (+ Y 1))(STR   (- X 1)   (- Y 1))(STR   (+ X 1)
(+ Y 0))(STR   (- X 1)   (+ Y 0))(STR   (+ X 0)   (+ Y 1))(STR   (+ X 0)   (- Y 1))"
/>

<WEAR    arg0="ITEMID"    action='(IF    (SEQ    (ITEMID    user)    &quot;&quot;)
{   (DO   (ITEMID   my_use))   (UPDATES   ITEMID   user   TURN)   (SOUND   PUBLIC
```

```
&quot;battle\wearon.wav&quot;)}
(IF          [SEQ              (ITEMID           user)          TURN]
{    (DO   (ITEMID   my_unuse))(UPDATE    ITEMID    user)(SOUND    PUBLIC
&quot;battle\wearoff.wav&quot;)                                          }
{ (TEXT PUBLIC &quot;Someone else is wearing that&quot;)})) ' />
    <LOG arg0="STR" action="(SETATT logger:log STR)" />
</GAME>
```